# MINNEAPOLIS IN THE TWENTIETH CENTURY

# MINNEAPOLIS
## IN THE TWENTIETH CENTURY

*The Growth of an American City*

## IRIC NATHANSON

MINNESOTA HISTORICAL SOCIETY PRESS

Versions of select chapters have appeared previously:
"A Tale of Two Cities: Charter Reform in Minneapolis and St. Paul." *Hennepin History* 65.1 (Winter 2006): 4–17.
"Revolution Redux: Don Fraser as Napoleon and Other Tales of City Reorganization Folly." *Minneapolis Observer* 2:2 (February 2005).
"The Shame of Minneapolis: Civic Corruption 100 Years Ago." *Hennepin History* 62.1 (Winter 2003): 12–33.
"Housing and Redevelopment Authority: Clearing Urban Blight." *Hennepin History* 57.1 (Winter 1998): 4–23.
"Handwritten Map Marks Inception of Community's LRT Vision." *Longfellow Nokomis Messenger* (July 2004): 1, 9, 12, 14, 16.
"LRT Vision Realized Despite Myriad Hurdles Along the Route." *Longfellow Nokomis Messenger* (August 2004): 1, 2, 7, 12.

www.mhspress.org

The Minnesota Historical Society Press is a member of the Association of American University Presses.

Manufactured in the United States of America

10 9 8 7 6 5 4 3 2 1

∞ The paper used in this publication meets the minimum requirements of the American National Standard for Information Sciences—Permanence for Printed Library Materials, ANSI Z39.48-1984.

International Standard Book Number
ISBN-13: 978-0-87351-725-6 (cloth)
ISBN-10: 0-87351-725-3 (cloth)
Library of Congress
Cataloging-in-Publication Data

Nathanson, Iric.

Minneapolis in the twentieth century : the growth of an American city / Iric Nathanson.
  p.  cm.
Includes bibliographical references and index.
ISBN-13: 978-0-87351-725-6
  (cloth : alk. paper)
ISBN-10: 0-87351-725-3
  (cloth : alk. paper)
1. Minneapolis (Minn.)—History—20th century.
2. City and town life—Minnesota—Minneapolis—History—20th century.
3. Minneapolis (Minn.)—Social conditions—20th century.
4. Minneapolis (Minn.)—Economic conditions—20th century.
5. Minneapolis (Minn.)—Biography.
6. Cities and towns—Minnesota—Growth—Case studies.
I. Title.
F614.M557N38 2009
977.6'579—dc22          2009023491

# Contents

*To Marlene Nathanson*

## Author's Note and Acknowledgments

In the spring of 2007, I had the opportunity to teach a course on Minneapolis history for the University of Minnesota's Osher Lifelong Learning Institute (OLLI). As a history buff with journalistic rather than academic proclivities, I had written about life in Minneapolis during the previous hundred years for a number of Twin Cities publications. Now, with the OLLI course, I had a chance to draw on my earlier work and take a more comprehensive look at my hometown and its rich past.

Initially, I planned to organize the course chronologically, with each session devoted to a separate historical period during the twentieth century. But the more I thought about the structure, the more I realized this traditional approach did not adequately convey the turmoil, energy, and sense of civic optimism that had helped define Minneapolis during the previous century. I discarded my original outline and decided to focus instead on a series of key episodes that had influenced the course of history in the City of Lakes over the longer term. I hoped this episodic approach might make Minneapolis's story more vivid and engaging for my students. My 2007 OLLI course—"Milestones in Minneapolis History"—provided the framework I have adapted for this book. I am indebted to my students and fellow elders, whose positive response encouraged me to proceed with this project.

I recognize that this framework has limited my ability to examine Minneapolis's history in a more comprehensive way. By necessity, I have not been able to give adequate attention to many broad topics, including the history of our local community institutions—particularly the schools, parks, and libraries—that helped provide continuity and stability in Minneapolis throughout its history. Their stories have been told, in part, in earlier works. Hopefully their important contributions to civic life will continue to interest local writers and historians.

*ix*

The more I immersed myself in twentieth-century Minneapolis history, the more I realized I would not be able deal with this topic with the objective detachment usually expected from authors of more traditional historical works. Writing as a lifelong Minneapolitan who has great affection for his hometown, despite its warts and blemishes, I have filtered the events described in this book through my own perceptions and outlook on the world.

Indeed, at several points, my life has intersected with these events. As a young Jew growing up on Minneapolis's near North Side, I and my family experienced the anti-Semitism examined in "The Curious Twin." During my adult years, I spent more than a decade working for congressman Don Fraser, who appears at several key points in "Struggle over Structure" and "Reimagining the Riverfront." Later, I spent twenty-two years with the city's development arm, then known as the Minneapolis Community Development Agency, which played a significant role in the events described in "Reimagining the Riverfront" and "Downtown Revival." Currently, I am on the staff of the Metropolitan Consortium of Community Developers, a nonprofit organization that deals with the housing and economic development issues discussed in the epilogue.

These many personal connections, far from limiting my understanding of Minneapolis's recent history, have made the stories I am able to tell here all the richer.

This book would not have been possible without the assistance of many friends, associates, and colleagues.

The following people reviewed and commented on sections of this book and/or provided firsthand accounts of the events described in its eight chapters: Peggy Lucas, Dick Brustad, David Riehle, Lois Binder, Georgia O'Brien, Jackie Cherryhomes Tyler, Linda Mack, Keith Ford, Don Fraser, Wally Bratt, and Jim Tennessen.

Steve Benson and Judy Schuck with OLLI encouraged me to proceed with that 2007 course on Minneapolis history.

JoEllen Haugo, Ian Stade, and Heather Lawton at the Minneapolis Central Library were always ready to help me track down that next reference to illuminate another facet of Minneapolis history.

Ellen and Ken Green, my longtime editors at *Hennepin History*, worked with me on more than a dozen local history articles. Anne Kaplan, my editor at *Minnesota History*, brought me into the MHS fold. Shannon Pennefeather, my editor for this book, kept me focused on the facts that are the building blocks for all historical works.

And finally, I want to thank my wife, Marlene. Her support and encouragement provided the inspiration that made this book possible.

# MINNEAPOLIS IN THE TWENTIETH CENTURY

# Introduction

THE TURN OF A NEW CENTURY was greeted with little fanfare in Minnesota's largest city.

"So far as Minneapolis is concerned, the year 1900 was ushered in with no more ceremony that any former year of the series 1800," the _Minneapolis Times_ observed on January 1. "The whistles steamed forth their tidings of the glad new year, the bells in the courthouse tower clanged a bit more industriously, and the policeman walking the beat allowed all sober disturbers of the peace to make just as much noise as they wanted."[1]

One hundred years later, the same courthouse bells clanged to welcome a new millennium, but there was considerably more excitement in the city's streets. "At midnight, fireworks blossomed and boomed over downtown Minneapolis alongside swaying searchlights," the _Star Tribune_ reported on January 1, 2000. "As the clock chimed 12 times at City Hall, the 'Auld Lang Syne' from the building's carillon wafted over the city."[2]

Ten decades separated those bell soundings in the courthouse tower on Fourth Street. During that time the city's population would rise and fall, two world wars and a depression would intervene, and the broad economic, social, and political waves of the twentieth century would wash over the state's largest city. Yet, despite dramatic changes occurring over a span of one hundred years, the century's beginning and its ending in Minneapolis were characterized by some remarkable similarities.

In 1900, times were good. The city was undergoing an economic boom, and jobs were plentiful—at least for men with strong backs. "Minneapolis has prospered as never before," the _Minneapolis Journal_ declared in January of that year. Then, the city's economic engine was powered by St. Anthony Falls, where a riverfront industrial district made Minneapolis the flour-milling capital of the world.[3]

One hundred years later, Minneapolis was enjoying another economic boom. The milling industry had long since disappeared, but a vibrant new urban community had taken its place on the banks of the Mississippi. All over town, paychecks were fuller than they had been in a long time, and the newspapers' classified sections were bursting with help-wanted ads.

In 1900, the city's streetcar system was poised for an expansion that would soon bring about a golden age of mass transit. One hundred years later, plans were in place for a new, more modern transit system that would operate in one of Minneapolis's most historic transportation corridors.

The century's early years also saw a burst of energy on the city's cultural front, with the establishment of a world-famous orchestra and, a decade later, the opening of an elegant new museum for the Society of Fine Arts. By 2000, the museum, now known as the Minneapolis Institute of Arts, had completed two major expansions and was planning a third. Also by then, other cultural institutions were making their own plans for dramatic new facilities which would soon become nationally acclaimed architectural landmarks.

The twentieth century may have started and ended on a high note in Minneapolis, but the intervening years saw periods of decline into the lower registers. One shift in economic fortunes occurred soon after the turn of the last century, just as a labor shortage in the skilled trades was providing a small boost for the city's fledgling labor movement. This modest advance by organized labor led the city's major employers to organize themselves in order to thwart union efforts. The employers' union—the Citizens Alliance—maintained a decades-long grip on the city's economy, until the workers' pent-up frustration exploded in violence at the height of the Great Depression.

During the early decades of the twentieth century, Minneapolis struggled not only with contentious labor relations but also with difficult social relationships. Throughout much of its history, ethnic and religious minorities were, by and large, shut out of the city's civic life. While social and economic barriers based on religion would eventually disappear, those based on race remained. Eventually, smoldering resentment over racial exclusion exploded during the turbulent decade of the 1960s, just as rancor over economic exclusion had thirty years earlier.

This book examines the high and low points of Minneapolis's history in the twentieth century by considering a series of key episodes that serve as important historical landmarks. Some of these episodes made the front pages of the daily papers and captured public attention for weeks at a time; others were all but ignored in their moment and in the years that followed. Certain of these landmarks were journalistic in nature and trained a national spotlight on serious local problems. Others involved economic events outside the city's municipal boundaries that nevertheless profoundly affected local commercial life.

Often, the responses to these difficult issues were shaped by local public and private institutions that worked in partnership to deal with serious affronts that threatened to disrupt community life. In some cases, Minneapolis was successful in overcoming the challenges it faced—particularly those physical in nature or dealing with the built environment. In others, success was more elusive as the community and its leaders grappled with endemic social and economic problems.

Throughout the last century, events were propelled by a large cast of characters, many now forgotten. There were fearless heroes who rooted out municipal corruption, charismatic leaders who challenged the economic establishment, and farsighted politicians who promoted progressive public policies. But there were also scoundrels and villains who plundered the public treasury, presided over criminal syndicates, and advocated hatred and disdain of those who did not share their religious and political views.

While the following chapters deal with a variety of social, cultural, and economic issues, this book at its core is a political history. During the last century, the massive Richardsonian Romanesque city hall on Fourth Street was at the center of Minneapolis's civic life. Through the decades, outside forces have swirled around this impressive building, buffeting its inhabitants from all directions. Those forces have emanated from the heights occupied by the city's political elites; they have also emerged from the depths of the city's shadowy underworld. Throughout the last century, a broad range of local interest groups have used election day ballots, appeals to civic virtue, intimidation, bribery, and even street violence in an effort to achieve their desired ends.

Those seeking to exert influence at city hall generally have been inspired by economic motives. Immediately after the turn of the last century, the city's crime lords successfully elected a mayor who was able, at least for a brief time, to protect their highly profitable but illicit business operations. Within a few years of that dark episode, financiers and industrialists from the very highest ranks of Minneapolis's social structure pooled their resources to thwart union organizing efforts and curb labor costs. At the height of the Great Depression, these men were able to enlist the Minneapolis Police Department to assist in suppressing labor agitation.

Following World War II, a new generation of business leaders moved away from the earlier generation's preoccupation with issues of immediate economic self-interest, instead voicing broader civic concerns focused on the need to revitalize the city's aging downtown and its obsolete industrial riverfront. Starting in the 1950s, they pressed the city's elected leaders to move more aggressively to deal with these development challenges.

Even so, day-to-day bottom line concerns had not always been the primary motivating force for Minneapolis's business leadership, even during an earlier era. At the turn of the last century, many of the city's "movers and shakers," who may have been viewed as economic reactionaries, considered themselves political reformers. In 1900, they initiated a concerted effort to overhaul Minneapolis's antiquated charter and create a strong mayoral system in city hall. Unable to overcome the substantial political forces arrayed against them, they were ultimately unsuccessful. Those same forces continued to resist moves aimed at strengthening the Minneapolis mayor's power throughout much of the twentieth century.

Soon after the end of World War II, a new constellation of interests—drawn from the city's disenfranchised ethnic and racial minorities—was able to achieve some modest political gains thanks to the support of an energetic new political leader. And later, a new political force emerged from the city's neighborhoods when local activists began demanding a role in shaping the development and transportation plans that affected their communities most directly. A high point in the citizens movement came in the 1980s, when thoughtful and politically sophisticated community leaders were able to reshape a major highway project and lay the groundwork for a whole new approach to public transportation in the Twin Cities region.

The city's elected officials often did little more than react to the outside forces pressing in on them, but some showed great resolve in chartering their own course of action in the face of such stress. Indeed, several mayors pushed back against the structural limitations of their office in order to have a broader impact in city hall.

Soon after the turn of the last century, the long-forgotten David Percy Jones faced down the city's crime lords after he succeeded the notoriously corrupt Albert Alonzo Ames as mayor in 1902. More than fifty years later and before a turn on the national stage, Hubert Humphrey had to confront the same dark forces when he occupied the mayor's office.

Farther along into the twentieth century, Humphrey's protégé Arthur Naftalin dealt with another outside force, this one propelled by street violence, when Plymouth Avenue erupted in flames during the turbulent era of urban unrest in the 1960s. Naftalin's successors faced substantial challenges, yes, but ones lacking the dramatic intensity of the Plymouth Avenue conflagration. In the 1980s, Donald Fraser, Minneapolis's longest-serving mayor, was able to combat substantial resistance to charter reform in city hall and bring about subtle but significant changes in the city's governmental structure. Fraser was succeeded by Sharon Sayles-Belton, the city's first female and African American mayor, who worked effectively behind the scenes to halt the continued decay of the city's riverfront and to promote a dramatic revival in the former milling district.

Minneapolis and its history are the focus of this book. In some cases, however, that history can be more fully illuminated by looking across the river to the city's older, more established sibling. For years, the younger of the Twin Cities has struggled to reinvent itself; meanwhile, St. Paul seems perpetually to be more comfortable in its own civic skin.

Time and again, reformers in Minneapolis tried but failed to create a new, more highly centralized governmental structure for the city. Eventually, they compromised by creating a complex system that diffused political power in city hall. At the same time, St. Paul moved almost effortlessly from one municipal arrangement to another, finally settling on a more straightforward, strong mayoral system.

Controversy and conflict have characterized Minneapolis's social and economic relationships, leading to occasional eruptions in street violence during the last century, while St. Paul can claim a much deeper tradition of racial, ethnic, and workforce harmony.

Minneapolis rebuilt its urban core, in the process obliterating a significant share of its architectural heritage, while St. Paul, less ambitious in its urban development goals, has more successfully used its built environment to preserve its sense of history.

While critics may disparage Minneapolis's reinvention efforts, supporters can counter that these efforts and the energy they generated have made urban life more vibrant there. Considering their different outlooks, Minneapolis and St. Paul seem less like twins and more like cousins who share a common lineage but have made their separate ways in the world.

One local observer in particular has attempted to explain why Minneapolis and St. Paul have moved along such separate paths, even with their adjoining geographies. Minnesota historian Mary Lethert Wingerd traces the origins of those separate paths to widely divergent social and economic conditions in the two cities at the turn of the last century.

"[In Minneapolis] a small cohort of powerful capitalists—families of the original New England settlers—jealously guarded control of the city which had been the preeminent milling and manufacturing center of the Northwest," Wingerd writes. "They dominated politics, finance, and business and successfully dictated the terms between business and labor. As a result of such closely held power and social exclusivity, class and ethnic tensions made Minneapolis a divided city, where claims of common civic community rang hollow."[4]

In contrast, "an uncertain economy and a more permeable stratum of elites created a different set of social dynamics [in St. Paul]. These dynamics in turn relied on negotiation and compromise among a broad set of players—including working people—to keep the city functioning."[5]

Wingerd's observations point up a central paradox that has defined much of Minneapolis's history during the twentieth century. The city's early leaders brought with them from the East an ideal of civic engagement based on the New England model of participatory town hall democracy. Yet these leaders put those same ideals into practice only within their own elite group, excluding those who did not share their common ancestry. With this exclusionary pattern in place during the early 1900s, Minneapolis faced troubled times as labor strife and social divisiveness impeded civic unity at a time when the collapse of the milling industry was causing economic decline. Only after World War II, as many barriers began to disappear, did the early leaders' ideals take root and flourish. The postwar years saw the creation of one of the nation's first municipal fair employment agencies and ambitious plans to stem urban blight and revive the city's central business district.

While exclusion had once been one of the city's defining characteristics, inclusion now became a recognized objective. Indeed, during the postwar era, civic engagement on a broad range of fronts became a driving force for improvement in Minneapolis. Urban historian Jon Teaford might well have been referring to this city when he wrote in 1986, "in response to every urban problem there were a dozen proposals promising a better future. Scholars, architects, planners and civic minded citizens did not throw up their hands in exasperation and conclude that the unsatisfactory status quo was the best of all possible worlds. Instead, a degree of optimism and willingness to adapt and reform prevailed."[6]

From a vantage point at the end of the first decade of the new millennium, this book looks back at an earlier era, when civic optimism prevailed and civic engagement contributed to a quality of life that made Minneapolis one of the preeminent American cities of the twentieth century.

# Struggle over Structure

T. B. WALKER could barely contain his anger. Minneapolis was about to get a "dictator," Walker thundered in a letter to the editor of the *Minneapolis Tribune*. The influential civic leader's strong words were provoked by an ambitious plan in 1900 to overhaul the city's charter. A passionate opponent of charter reform, Walker had parted company with fellow members of the local elite who were determined to overhaul what they viewed as the city's outmoded governmental structure and replace it with a system that centralized political power in the hands of the mayor.[1]

Throughout the next one hundred years, the seemingly arcane issue of governmental structure would continue to arouse passions like Walker's. More than once, the term *dictator* would be used by opponents of the various plans to establish a strong mayoral form of government for Minneapolis.

## Striving for Home Rule

The origins of the city's governmental structure extend back to 1856, when the frontier settlement of Minneapolis, on the west bank of the Mississippi River, received its act of incorporation from the Minnesota Territorial Legislature. A year earlier, the town of St. Anthony, across the river on the east bank, had been incorporated by the legislature.

Following the Civil War, Minneapolis soon overtook St. Anthony in size and prominence. Seventeen years after it was first incorporated, St. Anthony lost its separate civic identity and was swallowed up by its west-side neighbor in a new municipal charter established by the Minnesota Legislature in 1872.

During the latter decades of the nineteenth century, as Minneapolis and St. Paul experienced explosive growth, both cities faced the need to revamp their governmental structures to accommodate this rapid change. But each time a charter change was proposed, the cities were required to approach the Minnesota Legislature, hat in hand, requesting legislative authorization to make changes. The state's major cities found that they were at the mercy of a statewide legislative body not always responsive to their needs and interests.

Finally, in 1896, the cities were able to lift the heavy hand of the legislature through a "home rule" amendment to the state constitution, which enabled them to adopt and amend their own charters through a local election process, without first seeking state legislative approval. The home rule amendment set Minneapolis and St. Paul on separate paths that would continue to diverge for more than one hundred years. Even though they would all but merge in a geographical sense, the two cities would create quite different governmental structures for themselves—a difference which would continue up through modern times.

In 1898, Minneapolis and St. Paul both sought to take advantage of the new home rule amendment but both failed to gain voter approval for their charter changes. "It was a great mistake to have incorporated so many desirable reforms in this first edition of the new charter . . . it invited attack at so many points from such an array of interests as to make its defeat almost certain," the *St. Paul Pioneer Press* editorialized.[2]

Two years later, Minneapolis and St. Paul were ready to try again to achieve home rule. The start of a new century proved a pivotal year in the history of municipal government in both cities. In 1900, St. Paul charter advocates successfully sought to implement reforms, adopting in May a new charter with overwhelming popular support and setting in place a strong mayoral system for Minnesota's capital city. Seven months later, Minneapolis voters rejected their own home rule charter—an electoral outcome repeated throughout most of the twentieth century, as one charter reform plan after another went down to defeat in the larger of the adjoining cities. These electoral defeats left Minneapolis with a municipal structure once described as a "hodgepodge" by the city's own charter commission.[3]

### Moving Ahead in St. Paul

In April 1900, as the charter election drew near, the *St. Paul Pioneer Press* gave its readers a series of reasons why they should vote for the new civic document. The first and most important reason, according to the *Pioneer Press*, was the charter's home rule provision. "Even if the charter contained objectionable features, this one consideration would far outweigh any conceivable objection to it," the paper maintained. "Once adopted, it can be easily amended without asking permission of Minneapolis and Duluth, which is now necessary . . . It makes St. Paul a self-governing autonomy, with all necessary powers within the limits of the constitution and the general laws of the state vested in the people of the city for managing their own affairs."[4]

In addition to conferring home rule authority on the City of St. Paul, the 1900 charter broadened the appointment power of the mayor, who was given direct control over the city's public works department. The commissioner of public works, previously appointed by the quasi-independent public works commission, would now become a mayoral appointee. The charter also diminished the authority of individual aldermen. In the past, they were able to authorize the placement of streetlights in their wards; in the future, this function would be performed by the citywide public works department.

A key charter provision established ground rules for the allocation of public franchises, including that of the Twin City Rapid Transit Company. This latter provision did not sit well with leaders of the powerful, privately owned transit company, which controlled public transportation in both cities. The *Pioneer Press* surmised that the company and certain other local franchises would, "in all probability," like to see the charter defeated. "But," it noted, "if they are doing anything in that direction they are doing it so quietly that it has escaped observation."[5]

The week before the charter election, one of St. Paul's other major dailies, the *Globe,* noted that "no opposition has been openly made to the Charter . . . No interest in the city, political or otherwise, is concerned in its defeat. On the contrary, the entire commercial community is profoundly interested in its success." On May 2, the day after the election, the *St. Paul Dispatch* declared that the charter had carried overwhelming, winning support in every city precinct. "Comparatively Few Votes," fewer than three thousand, "Recorded Against It," the paper reported.[6]

### An Unsuccessful Campaign in Minneapolis

The Minneapolis Charter Commission represented the pinnacle of the city's political and economic power structure. The fifteen-member commission included men like Alexander Ankeny, William Hale, Fred Bell, and August Darelius—many of whom were born in New England and most of whom shared a Waspish pedigree. None of the names on the commission's membership list indicated any direct ties to the huge number of foreign born

*St. Paul voters approved a new charter in 1900, but Minneapolis voters rejected their proposed charter that same year. "Minne" gazes enviously at St. Paul in a* Minneapolis Journal *cartoon.*

who constituted more than 30 percent of the city's population. The commission's complex charter, unveiled in the summer of 1900, contained thirty-two separate sections. The document's main thrust was to tip the balance of power in city hall away from the city council and toward the mayor. Under the 1881 charter, then in effect, the mayor did little more than appoint the police chief and hold seats on several local boards. Under the new plan, he would appoint the city engineer, the fire chief, the superintendent of the water department, and the building inspector, along with the members of half a dozen key city commissions.

The plan limited the city council to a mainly legislative role, stripping away its power to hire and fire city department heads.

The twenty-six-member council itself was also restructured. In 1900, the council comprised two members from each of the city's thirteen wards. The new plan added a fourteenth ward but also called for a single member from each district. In order to gain a citywide perspective, the charter added six at-large positions, for a total of twenty council seats.

Almost immediately, the city's major daily, the *Minneapolis Journal*, began a concerted effort to generate support for the proposed charter. The paper published a series of guest editorials by noted local historian Horace B. Hudson, who used a question-and-answer format to explain the charter's merits to the *Journal's* readers. In an early editorial, Hudson examined the form of municipal organization then in effect in Minneapolis. The city had what was considered a council form of government, he explained:

> [In a "council" government] the city council is the chief authority—both legislative and executive. The council not only passes ordinances, appropriates money and determines how it is to be spent, but it also spends it, lets its contracts and carries out the work and finally approves its own bills. The council also manages the several departments of the government, through committees, and appoints and removes the heads of such departments at pleasure. The mayor remains something of a figurehead. At present the mayor of Minneapolis has practically no appointive power except in the police department. The charter makes him accountable for the conduct of the departments, but gives him absolutely no power to enforce such authority except through legal proceedings.[7]

Hudson's analysis, by and large, accurately described charter arrangements in Minneapolis for the next eighty years. The *Journal* and its allies knew that the 1900 charter faced strong opposition from the city's labor interests, who believed the current council system gave them more political leverage. In 1900, local labor unions were engaged in a series of bitter battles with a group of Minneapolis industrialists who would soon form the virulently antilabor Citizens Alliance. "Some of the self-appointed guides and leaders of working people, in respect to this charter matter, are doing all they can to secure the defeat of the proposed measure," the *Journal* declared. But Minneapolis workers were being misled by their leaders, the paper maintained: "Working

people . . . secured the incorporation into the charter of everything that they asked for . . . labor will make the mistake of its life
if it turns down this charter."[8]

Despite the *Journal's* exhortations, Minneapolis labor leaders,
guided by their own economic interests, believed they did not err
by opposing the proposed charter. In later years, these labor activists would take a hard line against charter reform, knowing
that many of the reform advocates were the same men who lined
up against the unions at the bargaining tables and worked behind
the scenes in the Citizens Alliance to thwart the aims of organized
labor.[9]

In 1900, the *Journal,* like other newspapers of its day, felt no
obligation to provide editorial space to those who did not share its
views. During the weeks leading up to the city charter election, labor leaders and other charter opponents were not given an opportunity to reply to Hudson and to the *Journal's* own unsigned
editorials. Charter opponents found an outlet in another city daily,
the *Minneapolis Times,* which took a measured approach to the
issue of charter reform, finding some merit in the proposed civic
documents. In an editorial published during the week prior to the
charter election, the *Times* commented on the "desirability of a
new charter which would fit the adult city better than the current
one." Initially, the *Times* had been prepared to support a new
charter, but the paper had found one "fatal flaw" in the new document: the concentration of excessive power in the mayor's office.
"The mayor is given dangerous and autocratic power. Denial of
this, no matter how vociferous and insistent does not, cannot, alter the facts," the paper maintained.[10]

T. B. Walker, probably the city's most influential charter opponent, made an even stronger case against the reorganization proposal. Walker rejected the proponents' claim that the charter
would take the police department out of politics by bringing the
members of the force into the civil service system. "This charter
provides that the mayor shall appoint chief of police, and this chief
of police, which means the mayor, himself, shall appoint the whole
force," Walker noted. "The Mayor appoints the civil service commissioners, and they make rules on which he may make new se-
lections or fill vacancies. This [police] department is just as much

in the hands and control of the mayor under the new charter as under the old one."[11]

Walker was also skeptical about the reformist impact of a civil service system. "In a rightly conducted government civil service rules are not much needed, and in a corrupt government they place but a very limited amount of check upon corrupt deals and official patronage. This provision was brought into this charter to try and make people believe that all the vast power placed in the hands of the mayor, which everywhere else has been used for corrupt purposes, would be so checked and limited," he maintained.[12]

In 1900, as he marshaled his arguments against the charter, Walker had no way of knowing that municipal corruption of astounding proportions would soon take hold in city hall with the election of Albert Alonzo Ames as mayor. In the end, the charter went down to defeat on November 6, gaining only 43 percent of the vote. In a voting pattern repeated in later elections, the new charter carried in southeast's Second Ward and in the silk-stocking lake district wards but lost by large margins in the heavily working-class North Side and Northeast wards. The *Minneapolis Journal,* a staunch advocate for a losing cause, was clearly envious of progress made on charter reform across the river. "We shall be at a disadvantage," the paper observed, somewhat ruefully.[13]

## *Looking Back at the Political and Social Dynamics*

By the close of the first year of the new century, Minnesota's two largest cities had approached the issue of municipal organization quite differently. More than one hundred years later, the question remains: why did charter reform succeed in St. Paul but fail in Minneapolis in 1900? Two political cartoons from the period could help explain the difference. The first, in the *St. Paul Pioneer Press,* shows three symbolic figures working together to roll the new charter down the municipal highway. Each represents one of the three major voting blocs: the independents, the Republicans, and the Democrats. A second cartoon, this one in the *Minneapolis Journal,* shows a quite different scene: a disreputable gang of opponents throwing rotten eggs and vegetables at the new charter.

Clearly, civic leaders in St. Paul had been able to achieve a broad political consensus in support of charter reform, but con-

PUSHING A GOOD THING ALONG.

*In St. Paul, civic unity prevailed as the city's various political forces, illustrated here in a* Pioneer Press *cartoon, worked together to approve a new charter in 1900.*

sensus was not possible in Minneapolis. In 1900, reformers in Minneapolis had persuaded themselves that they were "good government" advocates, operating above the political fray. In fact, they were proposing to alter the distribution of local political power, and this effort at redistribution provoked a strong reaction, as similar attempts would throughout the twentieth century.

Writing in 2001, historian Mary Lethert Wingerd explored the political and social differences between Minneapolis and St. Paul at the start of the last century. While Wingerd did not deal directly with municipal organization in the two cities, her analysis could help explain why the charter campaign succeeded in St. Paul but failed in Minneapolis. By the turn of the

HIS FRIENDS THE ENEMY.
Minneapolis—I Love You for the Enemies You Have Made.

*In Minneapolis, charter reform was embroiled in controversy in 1900
as reform opponents, depicted in a Journal cartoon, attacked the plan
to establish a strong mayoral system in city hall.*

last century, the economies of the two cities were diverging significantly. Minneapolis had become an economic powerhouse,
one of the country's major milling centers. But St. Paul was not
keeping pace with its more robust twin. Since its founding
more than fifty years earlier, Minnesota's capital city had been
a regional trading center with an economy fueled by commercial connections throughout the Midwest. However, those connections were starting to fray as Minneapolis began elbowing
its older sibling out of the wholesaling and transportation business. At the same time, St. Paul's manufacturing sector was
languishing. By 1900, St. Paul lagged substantially behind
Minneapolis in terms of total economic output.[14]

Building on this analysis, Wingerd noted,

Faced with such hard facts, St. Paul civic leaders were forced to discard metropolitan aspirations and focus their energies on a defensive strategy to keep the city's position from eroding further—a project that would require interclass investment in civic loyalty. Boosterism was redirected at a new audience— the residents of St. Paul—in a campaign to turn the city's liabilities into virtues. Smaller was better, so the rhetoric went. St. Paul, unlike its rival across the river, cared about its citizens. St. Paul was not a heartless industrial machine; it was a community. The bonds of community then logically demanded that St. Paulites patronize local businesses, support the Democratic Party and keep their dollars and their votes out of the grasping hands of Minneapolis. The other side of community accountability required businesses to make considerable concessions to working-class residents of the city. Both business and labor had much to gain from such a pact, and they worked together to construct a fortress of localism that would engage St. Paulites, across class and ethnic differences, in a common loyalty to the city.[15]

This interclass solidarity was not at all the case in Minneapolis, where the city's economic elite had little incentive to make concessions to their largely immigrant workforce, according to Wingerd. In Minneapolis, "the milling, manufacturing and machine tool industries that powered its economy served a national rather than a local market. These industries depended on a large-scale industrial work force—people primarily of immigrant stock who shared few common bonds with their employers. The corridors of power in Minneapolis remained the exclusive province of the Old Stock families. All of this fostered economic and social priorities quite unlike those of St. Paul," she noted.[16]

Wingerd's observations, more than a century later, could help explain why labor and ethnic interests in St. Paul largely acquiesced to that city's new charter in 1900 while similar interests strongly opposed charter reform just across the river in Minneapolis. Minneapolis civic leaders would propose new governmental organizational plans in 1904, 1906, 1907, and 1913, but each time they were rebuffed by voters. Finally, in 1920, the local electorate agreed to a charter plan which gave Minneapolis home rule—but at a price. In order to win popular support, the city's charter commission merely codified the existing municipal governmental system into a new charter and abandoned any attempt to overhaul and reform it.

Nine years later, the *Minneapolis Journal* editorialized again on the need for charter reform—this time in the wake of the 1929 city council corruption scandals that sent four aldermen to jail. "Our municipal government in Minneapolis is carried on, down to the minutest details, by Council committees," the *Journal* noted.

There is a Purchasing Agent, but he is not permitted to purchase. He makes recommendations, after getting bids or prices, but the committees do as they please. So with licenses or permits. They are granted under the operation of no system of standard rules, but each case is passed on by some committee according to the whims or desires of its majority.

We have a council form of government, in which the Council not only legislates, but administers. Not only is such a system wrong in principle and thoroughly unbusinesslike, but it multiplies opportunities for corrupt deals. Where there is opportunity, it is all but certain there will be graft.

The remedy? Divorce the administrative functions from the legislative functions. Give the legislative work to the Council, and the administrative work to a City Manager, working through subordinates appointed by and responsible to him, and dependent for retention of his position on his record of honesty and efficiency.

That, after all, is the supreme lesson of this graft investigation for the people of Minneapolis. Let them follow the example of more than three hundred American cities, and set this City free from the evils and abuses of the present municipal system. Let them order administrative authority concentrated in one man—and then watch that man.[17]

Despite the determined editorial efforts of the city's leading papers, Minneapolis retained its weak mayoral system, in which the city's chief executive had little direct control over the machinery of local government. After 1920, reformers continued—unsuccessfully—to push for a full-scale, strong mayoral system in Minneapolis. Throughout the twentieth century and into the twenty-first, Minnesota's two largest cities continued to differ in their approach to municipal organization. St. Paul overhauled its charter in 1914, adopting a commission system that gave individual city council members administrative authority over city departments. Fifty-six years later, in 1970, St. Paul abandoned the commission system and returned to a strong mayoral form of local government.

## A Failed Attempt in 1948

In the mid-1940s, Minneapolis mayor Hubert Humphrey was able to use his charisma and his considerable powers of persuasion to overcome the structural limitations of his office—at least in part. But even Humphrey realized he needed more than the bully pulpit to accomplish everything he wanted to do in city hall. When he ran for reelection in 1947, he made charter reform a key plank in his platform. As a candidate, Humphrey won widespread support from a broad array of the city's political forces. Organized labor backed him enthusiastically, as it had in 1945. The heads of the major business groups served on his campaign committee, and all the city newspapers endorsed his reelection bid. In June, he demolished his opponent by a vote of nearly two to one, an all-time city record.

But many of Humphrey's supporters knew his seat in the mayor's chair was not permanent, and they were reluctant to expand the powers of his office. Some Republican business leaders, while applauding the work he had done in city hall, were not sure they wanted to give him another political victory that he could use to boost his campaign to defeat the state's incumbent Republican senator in the 1948 election.

Humphrey's biographer, Carl Solberg, would later write, "The blue-ribbon committee [Humphrey] had named to draw up a restructured government for Minneapolis held more meetings than any other. But labor had misgivings from the first. The council members, many of whom had union ties, figuring their friend would not always be mayor, drew back from enlarging the powers of the mayor's office."[18]

Humphrey, hoping to outmaneuver charter reform opponents, decided to force the issue when a financial crisis at the board of education threatened to curtail school services. The mayor pushed for a vote on the new charter as frustration was building over proposed school cutbacks. But his push only served to strengthen the resolve of city council and labor leaders aligned in opposition to Humphrey and his charter overhaul plan. One of those leaders told the popular mayor that, because of charter reform, "the relationship between you and the CIO and AFL is to say the least considerably strained." Opponents sued to block the charter reform referendum and got backing from a state supreme court ruling that declared the charter language improperly drawn. Humphrey and his supporters reworked the charter plan to comply with the court order and submitted it for a vote in the fall of 1948, when it went down to defeat. The mayor expressed disappointment, but in truth he had become more concerned about other, more sweeping issues as he prepared to move on to Washington, DC, and the U.S. Senate.[19]

### A Bitter Fight in 1960

Twelve years later, charter reform proponents were ready to try again to revamp the city's governmental structure. By now, a Republican, P. Kenneth Peterson, occupied the mayor's seat in city hall. Reformers organized the Charter Improvement Volunteer Information Committee, or CIVIC, to push for an ambitious plan which would make the mayor the city's chief executive officer. The CIVIC charter stripped the city council of its appointment powers and gave the mayor the authority to select the city attorney, fire chief, director of public works, and planning director, among other offices. The charter also eliminated the park board, the library board, and the board of estimate and taxation as independently elected bodies and made their members mayoral appointees.

Under the reform plan, the city council would become a legislative body with the ability to appoint little more than its own staff. Not surprisingly, the city council, unwilling to see its powers sharply curtailed, campaigned vigorously to defeat the CIVIC charter. The *Minneapolis Tribune*, by then the chief public advocate for charter reform, took note of the council's opposition in a May 31 editorial: "The amazing aspect of the Minneapolis charter revision campaign is the frantic opposition of the alderman and some other city hall officials," the paper declared. "[They] want no tinkering with the status quo."[20]

When the city's police federation joined forces with the city council in a campaign to defeat the CIVIC plan, the *Tribune* hinted that the group was acting inappropriately. "Police Foes of Charter Use City Hall Facilities," a *Tribune* headline declared as the vote on the plan drew near. The paper's story revealed that "Vote No" signs were being stored at police headquarters: "About 100 signs mounted on stakes were seen over the weekend stacked in the police roll call room on the ground floor of city hall." Next to the signs in the roll call room, the head of the police federation, Carl Johnson, had posted a notice urging members to oppose the charter: "the campaign to deprive you of the right to vote for a number of candidates for public offices . . . is now in full swing. We who are opposed to this dictatorship charter must now, in the last week of the campaign, put on an all out effort to get out the vote and vote no."[21]

The theme of dictatorship was played up by the *Minneapolis Labor Review*, a vigorous opponent of the CIVIC charter. "Read-Study Dictator Charter Column 7 This Page" a *Labor Review* headline called out during the week before the charter election. In the story accompanying the headline, the *Review* reported on a statement by Walter H. Wheeler, identified by the paper as "a nationally-known consulting engineer." Wheeler told the labor party that the proposed charter would make the mayor "the absolute dictator of the city hall in reality, and as a matter of practical politics."[22]

On the editorial pages of the *Tribune*, the pros and cons of charter reform were debated in more moderate terms. "A charter should be sound and up to date at the outset, for once a provision is adopted it is very difficult to change. The proposed charter does not possess these attributes," noted Mrs. T. O. Everson, a member of the "Vote No" Committee. But J. Leonard Erickson had a different view: "On June 7, we will have a once-in-a-decade opportunity to modernize Minneapolis city government . . . Let us go to the polls on June 7 and vote 'yes' for the CIVIC charter," he declared.[23]

In the end, the CIVIC charter was decisively defeated by a vote of 54,730 to 43,819, virtually the same margin suffered by the Humphrey-backed plan in 1948. And, in a pattern extending back to 1900, the wards in the lake district and in the neighborhoods around the university voted "yes" while the labor wards on the north and south sides voted "no." The *Tribune* was disappointed with the results but hopeful for the future. "The campaign for better government and a better city of Minneapolis will continue in spite of Tuesday's setback," the paper observed. "The campaign simply will have to be waged with better educational programs and with a broader base of support."[24]

The *Tribune* may have been hopeful, but the *Minneapolis Labor Review* was triumphant. In a slap at the daily paper's editorial position, the *Review* declared, "Minneapolis Voters Smash News Trust City Dictator Plan!" It went on to report, "Minneapolis voters Tuesday once again registered their emphatic protest against an attempt to put over a dictator charter for Minneapolis that would rob the people of their right to vote for practically all offices in city government." Eventually, passions would subside and charter reformers would try again in 1967 to win support for a strong mayoral plan. Once again they would fail.[25]

## Reviving the Reform Campaign

In the 1980s, as the scars of battle began to heal, a new generation of advocates took up the cause of charter reform, only to rub raw those earlier wounds. Often in the past, various groups of self-appointed local civic leaders, considering themselves "good government" crusaders, had spearheaded charter reform. But the new efforts in the eighties were organized not by unelected leaders but by the city's mayor, former Fifth District congressman Donald Fraser, who was first elected to the city hall post in 1979. The year before, while still serving in the U.S. House of Representatives, Fraser had run for the U.S. Senate and been upset in the DFL primary by a maverick local businessman, Bob Short. The defeated senatorial candidate had come back to his hometown, bringing with him a huge reservoir of good will built up during sixteen years as Minneapolis's congressional representative.[26]

In the DFL Party's 1979 endorsing convention, Fraser had elbowed aside city council president Lou DeMars, who had hoped to succeed the city's incumbent DFL mayor, Al Hofstede. Hofstede had taken the DFL establishment by surprise when he announced that he would not be a candidate for reelection. Once Fraser arrived in city hall in January 1980, he found the environment anything but welcoming. Almost immediately, he became involved in brawls with city council leaders who were not in the least awed by

Fraser's national credentials as a courageous liberal and early opponent of the war in Vietnam.

By May, five months after Fraser had taken office, First Ward
alderman Walt Dziedzic was describing mayor-council relations
as a "war." For his part, the new mayor complained about the levels of "pettiness" and "paranoia" in his dealings with the council.
The city hall conflicts inspired more than name-calling. Serious issues involving the future of the city's economic development
efforts were at stake. A citizens task force headed by local banker
John McHugh had recommended consolidation of Minneapolis's
fragmented economic development programs under the authority of a city council appointee, the city coordinator. But this reorganization would have shifted power and authority away from the
mayoral appointees who oversaw the city's industrial development
commission and its housing and redevelopment authority. Fraser
was not at all pleased with the task force recommendations: "It is
very difficult for me to argue that [the task force proposal] advances our effort to resolve our internal problems," the mayor observed. In the end, the council and the mayor were able to work
out their difference over economic development, but tension remained in their relationship. "I think the Mayor is a little over-
sensitive," remarked council president Alice Rainville when asked
to comment on Fraser's paranoia statement. "He'll have to develop
a thicker skin. This is a proud City Council, and history has shown
that we managed this city very well. I don't think he was prepared
for this."[27]

During his early years in city hall, the usually mild-mannered
Fraser became increasingly frustrated by the council's ability to
use its considerable institutional powers to thwart his agenda.
Like Humphrey and fellow DFLer Arthur Naftalin, Fraser eventually realized that he needed to strengthen his office if he was going
to be a significant force in city hall. Not until his ninth year as
mayor did Fraser begin a concerted effort to overhaul the city
charter.

In his January 1988 state of the city address, Fraser proposed
two alternative plans to substantially increase the mayor's power.
One awarded the mayor sole appointing power over all department heads, subject to council approval. The second made the
mayor the council's chief presiding officer, lacking a vote but with

the power to veto council actions. Once again, as T. B. Walker had done in 1900, a charter reform opponent raised the specter of dictatorship. "He wants a Napoleon style of government," First Ward council member Dziedzic thundered, brushing his hair down over his forehead and thrusting his arm across his chest in imitation of the nineteenth-century French military leader. City council president Rainville used more temperate words to dismiss Fraser's plan: "A strong Council close to the people of Minneapolis is a great strength. To dilute that would be a great loss." "Leave the tinkering to the Humphrey Institute," declared Third Ward council member Sandra Hilary disdainfully.[28]

The Fraser plan unleashed a major battle that would preoccupy city leaders for much of 1988. "The thunder claps rolling out of

*Don Fraser, imagined in a 1988 Twin Cities Reader sketch, was accused of acting like Napoleon and fostering a dictatorial regime in city hall because he sought to increase the mayor's powers.*

City Hall are the sounds of battle among politicians who are either zealously guarding their turf or seeking additional authority," *Minneapolis Tribune* reporter Dennis McGrath later wrote.[29]

When the time came for Fraser to present his overhaul plan to the Minneapolis Charter Commission in May, he backed off from the more ambitious of the two proposals outlined in his state of the city address. Rather than consolidating appointment power in the mayor, as he had suggested in January, Fraser urged the commission to approve a charter change that would make the mayor presiding officer of the city council. The Fraser plan would give the mayor indirect authority over city department heads through authority to nominate them to the council's executive committee. The committee, whose members included the mayor, would vote up or down on the mayor's recommendation but could only consider nominations made by the mayor. Fraser's charter overhaul plan was intended to move Minneapolis closer to St. Paul's version, in which the mayor appointed municipal department heads.

Fraser described his plan as a "strong mayor–strong council option" and "a modest, incremental step in clarifying responsibility for running City Hall," but council members saw the plan as anything but modest. "If the mayor came up to the third floor more often, we would have more collaboration," observed Rainville, who viewed the charter proposal as an unwarranted attempt to dilute council authority.[30]

The city's charter commission agreed with Rainville and declined to approve Fraser's plan. "I kind of get gun shy on changes," one commission member observed. "I always thought we were so much more progressive than St. Paul. To go into their way of doing business, I figure it might be a step backwards." Without the backing of the fifteen-member commission, Fraser and his supporters were forced to circulate petitions in order to place the proposal on November's general election ballot.[31]

Fraser was not the only Minneapolis politician who circulated charter petitions during the summer of 1988. Twelfth Ward council member Dennis Schulstad had come up with his own three-part plan to overhaul city hall. Schulstad proposed reducing the size of the council from thirteen to nine members, eliminating party designation for city offices, and staggering the terms of the mayor and the council so they would not run in the same year.

Like Fraser, Schulstad had been rebuffed by the charter commission, leading him also to take to the streets to petition his way onto the Minneapolis election ballot.

Both city hall politicians had no difficulty gathering the five thousand-plus signatures that assured them a place on the November ballot, but a vote was all the petitioning got them. According to the charter amendment process, the city council, not the proposals' authors, determined the language of the amendments. When Fraser saw the council's initial draft of his proposal, the usually even-tempered mayor flew into a rage. Fraser charged that the council's language was misleading and deliberately designed to defeat his proposal. He was also angry about the council's plan to position his proposal on the ballot in a way that, he said, would make it difficult for voters to distinguish between his plan and Schulstad's. After threatening to sue the council and trading barbs with several of its members, Fraser was finally able to have some new language more to his liking inserted, but he was still not completely mollified. "If somebody's about to shoot you and you're able to avoid being shot and that's a victory, then I guess I won," Fraser said after the language controversy had finally been settled.[32]

This skirmish in the 1988 charter battle came only a few days after a brouhaha over a letter circulated by Peter Hutchinson, then a vice president with the Dayton Hudson Company. Hutchinson's letter, written on Dayton Hudson letterhead, urged downtown business leaders to endorse Fraser's charter plan and to make contributions to a campaign organized to win votes for it. Hutchinson's letter angered city council leaders, who charged that it represented a possible violation of state campaign finance laws. "If the letter isn't illegal, it's improper and represents an attempt by the city's large corporations to decide the outcome of the city election," one council member declared. Fraser fired back: "This seems to be part of a guerrilla war. A number of people are being called by Council members with the intimation that they have to do business with the City Council and they ought to take that into consideration. That's intimidation."[33]

In the weeks leading up to the November 8 election, Fraser campaigned furiously for his amendment, saying that he "would be all over this city talking to people," trying to explain the amendment to them. In response, the council fielded what it called "a truth squad" to counter the mayor's criticisms of the current city hall system.[34]

In the charter battle's final days, the Hutchinson letter continued to draw sparks. Some council members, backed by several of the city's major labor leaders, saw Dayton Hudson's involvement as an effort by downtown business interests to cut the council's power. "It's all rich people. They're trying to buy an election which will center control on one person," declared Dziedzic. Council vice president Tony Scallon called on Fraser to disclose why his campaign had received such a sizeable contribution from the Dayton Hudson Company. "He should be embarrassed by that. Dayton's wants something back," Scallon charged. "What [the Council] say[s] is complete and utter nonsense, and they know it," Hutchinson replied. "What they're saying looks good in print and makes them feel better, but it has no relation to our role in the community." In the end, neither Fraser nor Schulstad was successful in wining support for his proposal at the polls on November 8, the same day George H. Bush defeated Michael Dukakis for the U.S. presidency.[35]

Schulstad's amendment to reduce the size of the city council lost by a vote of nearly two to one, and his proposal to eliminate party designation on the city ballot lost by an even larger margin. Fraser's amendment did much better, garnering a respectable 47 percent of the vote. The mayor, encouraged by this showing, indicated that he would continue working to restructure city government. The next year, Fraser returned with a new, more focused plan to revamp the city charter. Fraser's 1989 amendment made a subtle but significant change in the authority of the city's executive committee, the five-member group that included the mayor, the city council president, and three other council members. Fraser had spurred creation of the committee during an early term as a way of managing the appointment of city department heads. His 1989 amendment allowed the mayor to continue the practice of recommending appointments to the executive committee, which in turn could forward these recommendations to the full council for a confirmation vote.

Under Fraser's revised charter language, the executive committee could vote the mayor's recommendation up or down, but it could not substitute any other names. In other words, the mayor controlled the department head selection process. If the executive committee was displeased with the mayor's nomination, it could only stand by and wait to receive a name more to its liking. While the mayor did not have the direct power to fire a department head, he could refuse to recommend reappointment of that person at the end of his or her two-year term. In effect, the amendment gave the mayor the power to hire and fire, albeit indirectly.

This new plan was not eagerly embraced by many on the city council, who saw it as another, more camouflaged attempt to dilute their power. Led by Ninth Ward council member Scallon, the council drafted its own competing charter amendment, which would have weakened rather than strengthened the executive committee's authority. This time, Fraser prevailed. In the 1989 city election, which earned him a fourth term, Fraser's amendment was approved with 60.4 percent of the vote. Scallon's competing amendment lost by a margin of nearly two to one.

### Assessing the Charter Battles of the 1980s

Looking back at his fourteen years in city hall, Don Fraser notes that he got much of what he wanted in the way of charter reform: "I think the Executive Committee system has worked pretty well. The Mayor does have the power of appointment even if it is indirect. There is a public perception that we have a weak mayor system, but people can't tell me what that means." Dennis Schulstad agrees. "The Mayor has immense power in Minneapolis," says Schulstad, who gave up his Twelfth Ward council seat in 1997. "Every department head in City Hall knows that the Mayor controls their fate, so they are going to pay attention to what he says. It may not look that way, but we really have a strong mayor system."[36]

But into the twenty-first century, the perception persists that Minneapolis lacks a strong mayoral system. This misreading has influenced reality, notwithstanding claims by Fraser and Schulstad that the mayor's office has more inherent powers than it did prior to the charter changes of the mid-1980s. To accomplish business in city hall, groups and individuals believe they need to lobby the mayor and the city council on equal terms—and this conviction continues to preserve and enhance the council's role. The executive committee system, institutionalized by Fraser, requires a strong degree of collegiality between the mayor and council leaders. In the absence of such a friendly relationship, the system could lead to a stalemate between opposing political forces in city hall.

Even though the charter changes of the 1980s have strengthened the mayor's ability to oversee the operation of various city departments, those changes have not provided the clear chain of command seen in a city manager system, where administrative responsibilities are centralized in one appointed official—the city manager—who answers to a local government's political leadership. Despite some administrative reorganization in recent years, the executive committee continues to oversee the work of nine separate department heads. Meanwhile, a complicated network of independent boards and commissions operates outside the executive committee's direct control.[37]

At the turn of the last century, charter reformers hoped to establish what they viewed as a clean, orderly form of local government for Minneapolis that would consolidate power and authority in the box at the top of the organizational chart marked "Mayor." More than one hundred years later, that goal remains elusive. Back then, charter reform failed, but Minneapolis politics moved in a direction that reformers had not anticipated. In 1900, the city elected a mayor who was clearly not a reformer: Albert Alonzo Ames. Ironically, had charter reform passed in that year, the results, at least in the short term, would have been anything but the clean, orderly government a strong mayoral system was intended to deliver.

# MINNEAPOLIS:
# Who's in charge?

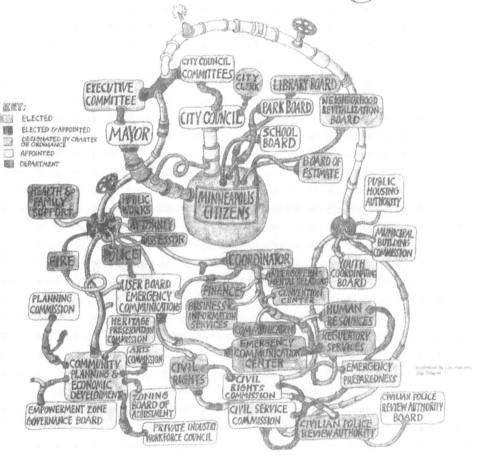

In 2004, the Star Tribune depicted Minneapolis city government as a Rube Goldberg machine comprised of convoluted and confusing parts.

# The Shame of Minneapolis

THE CRUSADING CIVIC REFORMER was seething with outrage when he confronted the mayor of Minneapolis on the steps of city hall. "Yes, Doc Ames . . . I'm after you," Hovey C. Clarke declared angrily. "I've been in this town for seventeen years, and all that time you've been a moral leper . . . Now, I'm going to put you where all contagious things are put—where you cannot contaminate anyone else." The object of Clarke's wrath, Albert Alonzo Ames, would soon be driven out of town in disgrace as a municipal corruption scandal of amazing proportions unfolded in city hall in 1902.[1]

Two years earlier, Minneapolis voters had defeated the strong mayoral charter supported by many of Clarke's fellow reformers. If it had passed, the new charter would have enabled Ames to cause even more damage than he managed to during his eighteen months in office.

In 1902, the scandal was merely a local story, but soon the entire country learned about "The Shame of Minneapolis." In January 1903, Lincoln Steffens, a New York journalist, turned a national spotlight on Minnesota's largest city when he published an account of the Ames scandal in *McClure's Magazine.* Steffens's "Shame of Minneapolis" recounted the events of 1902 in painful detail. His article, and others like it in *McClure's,* was part of an early wave of muckraking journalism that helped propel progressive reforms in the early decades of the new century.

The word *shame* caught the public eye, but Steffens's article had a subtitle that received less attention: THE RESCUE AND REDEMPTION OF A CITY THAT WAS SOLD OUT. In the end, "The Shame of Minneapolis" was a classic morality tale, with good triumphing over evil, as a group of courageous reformers, led by Clarke, ousted the crooks from city hall and restored decency and morality to Minneapolis city government.

Clarke accomplished a heroic feat in 1902, but he was not able to banish the crooks permanently. Over the succeeding decades, the twin evils of crime and corruption would continue to plague municipal life in Minneapolis.

## The Genial Reprobate

The story of "Shame" begins with Ames, the genial reprobate who served off and on as mayor of Minneapolis over a twenty-five-year period, starting in 1876. Born in Illinois in 1842, Ames moved to Minnesota as a young boy with his family in 1851. His father, Dr. Alfred Elisha Ames, was a well-known pioneer physician. The younger Ames received his own medical degree at the age of twenty from Chicago's Rush Medical College. After medical school, he enlisted in the Ninth Minnesota Volunteer Regiment, rising to the rank of surgeon major during the Civil War.

After the war, "Doc" Ames parlayed his medical credentials and military background into a successful political career. In 1867, he was elected on the "soldier's ticket" to represent Minneapolis for one term in the Minnesota House of Representatives. After the legislative term, he moved to California, where he began a new career as a journalist before returning to Minnesota in 1874 to resume his medical practice.

Mayor Albert Alonzo Ames was at the center of a municipal corruption scandal, dubbed the "Shame of Minneapolis" by the crusading American journalist Lincoln Steffens.

Something of a Jekyll and Hyde, Doc Ames drew praise from Steffens in the 1903 *McClure's* article. "Skillful as a surgeon, devoted as a physician, and as a man kindly, he increased his practice till he was the best-loved man in the community," Steffens wrote. "He was especially good to the poor. Anybody could summon 'Doc' Ames at any hour to any distance. He went, and he gave not only his professional service, but sympathy, and often charity. 'Richer men than you will pay your bill,' he told the destitute." But there was another side to the compassionate doctor. "Ames was sunshine not to the sick and destitute only," Steffens continued. "To the vicious and depraved also he was a comfort. If a man was a hard drinker, the good Doctor cheered him with another drink; if he had stolen something, the Doctor helped to get him off."[2]

Over time, the upstanding citizens of Minneapolis came to criticize the politician-physician. "His loose life brought disapproval only from the good people, so gradually the Doctor came to enjoy best the society of the barroom and the streets. This society, flattered in turn, worshiped the good Doctor, and, active in politics always, put its physician into the arena," Steffens wrote.[3]

As Ames began his third term as mayor in 1886, the genial doctor could still draw on a reservoir of good feeling from a large part of the local population. "He ran the city government with a casual indifference, spending little time behind his desk and long hours with his foot on the bar rail at one or another popular drinking establishment. He traded stories and joked with companions, and dispensed patronage to any who required his assistance. Many citizens of Minneapolis considered him more a colorful curiosity than a seriously corrupt or dangerous public official," one historian later wrote. By the end of Ames's third term, however, the tide of public opinion had started to turn. The *Minneapolis Journal* railed against Doc, describing his stint in office as a "stench, an offense against honesty, decency and over the ordinary safety of the common citizen."[4]

Ames had run successfully for higher office as a Democrat in the 1880s. When his term as mayor concluded in 1892, most observers thought his political career was over, but they were wrong. In 1900, Ames resurfaced, this time as a Republican. Doc and his supporters knew that a new state law substituted an open direct primary election for the political convention system previously used to nominate candidates for public office. The new law permitted crossover voting, meaning voters need not limit themselves to their own party's primary. Ames won the Republican primary for mayor with the help of his Democratic supporters and went on to win the general election, part of a national sweep that returned William McKinley to the White House.

### An Economic Boom

Ames returned to office during a period of great prosperity for a city that was experiencing explosive growth. Between 1880 and 1900, Minneapolis had quadrupled in population, from 50,000 to over 200,000 inhabitants. "Here in Minneapolis and through the northwest fortune has smiled upon the people," the *Minneapolis Times* noted in January 1900. "The keynote in the year 1899 in the Northwest has been PROSPERITY . . . Some of the grand totals of business . . . show that Minneapolis has prospered as never before," the *Minneapolis Journal* declared that same month.[5]

While many among the great mass of working people were still largely impoverished, the lucky ones—those with strong backs—were able to benefit from trickle-down economics. In November 1899, the *Minneapolis Tribune* observed, "Never before in the history of the city was there such a demand for labor as at the present time, and never before in the history of the Northwest has it been so hard to induce men to take positions that are offered. Nearly all the men who are looking for work have a few dollars in their pocket and they will not take the positions that are offered because there is not enough money in it."[6]

Quite a few of those dollars were probably spent at the city's 324 saloons, which outnumbered the churches in Minneapolis by almost two to one at the turn of the century. Downtown, in the Gateway neighborhood along the riverfront where many of the saloons clustered, the city had a recognized vice district, with houses of prostitution and gambling dens operating behind closed doors, often with tacit approval from the local police. With that economic boom under way, the vice industries flourished, setting the stage for the scandal that would soon unfold in city hall.

### Grabbing for the Spoils

During his previous three terms as mayor, Doc Ames may have been morally lax and indifferent to petty corruption in city hall, but he himself had not committed any openly criminal acts. Now, nursing resentments over his earlier public rejection, the newly elected mayor was determined to get some of the spoils for himself when he returned to office in 1901. Doc's power grab came through control of the police department. First, he installed his brother Fred, a disgraced former army officer, as chief of police. Then, the brothers brought into the department a group of men with underworld ties. One of the Ameses' key agents, "Coffee John" Frichette, who had earned his nickname as owner of a restaurant that served as a criminal hangout, became the senior police captain and assigned two junior captains, Fred Malone and Charles Brackett, to shake down the city's known criminals and vice lords. To make sure the police would fall into line, the Ames brothers fired half the force, including all officers who were considered incorruptible.

Under the direction of Norman King, a professional gambler who became chief of detectives, the police organized "big mitt" poker games. The big mitt used a stacked deck to swindle unsuspecting card players, the "suckers," who were lured into the games by men known as "steerers" and "boosters." If the suckers complained, they were threatened with arrest by a compliant police officer and told to leave town. The new Ames administration turned the Minneapolis police department into its collection agent for all forms of graft. "The administration opened with a revolution on the police force," Steffens reported. "The thieves in the local jail were liberated, and it was made known to the Under World generally that 'things were doing' in Minneapolis. The incoming swindlers reported to King or his staff for instructions, and went to work, turning the 'swag' over to the detectives in charge. Gambling went on openly, and disorderly houses multiplied."[7]

Revenue from various illegal sources poured into city hall, but "it only whetted the avarice of the mayor and his Cabinet," according to Steffens. Illegal slot machines alone netted Doc Ames $15,000 a year as his share. Opium dens and unlicensed saloons, known as blind pigs, provided another stream of protection money. Even the city's prostitutes had to pay: they were forced to make protection payments to a group of collection agents working under the direction of Mayor Ames's secretary, Irving Gardner. The payoffs came on top of a $100 monthly fine paid directly to the city. But Doc Ames, greedy for a larger share of the graft, devised a plan to milk even more money from the women. Manipulating his image as champion to the oppressed, the mayor declared that the monthly fine constituted too much of a financial burden for the prostitutes. Henceforth, they would be required to pay the fine only every other month. Doc's professed compassion was only a cover for his greed, however: on the alternate months, Gardner collected another $100 that went straight into the mayor's pocket.[8]

"In a general way all this business was known," Steffens reported. "It did not arouse the citizens, but it did attract criminals, and more and more thieves and swindlers came hurrying to Minneapolis. Some of them saw the police, and made terms. Some were seen by the police, and invited to go to work. There was room for all. This astonishing fact that the government of a city asked criminals to rob the people is fully established. The police and the criminals have confessed it separately. Their statements agree in detail."[9]

While the drama was unfolding in city hall during the early months of 1902, prior to the indictments issued by Clarke's grand jury, the growing scandal did not earn coverage in the local press—at least not directly. But reading between the lines reveals early hints of problems in the police department. "The records of the municipal court tell some interesting stories of police management during the present year," the *Minneapolis Journal* observed somewhat obliquely on January 1. "On the score of gambling, the year's record of arrests was exceedingly slim, the total number of arrests being but eight, and all of them were boys of tender years charged with shooting craps. The many responsible adults who have been doing the 'real thing' all this year escaped entirely," the *Journal* noted. "Another significant fact told by the figures of the year is the large number of people arrested who were found not guilty of the offenses charged. The explanation is found, it is asserted, in the lack of experience and judgment on the part of the police."[10]

While the crooks were taking over the police department, other units of local government not under the mayor's control were conducting business as usual. With the defeat of the strong mayoral charter in 1900, the city council continued to oversee most municipal functions—as it would throughout much of the twentieth century. In 1901, the city attorney defended Minneapolis against thirty-two personal injury suits, the city clerk issued 4,492 dog licenses, and the city engineer issued 4,915 sidewalk permits. The *Minneapolis Journal* gave these municipal units a clean bill of health in an editorial on the Ames scandal published in July 1902. "We have lost no public funds here through malfeasance," the paper noted. "Our council is not corrupt. The city government is administered with a fair degree of economy. Even the police scandal, black and white as it is, has not cost the city a cent of wasted or stolen public money."[11]

During his abbreviated fourth term, Ames tangled off and on with the twenty-six-member council. In January 1902, he went to court in two disputes with the council and lost on both counts. In one, the court compelled Ames to sign $150,000 in public improvement bonds that the council had approved. He had no discretion in the matter, the court ruled, and thus was required to sign the bonds despite any disapproval he might feel concerning them. In this case, Ames may have been looking for kickbacks, but he may have had more positive motives. Apparently, Ames preferred that the money be spent in neighborhoods most in need of repair, but the final decision was made by the council's paving and sewer committee. Ames also lost in his bid to compel the city council to appropriate $5,000 for the mayor's contingency fund, with the court leaving that decision in the council's hands.

As the Ames scandal continued to unfold, Minneapolis's upstanding citizens went about their business, apparently unaffected by the rampant corruption under way in city hall. In early January 1902, the Portland Avenue History Club held its annual banquet, the Hoevel String Quartet performed at the Unitarian Church, and Goodfellows Store on Nicollet Avenue prepared for its winter linen and muslin sale.

### The Thieves Fall Out

Doc Ames may have been venal and corrupt, but he was not an enforcer. He made no concerted effort to control his rapidly expanding criminal empire. Soon "his followers began to quarrel among themselves. They deceived one another; they robbed the thieves; they robbed Ames himself. His brother became dissatisfied with his share of the spoils, and formed cabals with captains who plotted against the administration," Steffens reported.[12]

All of this provided an opening for Clarke, a crusading local businessman outraged by the criminality of the Ames administration. In April 1902, Clarke was appointed to the summer term of the Hennepin County Grand Jury. The grand jury was empowered to hear complaints and accusations of criminal acts and to determine if and when indictments were warranted. This citizen group had considerable latitude to act on its own, and it was not required to take direction from the county attorney. Like many of the city's elite, Clarke was a transplanted New Englander with something of a Puritan streak. A successful, hard-driving businessman, Clarke was not about to be intimidated by the Ames clique. "He had the habit of command, the impatient, imperious manner of the master, and the assurance of success which begets it. He did not want to be a grand juryman, he did not want to be a foreman; but since he was both, he wanted to accomplish something," Steffens noted.[13]

When the county prosecutor refused to move against the Ames administration, Clarke told him the grand jury would get along without him. "Do you think, Mr. Clarke, that you can run the grand jury and my office, too?" the prosecutor asked rhetorically. "Yes," said Clarke. "I will run your office if I want to; and I want to. You're excused." Clarke was on his own. After winning over a majority of his fellow jury members, the foreman devised a clever strategy to combat the Ames regime. Using his own funds, he put out a false scent by hiring some well-known detectives with ties to police department leadership, knowing they would blab about the investigation. Then he hired a second group of undercover investigators who were not known in Minneapolis to do the real work.[14]

Ames's agents tried to bribe Clarke and to threaten him— to no avail. They even sought to hire a hit man from Chicago—a "slugger"—to come to Minneapolis to murder the fearless jury foreman.

Of his own accord, Clarke visited the county jail to interview inmates who had griev-

A hard-driving reformer, Hovey Clarke led the effort to root out municipal corruption during Mayor Ames's final term in office.

ances against the current regime and were willing to testify against their former partners in crime. Soon Clarke and his investigators had enough evidence to begin issuing a series of indictments, including several against the mayor himself.[15]

## Justice Is Done

Chris Norbeck, a police detective who helped run the big mitt scam, was one of the first to be indicted. On June 2, the *Minneapolis Journal* announced in a blaring headline "EDWARDS TESTIFIES THAT DETECTIVE CHRIS NORBECK WAS DIRECTLY RESPONSIBLE FOR OPENING BIG MITT JOINTS IN MINNEAPOLIS." "'Billy' Edwards, big mitt man, card sharper and all around confidence worker, said on the stand in the Gardner case this morning, that . . . Norbeck, a detective in the pay of the city, and who is now under indictment for bribery . . . came to [Edwards] with a proposition to open a 'joint,' and asked how much he would pay the police for the privilege," the *Journal* went on to report. Later, the *Journal* disclosed the shocking news that Norbeck had disappeared in the middle of his trial. "Everyone knows why Norbeck disappeared. How did he go? What did he do? Where is he now?" the *Journal* asked.[16]

Rumors spread that Norbeck had caught a train for Duluth and was heading for Canada. Some even thought he may have committed suicide: just before he disappeared, he had been seen at a downtown cigar store, distraught over his trial and claiming he was ready to jump into the river. Eventually, the errant detective returned to Minneapolis and testified against Fred Ames during the police chief's trial on bribery charges. Norbeck's testimony directly implicated Mayor Ames, who had recently been indicted for attempting to bribe two county commissioners: "Detective Norbeck testifies: That the Mayor of Minneapolis, Dr. A. A. Ames, gave him specific orders to work under Gardner in the collection of 'protection' money from women whose characters render them amenable to police interference, and from crooks generally," the *Journal* reported on July 3.[17]

During the following weeks, pressure mounted on Doc Ames to leave office. Finally, on July 31, he gave in, resigning as mayor immediately after firing his brother as police chief. "THE MALODOROUS AMES REGIME COMES TO AN INGLORIOUS END," the

*Journal* announced on the day of the mayor's resignation: "It Is the Finish. Mayor Ames resigns . . . Colonel Fred Ames relieved from duty as chief of police. Thus ends the drama in which the action has been swift and thrilling. It has been a tragedy. The good name of Minneapolis has been trailed in the slime and all the sisterhood of cities has seen her shame."[18]

But the drama had not ended; one act remained to be played out. Following his resignation and still under indictment, Doc Ames quietly slipped out of town. He was spotted on a train heading east, "an unlighted cigar in his mouth, his face ashen and drawn." Fred Ames also fled but was eventually captured and returned to Minneapolis for trial. The former chief blamed his brother, saying he had merely taken orders from Doc, who had been the real chief of police. Fred Ames was convicted and sentenced to six and a half years in Stillwater State Prison. Norbeck and other Ames henchmen were also sent to jail. Doc Ames returned to Minneapolis to face a criminal conviction in May 1903, but the verdict was later overturned by the Minnesota Supreme Court. Never retried, he returned to his medical practice. On November 16, 1911, he died at the age of sixty-nine.[19]

## Despair and Hope

When Lincoln Steffens's article appeared in *McClure's* in January 1903, the story was already old news in Minneapolis. While Steffens did not cover new factual ground, he did reproduce a copy of the big mitt ledger, which documented the payoffs to Doc Ames. Until then, the ledger had been seen only by the grand jury and not by the public. Probably because the Ames scandals had been so widely reported in the Minneapolis papers, the local press did not acknowledge Steffens's article in the months following its publication.

Even before Steffens's article appeared in *McClure's*, newspapers around the country took note of the events in Minneapolis. In the summer of 1902, the *New York Times* declared, "New York never presented a spectacle quite so bad—its criminality never spread so far over the official circle, never involved so many men supposed to be respectable." The *New York Commercial Advertiser* was even more caustic, maintaining that "even in New York, where our experience with municipal corruption has not been limited, it is difficult to realize the extent of the rottenness of Minneapolis." The *St. Louis Star* wrote, "in police corruption, Minneapolis can give St. Louis cards and spades and still win the game."[20]

The *Minneapolis Journal* did not take kindly to the criticism from other big-city newspapers. "They dwell upon the loathsome malady from which Minneapolis is suffering . . . but they do not pay much attention to the heroic remedies now being administered," the *Journal* reminded its readers in July. "We are not so sure that New York never presented quite so bad a spectacle," the *Journal* went on to say,

> There have been times in New York when scarcely a department of city government was clean. We wish to remind the Times that it is only the mayor and his police force that are affected in Minneapolis, that the various other city offices and departments are generally strong and clean and not in the least affected by the inequity among the police. We would remind the St. Louis critics of this fact, too.
>
> And look at the stern measures we have taken to clean up the force. Indictments and convictions have for weeks been coming out so fast that we can scarcely keep track of them. What is left of the police department has a sterner determination to do right and eschew evil than any police force in Minneapolis ever had before.
>
> There has been a wholesale bracing up of the political atmosphere of the whole city. Good people have been aroused from their lethargy. There is a general determination to let no guilty man escape, to prove to the country that Minneapolis can exemplarily punish the crime it breeds, and to make itself as remarkable for the justice it metes out to its dishonorable employees as they had been made it by reason of their corruption.[21]

## A Postscript

Albert Alonzo Ames had been driven from office by the time "The Shame of Minneapolis" appeared in *McClure's*, but Steffens knew that corruption had not yet been permanently banished from Minneapolis City Hall. He concluded his widely circulated article by recording his interview with Ames successor and former city council member David Percy Jones. A well-to-do local businessman, Jones had been elected to the council as a reformer. As mayor, he had to act on his reform principles. "[Jones] was confronted at once with all the hardest problems of municipal government," Steffens noted. "Vice rose up to tempt or fight him. He studied the situation deliberately and by and by began to settle it point by point, slowly but finally."[22]

The new mayor began his term by cleaning house in the police department and appointing a trusted friend as chief, but then the gambling kingpins came stalking. First they offered to control the criminal elements in town if he let them run some gambling dens without interference. Jones told them he didn't need their help because he did not expect to see any upswing in crime. But then a rash of burglaries broke out, including an attack on the home of one of Jones's relatives. The gamblers came back, this time telling Jones they could recover the stolen goods for him. Prove it, Jones replied.

Soon the goods came trickling back, parcel by parcel, to city hall. When the crooks returned to collect their reward, Jones told them in no uncertain terms that there would be no gambling with police connivance in Minneapolis during his term. The new mayor told Steffens that he might have been tempted to reconsider his forceful approach had he faced a longer stay in office: "[Jones] believed he would decide again as he had already, but he would at least give studious reflection to the question—Can a city be governed without any alliance with crime?" Steffens concluded, "It was an open question ... [Jones] had closed it only for the four months of his emergency administration. Minneapolis should be clean

*Mayor David Percy Jones faced the question "can a city be governed without any alliance with crime?" and aimed to clear city hall and the police department of corruption during his brief term.*

and sweet for a little while at least, and the new administration should begin with a clear deck."[23]

Jones had helped close one chapter in an ongoing municipal saga, but others were still waiting to be written. Off and on during the succeeding decades, corruption continued to hover like a dark cloud over city hall.

### Vote Selling During the Roaring Twenties

A quarter century after "The Shame of Minneapolis," municipal corruption was once again front-page news. This time, the crusading reformer was a dynamic thirty-six-year-old county attorney who would later be elected governor. First appointed to his post by the Hennepin County Board of Commissioners in 1920, Floyd B. Olson made a name for himself as a high-profit prosecutor who did not shy away from battles with city hall politicians.

By 1927, rumors were swirling around Minneapolis mayor George E. Leach and police chief Frank Brunskill about alleged ties to certain underworld figures. That year, Brunskill was the subject of a grand jury probe initiated by Olson. While the grand jury was not able to assemble enough evidence to justify an indictment, court records indicate the jury was highly suspicious of Brunskill. One witness refused to answer when asked whether he had seen a local gangster give a roll of paper money to the chief. Even though Brunskill dodged an indictment, he did not escape the wrath of Mayor Leach, who fired him soon after the grand jury probe was finished.

Leach justified the firing by claiming that Brunskill had been disloyal, but some city hall denizens maintained that other motives for the mayor's action existed. One historian later wrote, "Word on the street offered a more elaborate version: While Mayor Leach was out of town, Brunskill had accepted Leach's weekly envelope. 'Leach didn't get his cut that week, and he put the burn on Brunskill to pony up . . . The mayor was so mad that he fired Brunskill.'" Leach and Brunskill may have eluded grand jury indictments, but other city hall politicians were not so lucky during the Roaring Twenties era in Minneapolis.[24]

For weeks at a time in late 1928 and early 1929, local newspapers were filled with front-page revelations of municipal corruption, much as papers during the Doc Ames reign at the turn of the century had been. With Floyd Olson spearheading the action, one alderman after another was outed for taking bribes in exchange for his votes on city business. In all, five were indicted while a sixth, Louis Ritten, turned state's evidence, implicated several of his former colleagues, and escaped a jail sentence through a grant of immunity.

With their juicy revelations of municipal misdeeds, the city hall corruption scandals of the 1920s came close to equaling the drama of "The Shame of Minneapolis" at the turn of the century. The spectacle was played up by the fiercely competitive local papers, whose editors sought to gain and retain readers. The *Minneapolis Journal* got the best of its rivals when it sent two reporters, H. A. Van Dusen and Edward Wallace, to track down Ritten, who had left town and gone into hiding after blabbing to the grand jury.

In a front-page expose, Van Dusen and Wallace told about receiving a tip that Ritten was on his way to Seattle, Washington, when most city hall insiders thought he was hiding out in Chicago. Soon, the reporters themselves were part of the story: "We had been working for several days on various angles more or less connected with the graft investigation . . . Our experiences in the last few days had convinced us that either we were being shadowed, or our movements were being reported by telephone to someone who immediately passed the information on to everyone likely to be concerned."[25]

In an effort to shake their pursuers, the two reporters brought tickets separately and hopped the train for Seattle in St. Paul. But they were unable to evade detection by an unknown underworld agent who had followed them aboard. As the Seattle-bound train sped through Montana, Van Dusen and Wallace were robbed of documents dealing with an investigation of racketeering in the Twin Cities' cleaning and dyeing industry. "Theft of these records had no apparent connection with our mission to Seattle, which was to find Ritten and to obtain from him a complete confession of his part in city hall graft," the *Journal* staffers reported. "For two hours after we arrived in Seattle it appeared that our tip had been wrong. The checkup of Seattle hotels, arranged by long distance telephone from Minneapolis had failed to show any trace of the man we were hunting."[26]

Then, Van Dusen and Wallace had a stroke of good luck when Mrs. Ritten was spotted at the Olympic Hotel. The *Journal* reporters hired private detectives to watch for Ritten at each of the hotel entrances, but seven hours later, he still had not appeared. Finally, the two men slipped a note under Mrs. Ritten's door indicating they needed to talk to her husband because of new developments that had occurred in Minneapolis since his confession to the grand jury.

At 7:30 that evening, Wallace and Van Dusen got word from Mrs. Ritten that her husband was on his way to the hotel. Finally, shortly before 10 PM, the two reporters were able to interview the elusive former alderman. "He came to our room, coming down the corridor just as one of us opened the door," they reported. "It was a strangely casual meeting for a former council president who had confessed to a long series of briberies . . . and two newspaper men, strangers to him, who had trailed him 1800 miles."[27]

The *Journal* reporters confronted the former city council president, telling him he did not have complete immunity from prosecution if he withheld relevant information from the grand jury. "No! That isn't true, is it?" Ritten cried. "I thought I was clean of everything up to the moment I went into the grand jury room. I'll be ruined. And I was just beginning to be able to sleep at night. This is terrible boys. It's a devil of a fix to be in." Then Ritten broke down in sobs and gave the reporters a full account of his involvement in city hall bribery. Under banner headlines on the front page of its Sunday, February 17 edition, the *Journal* reprinted a sanitized account of Ritten's statement, referring to his coconspirators as Mr. A. and Mr. B. and Alderman X and Alderman Y. The original statement, filed with the Hennepin County grand jury, included their full names.[28]

"Mr. A, representing the ___ Company of ___, gave me $700 to vote favorably on a hose contract," Ritten acknowledged. "I told him the money would be divided between Alderman X, Alderman Y, and myself. He said he didn't care how the money was divided, just so he got all or as much of the contract as possible for his company." Ritten feebly tried to justify his actions by pointing a finger at the people who offered him the bribes. "Aldermen are not alone responsible for the present situation in Minneapolis," he maintained. "Some of the blame should be placed on the shoulders of those business firms who solicit business by holding out a roll of bills to city officials."²⁹

"There are many responsibilities attached to the office of alderman," Ritten continued. "He puts in long hours in committee hearings, attending council meetings and to the business of the city. The routine of business follows him into his home in the evenings, on Sundays and holidays. The present salaries are too low; many of the aldermen cannot afford to give their position the time it demands. When bribes are offered for doing things they would probably do without money, it is a great temptation. They hear of others accepting bribes; after awhile they become involved themselves."³⁰

But one chapter remained to be played out in the Ritten saga. Fearing for his life, the former alderman left Seattle under an assumed name and came to St. Paul, where he registered at the Commodore Hotel as C. W. Farnsworth. As the two *Journal* reporters continued their interview with him, five men brandishing pistols burst into the room. "I thought they were sure after me," Ritten later said. But the five men turned out to be plainclothes policemen called to the Commodore to investigate "suspicious" behavior. After listening to Ritten's story and questioning the two reporters, the five left the hotel.³¹

As a crusading Hennepin County attorney in the 1920s, Floyd Olson prosecuted Minneapolis aldermen who received kickbacks from local businessmen seeking city contracts. Olson's high profile as a crime fighter helped him win election as Minnesota's first Farmer-Labor governor in 1930.

The *Journal* claimed the revelations in its February 17 edition would lead to further indictments, but it is not clear how much new information

Ritten's statement provided to the grand jury. Indictments against three aldermen—Frank Gibenhain, Fred Mauer, and John Ekberg—were returned prior to the publication of Ritten's confession. But later indictments were brought against two more aldermen, both from the Eighth Ward: W. H. Rendell and Jay Russell Sheffield. Gibenhain, Mauer, Ekberg, and Sheffield were later convicted and served jail time, but Rendell was freed when his two trials resulted in hung juries.

While Floyd Olson was clearly the driving force behind the city hall corruption probes, the dynamic county attorney was circumspect in his statements to the press. Only during Ekberg's trial did Olson's exhortation to the jury get full coverage in the local papers. Using impressive rhetorical skills he would later exhibit in his gubernatorial campaign, Olson told the jury,

> Well, ladies and gentlemen, here is a typical example of bribery. The occasion existed—books were juggled, checks destroyed. Ekberg lied to the prosecution, these other men lied. They all lied . . . I'm not going to appeal to you on the grounds that you are taxpayers. I'm not going to appeal to your emotions, but I will appeal to you with cold hard facts of the case. And then it will be for you to say. If you want to say that it is all right for a man to go about bargaining his vote in the city council away. If it's all right, say so. But . . . if you think a bribery was committed, then there is no logical reason why you should not return a verdict of guilty. And that, ladies and gentlemen, as far as I can see, is the only possible conclusion you can reach.[32]

Through late 1928 and into the early months of 1929, the city hall corruption probe took a heavy toll on Olson and his family. His wife, Ada, was harassed constantly by phone calls—many quite threatening. "While her husband is at the courthouse and elsewhere, Mrs. Olson has her troubles at home," the *Minneapolis Tribune* reported. "The telephone is never silent and the Olsons do not dare cut it off. All day long and far into the night Mrs. Olson is called to the phone. She is threatened and cursed. Men and women call her and tell her they wish she would use her influence with her husband to end the graft investigation . . . Others volunteer 'red hot' information." His reputation as a fearless prosecutor enhanced, the following year, in November 1930, Olson would be elected to the first of his three terms as governor of Minnesota.[33]

## A Man Called Kid

As Minneapolis entered the depression years of the 1930s, a cloud of corruption continued to hang over city hall. Olson had moved on to the state capitol, and the county attorney's office was no longer the center of an ongoing crusade against evildoing in the Mill City. Past municipal scandals had commanded a comic opera aspect, but the thirties were a more deadly serious time. Gangland slayings occurred regularly on the streets of Minneapolis, and hints of shady dealings between the local politicians and underworld figures abounded.

One of the most formidable of those figures was a man with the innocent-sounding name of Isadore Blumenfeld. Better known as Kid Cann, Blumenfeld, the son of Eastern European Jewish immigrants, grew up on the tough streets of north Min-

neapolis and became a successful bootlegger during the Prohibition era of the 1920s. When Prohibition ended in 1933, Blumenfeld used his considerable organizational skills to move into the retail liquor business. According to the Federal Bureau of Investigation, Kid Cann had a tight hold on liquor licensing in Minneapolis: "Every license must clear through him, for which he and his group get from $5,000 to $20,000 for police protection," FBI files disclosed.[34]

The bureau also noted that Blumenfeld's mob dabbled in local politics. Initially, the mob supported an outsider in the city's 1933 mayoral election but later switched its support to the candidate who ultimately won the election.

*Minneapolis's most notorious crime lord, Isadore "Kid Cann" Blumenfeld, used bribery and intimidation to gain influence at city hall during the 1930s and '40s.*

"In return, the gang was given practical control of the city," the
FBI reported.[35]

As his wealth increased through control of much of the local
vice business, Blumenfeld spent freely to buy influence for himself
in city hall. One local observer would later write, "[Blumenfeld]
shared wealth liberally with police and politicians, contributing
abundantly to campaign funds and politicians' pockets. For his
money he received ample value."[36]

Throughout the 1920s and 1930s, Blumenfeld was implicated
in a series of gangland-style executions but never convicted of
murder. The best known of these incidents involved the murder of
Walter Liggett, whose *Midwest American* newspaper had attacked
the Kid Cann gang for buying off city officials. Liggett was gunned
down as he unloaded groceries behind his south Minneapolis
home. "I'll never forget his leering face," Liggett's wife declared
tearfully as she identified Blumenfeld in a police lineup. But the
local crime boss claimed he was getting a haircut at a Hennepin
Avenue barbershop at the time of the shooting. Blumenfeld was
later acquitted of all charges in the Liggett case.[37]

By the 1940s, Blumenfeld was able to roll his considerable
wealth into more legitimate activities, including real estate in
Florida and Las Vegas. He gained a measure of respectability and
continued to cement his ties to local politicians. Eventually he was
convicted of bribery, spent time in Leavenworth Penitentiary, and
retired to Florida after his release. When Blumenfeld died in 1981,
more than two hundred people attended his funeral in Minneapolis, where he was lauded as a generous family man.

### An Exuberant Young Newcomer

During the war years of the 1940s, Blumenfeld was still very much
on the scene in Minneapolis, and his shadowy presence cast a pall
over local politics. In 1943, that politics revolved around the city
mayoral campaign, which pitted an exuberant newcomer named
Hubert Humphrey against the city's incumbent mayor, Marvin
Kline. A key issue separating Kline from his young challenger was
a proposed charter amendment, which would have given the city's
police chief civil service protection. Kline supported the amendment, but Humphrey opposed it, reflecting the views of his supporters in the local labor movement, who believed the amend-

ment would give anti-union forces in Minneapolis greater control over police department operations.

Both candidates knew police issues touched a raw nerve in Minneapolis because of widely circulated rumors of city hall ties to local underworld elements, and both tried to gain some mileage from the corruption issue. Kline charged that his opponent was backed by racketeers who had engineered Humphrey's endorsement by the city's Central Labor Union council. Not willing to passively accept a pounding from the incumbent, Humphrey took the offensive and charged into the mayor's office on May 26, challenging Kline to name the racketeers. The *Minneapolis Times* covered the event, calling it "the most dramatic meeting that Minneapolis politics have produced in many a year."[38]

Temporarily unnerved by his opponent's unannounced visit, Kline hesitated before responding to Humphrey's query. But then the mayor replied that racketeers were backing Humphrey, whether he knew it or not, and one of them was George Murk, president of the Musicians Union. Murk operated a nightclub that had been raided by the police during Kline's term as mayor. Humphrey denied that Murk was part of his campaign. Then, going on the attack, Humphrey challenged the mayor to explain why he had not permanently closed down Murk's club if illegal activity was occurring there. "Why didn't you keep his placed closed up?" Humphrey angrily demanded. "Why didn't you run him out of town?" The two candidates volleyed charges and countercharges at each other for a few more minutes before the debate wound down. "As the argument grew prolonged, each man inserted a word of personal respect for the other and tempers gradually cooled," the *Times* reported.[39]

In the 1943 election, Humphrey narrowly lost to the incumbent Kline. Almost immediately, the young challenger began preparing for a rematch at the next city election. Two years later, with municipal corruption still a major issue, Humphrey returned to challenge Kline. Having immersed himself in the issues facing Minneapolis, Humphrey was well aware of the impact crime and corruption had on his city. "For years, Minneapolis had been wide open," Humphrey later wrote in his autobiography. "Prostitution, gambling, liquor sales to minors and after-hours joints flourished openly in violation of the law. Since responsibility for those conditions rested on the mayor, I had inevitably made law enforcement the central issue of the campaign."⁴⁰

The political aspirant relied on a southeast Minneapolis neighbor, Ed Ryan, then a police detective, to educate him about conditions in the city's police department. Through Ryan and others on the force, he learned about the insidious effect petty graft was having on the department. "The cop on the beat or a member of the morals squad would be taken care of by a bartender or an owner who was staying open after hours. It wasn't big stuff, but it pointed to considerable corruption at higher levels," Humphrey observed. "I was never able to determine how much money was moving, but it was clear that owners of gambling houses or brothels operated as casually as they would have run a neighborhood grocery—with better police protection and security. They stood little danger of being robbed or burglarized."⁴¹

In the 1943 campaign, the city's business leaders had mainly sat on the sidelines, uneasy about the young man's left-leaning political views. This time the maturing candidate made a concerted effort to win them over. Humphrey favorably impressed John Cowles, publisher of the *Minneapolis Tribune* and *Star Journal*, who opened doors to other local business leaders. In meetings with the city's power elite, Humphrey stressed his determination to root out municipal corruption in Minneapolis. At one such session during the height of the campaign, he declared forcefully, "the gangsters of Chicago are out to take over the city and are on their way to doing so unless they are stopped. We are starting to see business move out of the city—and people are going too, to the suburbs. This must be halted if Minneapolis is to go on as a city." Earlier in the year, he told Cowles, "One is not worthy of respect and confidence of the community if he becomes a pawn or stooge for . . . some outside influences, some invisible government. I have no intention of letting some outside influence select the Superintendent of Police."⁴²

In 1945, corruption as a municipal issue had gained front-page notoriety when Arthur Kasherman, a local scandal sheet publisher, was gunned down in the street. Earlier, Kasherman had claimed that Mayor Kline's administration was "the most corrupt within memory—racketeers in complete control." On the day he was shot, Kasherman had reported to the Hennepin County sheriff's office that a downtown crap game was spinning off $75,000 a month for a Chicago crime syndicate.[43]

In the June election, Humphrey decisively defeated Kline, gaining over 60 percent of the vote and carrying eleven of the city's thirteen wards. Now the mayor-elect would have to put his brave words into action. "Even before Humphrey moved into City Hall he was tested," Humphrey's biographer, Carl Solberg, would later write, reporting on an exchange between Humphrey and a local racketeer named "Chickie" Berman. Berman had requested and received an audience with the victorious mayoral candidate soon after the election. Berman got down to business right away. "What do you want?" he asked impertinently. "What do you mean, 'what do I want?'" Humphrey replied.

> Berman said: "Well, what do you want so we can operate like we used to? I don't mean absolutely—we don't mind getting knocked off once in a while so you can keep your record clear. But you're going to ruin our business."
> Humphrey replied: "Well, what's your proposition, Berman?"
> Berman said: "Twenty-five percent of the take."
> Humphrey answered: "I don't think that's a good deal for me. Let's make it 75-25, my 75 and your 25."
> Berman was shocked and cried: "My God, that would break us."
> Jumping to his feet, Humphrey announced: "That's exactly right—and that's what going to happen to you."[44]

Humphrey did follow through on his vow to battle corruption, appointing a citizens committee headed by Pillsbury Mills executive Bradshaw Mintener to advise him on the appointment of the city's next police chief. Mintener's committee recommended Humphrey's neighbor Ed Ryan, who was widely thought to be honest and free of corruption. Humphrey installed Ryan as advised, even though the appointment was viewed with suspicion by some local labor leaders.

Once settled in his city hall office, the newly elected mayor quickly learned he would not have an easy time battling the forces of corruption in the Mill City. "Minneapolis mayors had never interfered with the livelihood of those people who ran prostitution, gambling and illegal liquor activities. When I closed up the town, there was first surprise, then anger," Humphrey noted. That anger showed itself directly one night when Humphrey was returning home from a late meeting with several city aldermen. He had just been dropped off by his police driver when he noticed the street light near his home was out. "I didn't think it significant," Humphrey later reported.

> I waved good-by to the car and walked quickly to the door, which Muriel had locked from the inside. As she was opening the door, three shots rang out. I ducked inside, wondering aloud, "Why would anyone shoot at me?" Being more aggravated then scared, after calling the police, I went back outside to poke around the bushes to see if I could find footprints or the used shells. It was a dumb thing to do, but I had decided that the shots were intended to scare me, not kill me—unless the gunman had been one of the world's worst shots.[45]

As a quasi-weak mayor under the city's charter. Humphrey knew he would have to employ the powers of persuasion if he were to make a difference in city hall. "While I tried to change the attitudes of the police by education and chastisement, I tried, too, to upgrade the image that the policemen and their families had of their work," Humphrey later wrote. "I spoke to the wives of the officers, telling them what I hoped to do—namely to make ours the most honest and effective police force in the country, taking away the stigma attached to the entire force because of the dishonesty of some." Instituting a number of reforms, the newly elected mayor increased the size of the force, raised salaries, and established a forty-hour workweek for the officers.[46]

Humphrey also dealt with people whose relationship with the police had, at times, crossed the lines of propriety. Soon after he took office, he called in bar owners and told them he wanted to increase their license fees so he could generate the revenue needed to boost police salaries. "I don't want to have a fight," he told them. "If you run an honest place, you no longer need to worry about a shakedown. You don't have to pay off anybody any more and it's going to stay that way." Then Humphrey told the bar owners to approach the city council and testify in support of an increase in their license fees. "I'd rather have you pay a little more at the City Treasurer's office than to pay much more to a mayor or the chief or the cop on the beat or the head of the morals squad," he explained. The bar owners did as they were told, and Humphrey got his license fee increase.[47]

After a successful first term, Humphrey was reelected mayor by a wide margin in 1947. Then, following in Floyd Olson's footsteps, the charismatic young politician used his crime-fighting credentials as a stepping-stone to higher office. In 1948, he was elected to the U.S. Senate and began his rise to the pinnacle of power in Washington, DC.

## End of an Era

In the latter decades of the twentieth century, as vice became more readily available and even legalized—at least in the cases of alcohol and gambling—the underworld crime syndicates of an earlier era began to fade away as a force in American life. The sex trade and drug dealing would persist, but crusading journalists were no longer gunned down in the streets. Those seeking to gain access to and exert influence over politicians would find new, legal ways to do so, through the use of political campaign contributions. Still, crime and corruption remained a fact of municipal life.[48]

In 1903, Lincoln Steffens posed the question, "Can a city be governed without any alliance to crime?" Throughout much of the last century, that question was never answered decisively in Minneapolis. Men like Hovey Clarke, Floyd Olson, and Hubert Humphrey fought hard to eliminate municipal corruption—sometimes at great personal cost to themselves and their families. They may not have succeeded in permanently banishing the cloud of corruption hanging over the city, but their efforts helped make Minneapolis a cleaner, more honest city than it might have been had they not taken up the fight.

Throughout the twentieth century, the clean-government crusaders received strong backing from the local business elite, who knew that endemic corruption could do much to tarnish the city's image. While these power brokers may have supported political reform, their reformist inclinations did not extend into the economic sphere, where they continued to exercise tight control up through the Great Depression. In that era, an economic struggle that escalated into street violence would tarnish the city's image, just as the Doc Ames scandal had more than thirty years earlier.

*Minneapolis swims in a cesspool of municipal corruption, wherein floats a ballot box dated November 1900, referring to the election that returned Albert Alonzo Ames to city hall as mayor.*

# Blood in the Streets

ON A SPRING MORNING IN 1934, a Minneapolis attorney named Arthur Lyman woke up, got dressed, pulled on a pair of leather mountain boots, and made his way down to the city's market district, just a short drive from his Lowry Hill home. Lyman was a member in good standing of the city's economic and social elite. Men like him had controlled the levers of power in Minneapolis since the city's founding seventy-five years earlier. At the turn of the century, the power brokers had rooted out municipal corruption in city hall and pushed unsuccessfully to overhaul the city's outmoded governmental structure. But more recently, they had focused on darker aims. For the last thirty years, they had come together with the expressed goal of suppressing the city's struggling labor movement. Now, at the height of the Great Depression, those efforts had pushed many working-class Minneapolitans to the breaking point.

Arthur Lyman would soon face great danger—more danger than he could have anticipated when he laced up his metal-cleated boots. That day, he was swept up in a wave of violence that erupted in the market district as the police and their volunteer deputies clashed with a determined group of striking truck drivers. Lyman was part of a group of local business leaders, some from Minneapolis's most elite families, who had volunteered to help break the strike that had paralyzed the city for a week.

The day before, fighting had broken out between the two contending forces on First Avenue North when a local wholesaling company had tried unsuccessfully to start moving its trucks through the district. By nightfall, the fighting had subsided as the two sides regrouped. The next morning, Tuesday, May 22, the police and their force of a thousand volunteer deputies were back in the market district. The trucking employers, supported by the virulently anti-union Citizens Alliance, had issued an ultimatum to the workers: the trucks would start to move again, strike or no strike. But the drivers and their union, the militant Teamsters Local 574, were defiant. They were determined to keep the district bottled up until their demands were met.

Each side eyed the other warily. Then, someone threw a crate of tomatoes through a window. The market erupted as the strikers rushed the police and their deputies. Labor historian William Millikan described the scene: "Armed with almost every conceivable improvised weapon, from large stones and machine bolts to baseball bats and wagon wheel spokes, the strikers concentrated their attack on the easily identifiable special deputies. Blood-soaked men fell to the street as the carnage quickly mounted. The employers' soldiers, outnumbered and beaten, fled for their lives."[1]

One unlikely observer stood on the sidelines watching the battle in astonishment as Lyman tried to make his escape. Mrs. George Fahr, wife of a university medical professor, would later recall the events of that day: "I saw Arthur ... being pushed forward by the crowd and trying to push the strikers back. The floor of the market was cobblestone, and Arthur had worn mountaineering boots with metal cleats in them. It was just as though he was skating on a waxed floor or on ice. Nothing would have been more lethal than those boots were, and the strikers pressed upon him and he slipped and went down and they were on him like a pack of wolves. I had never seen anything like it."[2]

Lyman would later die of a blow to his head, one of two fatalities to occur during what came to be known as the Battle of Deputies Run. The May 22 violence was only one skirmish in a summer-long strike that provoked full-scale class warfare in Minneapolis during the height of the Depression. By the time it had run its course, the 1934 Teamsters Strike had altered the balance of power in Minneapolis. A settlement negotiated by federal mediators incorporated many of Local 574's demands. The union could claim at least a qualified victory in its battle with the trucking owners and their supporters in the Citizens Alliance. Labor strife continued throughout the 1930s, but the alliance's tight hold on the city's economic life had finally been broken.

## An Anti-union Alliance

More than thirty years earlier, as Minneapolis prepared to greet the new century, business was booming and workers with strong backs were in great demand. During the latter decades of the nineteenth century, the city's fledgling labor movement had struggled to get a foothold in the local economy. But now, with a major labor shortage, the local unions began to show more economic muscle as the forces of supply and demand tilted in their favor—especially as they organized elite workers with high skills and economic value.

*The Teamsters Strike exploded in street violence in 1934 as militant union members clashed with police deputies backed by the anti-union Citizens Alliance.*

Union organizing gained momentum in the city's machine shops, whose owners struggled to keep up with orders from Minneapolis's burgeoning milling industry. In 1900, a group of machinists organized the first local affiliate of the International Association of Machinists, one of the country's largest and strongest national unions. By 1901, IAM Local 91 had organized workers at three foundries. "The machine-shop owners, who had lost only one small strike in their history, now had to contend with an aggressive local union backed by the powerful IAM," noted Millikan.[3]

But soon the balance of power would shift again. Faced with a growing economic threat, the leaders of the city's machining industry were not content to sit back and allow the IAM to constrain what they viewed as their management prerogatives. They organized themselves as the Twin City Association of Employers of Machinists and, with the backing of their national industry association, were able to break a Local 91 strike in the summer of 1901. Additionally, they successfully checked the IAM's progress as it tried to organize "closed shops," which would have required workers to join the union as a condition of employment in the city's machine shops.

The IAM's defeat demonstrated the effectiveness of the employers' collective action in blunting the thrusts of the labor movement. That lesson was not lost on the broader business community that came together in 1903 to organize itself as the Citizens Alliance of Minneapolis. For the next three decades, the alliance dedicated itself to maintaining the "open shop," where workers did not need to join a union when employed by one of the city's major industries or businesses. Alliance leaders used philosophical precepts embedded in the Declaration of Independence to bolster their case for an open shop, according to Millikan, maintaining that "the very organizational nature of unions violates the American spirit of liberty . . . Unions deny workers the liberty to work. Thus, the open shop protects the liberty and independence of the employee."[4]

## New Leaders Emerge

The alliance's leader for more than thirty years, Albert W. Strong, became the organization's chief advocate of the open shop and the concepts upon which it was based. Strong helped establish the organization in 1903, and he was still there, as one of the group's leaders, when the truckers struck in 1934. By then, the local industrialist had to deal with a group of men whose philosophy differed sharply from his own.

Their leader was a former lumberjack named Vincent Dunne, who had left his northern Minnesota home in his teens and migrated west to Montana's forests. There he encountered the radical Industrial Workers of the World and became imbued with the IWW's views about the class struggle between bosses and workers. After a few years out west, he returned to Minnesota and settled in Minneapolis, where he started working in the newly established trucking industry. Retaining his radical beliefs from his IWW days, Dunne later became a committed member of the Communist Party's Trotskyite wing. By the mid-1920s, the radical activist was working in the city's coal yards, where he met a driver named Carl Skoglund who shared his political views. Together, Dunne and Skoglund became union organizers, eventually working through Local 574 of the Teamsters Union. Later,

Dunne's two brothers, Miles and Grant, aided his organizing efforts.[5]

As the Depression took hold, there was some work to be had in the coal yards, but it was sporadic at best. One driver recalled his working conditions during the early 1930s: "The only time you worked was when the weather was cold . . . This was during the depression; people wouldn't order coal unless they needed it. The report would come in that there was serious weather coming, then they would order coal. Then you'd haul coal until 12 o'clock at night. Never got overtime. The yard workers that unloaded the boxcars and loaded the trucks, they were working for 20, 25, 30 cents per hour and the only time they would work too was when the weather was severe."[6]

Dunne and Skoglund believed the city's coal yards provided a good organizing opportunity, but they knew they needed to organize in a new way. Traditionally, the U.S. labor movement had been organized around occupational specialties, but the two Minneapolis activists believed the traditional approach would not succeed in the city's coal yards, where some workers were drivers who might own their trucks and others were sorters and loaders who might never leave the yards. Dunne and Skoglund wanted to bring them all together in an industrial model that would later become the foundation for the Congress of Industrial Organizations (CIO). While they won acquiescence from Local 574's leaders for their organizing approach, Dunne and Skoglund encountered continued hostility from Dan Tobin, the conservative head of the International Teamsters Union, who wanted to maintain the traditional craft specialties.

The two labor activists were rooted in their ideology and its focus on class struggle, but they were more than ideologues. Unlike other radicals who were preoccupied with abstract philosophizing, Dunne and Skoglund knew how to put their ideas to work furthering their day-to-day organizing efforts. Working side by side with the men they were trying to organize, the two were able to establish a bond of trust with their fellow workers. "They offered coal yard workers a coherent explanation for the difficult conditions under which they struggled, and they communicated that explanation to other workers forcefully, credibly and effectively," noted labor historian Philip Korth. The network of per-

sonal relationships developed by Dunne and Skoglund contributed greatly to their organizing effectiveness. "[Skoglund] was
generous and a nice fellow, and most of the fellas knew him, and
if he asked you to join a union, you pretty much had to," one coal
yard worker later recalled.[7]

During the early weeks of 1934, Local 574 had been rebuffed by
the local coal operators when it sought bargaining recognition, so
the union started making plans for a strike, with Dunne and
Skoglund as chief strategists and organizers. Initially, the weather
did not cooperate: a January thaw caused the coal business to lag.
But then the temperature dropped below zero in early February,
coal orders shot up, and the union called for a strike to begin the
following week. Feeling the pressure, the operators implemented
some modest wage increases but refused to bargain directly with
the union. In response, the union and its seven hundred members
walked off the job on February 7.

Although they never bargained directly, the two sides did negotiate in a fashion by working through a third-party mediator,
the U.S. Regional Labor Board. Eventually, the board worked out
an arrangement that proved to be face-saving for both the operators and the unions. While continuing to reject exclusive bargaining rights for Local 574, the operators did agree to negotiate
about wages and working conditions with union officials who
represented some but not all of their employees. While many of
the coal companies would later subvert the spirit of the agreement, the union could show that it had achieved a measure of
recognition as a result of the strike, which ended three days after
it started.

The *Minneapolis Labor Review* was quick to claim victory.
"With a dash and unity that electrified the city, Coal Drivers of
Minneapolis last week after a whirlwind strike of two days and a
half won recognition of the union," the *Review* declared. "It was a
short, sharp but effective engagement with employers who had
steadfastly maintained that their employees were not organized
and it sent shivers up the back of the Citizens Alliance bosses as
they witnessed the power of labor militantly organized."[8]

## Building on an Early Success

Despite its qualified nature, Local 574 viewed the February coal drivers' strike as a success. Wages had been increased, at least modestly, and a process was in place for future negotiations. Harry deBoer, a coal yard worker and union activist, later recalled the impact of the settlement at a time when the city's struggling labor movement could claim few victories:

> We went back to work and the news spread like wildfire. The workers, truck drivers mainly, went down to the coal yards. They wanted the leadership of the coal drivers to organize them, nobody else. They'd walk up to the Central Labor Union and the first thing they said was: "Where's that union that organized the coal drivers?" That was proven that they had a leadership that knew what to do and wouldn't sell them out. Up to that point there was a lot of unions that went on strike and got sold out by the leaders and let down.[9]

Korth commented on the significance of Local 574's strike for Minneapolis workers generally. The upholsterers union had conducted a successful strike shortly before the coal drivers settled, but it did not have a significant impact on union organizing. "Perhaps the mass of workers could not so readily identify with the upholsterers' narrower craft base; the skills employed in delivering coal were available to every worker. The average worker could easily see himself working in the coal yard, either driving or carrying," Korth wrote.[10]

By now recognizing that the bulwark against unionism had suffered at least some minor cracks, the Citizens Alliance began making plans to mobilize the city's business leaders in an effort to combat the newly resilient labor movement that threatened to organize the entire local trucking industry. Alliance leaders knew that Local 574 could potentially exercise a stranglehold on the local economy because trucking served as the crucial link between the various facets of the city's industrial operations. But Albert Strong and his allies believed they could achieve a strategic and tactical advantage over the union by broadening the scope of the conflict.

During the coal strike, "[Local 574] targeted a limited number of employers in an effort to focus the strike," Korth explained. "To conduct a broader strike against large numbers of employers would have required sophisticated organization, extensive resources and a large cadre of organizers. What was good for the union was bad for the targeted employers, whose chances of defeating the union would be improved by stretching the unions' resources as thin as possible."[11]

## Preparing for a New Battle

Dunne, Skoglund, and their supporters knew they needed to build on the momentum of the earlier strike by taking aim at a new and larger target—despite the risks entailed in doing so. With enthusiastic support from local truckers, Local 574 shifted its focus to the city's market district and its major employers, who dealt in perishable produce. On April 30, the union announced its demands for a closed shop and an average wage of $27.50 per week, with extra pay for overtime work.

The eleven market district firms targeted by Local 574 quickly called in reinforcements to deal with this new threat. Soon an informal committee, representing 166 local businesses with truck driver employees, had been formed to respond to the union's demands. Behind the scenes, Strong and the Citizens Alliance would plot strategy for this business group.

Almost immediately, the two sides began jockeying for position. In its opening shot, the committee charged, accurately enough, that Local 574 did not represent workers at all of the 166 firms. But the union had never claimed the broader representation; its target had been the eleven market firms that employed drivers. For its part, the business committee wanted to expand the scope of the conflict. "If [the committee] could transform a dispute between a few employers and their workers into a broad struggle between respectable community leaders, who rose up to defend their workers against a disreputable, revolutionary cadre, than they might generate public support that would assure successful resistance," Korth observed.[12]

After an inconclusive meeting between Local 574 and business committee leaders convened by the Regional Labor Board, the union dropped its immediate demand for a closed shop. Still, the business committee refused to negotiate, maintaining that the union lacked any legitimate claim to represent workers at the firms represented by the committee.

The Citizens Alliance sounded the alarm to its members, warning that the ultimate aim of Local 574 was "unionization of every truck driver in Minneapolis and closed union shop control of all primary transportation."[13]

Frustrated by the lack of progress on the negotiating front, the union called a strike to begin at midnight on May 14. The targeted business owners, backed by the Citizens Alliance, worked to rally public opinion by raising the stakes in the conflict. They attempted to portray the strikers as outside agitators who were a menace to the entire community, intent on fomenting civil unrest. For its part, the union sought to tone down the rhetoric by claiming that it was merely trying to resolve a dispute between the employers and their employees but that the employers had refused to come to the bargaining table.

While they were preparing for the strike, union leaders had to contend with a troublesome internal issue. Local 574 had decided to act on its own after the International Teamsters Union and its head, Dan Tobin, had refused to authorize the strike. The American Federation of Labor backed Tobin and warned its Minneapolis affiliate, the Central Labor Union Council, not to cooperate with Local 574. Individual CLU members strongly supported the local, but the council as a body did not take a direct role in the strike.

However, the CLU's weekly newspaper, the *Minneapolis Labor Review*, did not shy away from rallying support for the truckers. Under a huge banner headline on May 18, declaring "Unionists Report for Picket Duty to 1900 Chicago Ave.," the *Labor Review* told its readers, "Minneapolis is gripped with the most powerful and far reaching strike in its history." The paper went on to praise the courage and tenacity of Local 574, declaring, "they have held the line. They have done their part nobly. It is now for all of organized labor to rally to their support and change Minneapolis from a plague spot of industrial slavery to a place of economic freedom."[14]

Minneapolis at large was split in its views about the strike. About 95 percent of the workers—65 percent of the city's population—were supporters according to Charles Walker, a union sympathizer and journalist who interviewed key leaders on both sides of the labor struggle. Walker reported that about two-thirds of Minneapolis employers strongly supported the Citizens Alliance and its business committee allies, but the remaining one-third,

# ⋆THE MINNEAPOLIS JOURNAL

WEATHER <small>Partly cloudy to-night tonight</small>      FRIDAY EVENING MAY 18, 1934

# 84 Pickets Jailed, Strike Climax Nearing; Huge Mass Meeting Acts to Restore Order

| Board of 40 Named to Aid Police Heads | TRUCK OVERTURNED AS VIOLENCE BREAKS OUT | Salt Boy on Stand Against His Mother | Summary of Moves in Strike . . . . . . . . Quick End of Dispute Urged | Olson Begins Overtures for Peace Meet |
|---|---|---|---|---|

The anti-union *Minneapolis Journal provided one-sided coverage of the 1934 strike in an effort to discredit the Teamsters.*

while opposed to the strike, were nonetheless opposed to the alliance's inflexible, hard line.[15]

Many Minneapolis families found themselves caught in the middle between the contending forces. One included a ten-year-old boy named Sam Hynes. Years later, Hynes recalled the distress the strike had caused his father, then a salesman for Shell Oil Company. During the strike, the elder Hynes had been assigned to follow one of Shell's delivery trucks in a company car. He had the bad luck of following the strike-breaking truck to a gas station just a block away from CLU headquarters. As he was getting out of the car, Hynes saw a mob of angry strikers racing toward him, waving clubs and ax handles. He ran into the gas station, climbed through the bathroom window, jumped back into his car, and sped away, the mob in hot pursuit. "It wasn't an adventure for my father, or a funny story to be told," Sam Hynes remembered.

> It was a humiliation. He had been given a job to do, and had tried to do it, as a man should. But he couldn't, he had to run away . . . He was ashamed.
>
> I began to understand my father's distressful place in the strike. He was on both sides, and on neither. He respected the

authority of the employers—they had a right to tell their workers to go back to work—but he despised their upper-class ways . . . their rich men's arrogance. He thought workers should be loyal to the men who paid them, but he understood why the truck drivers wanted more money; fifteen bucks a week wasn't much to feed a family on. And he hated both sides when they acted violently in mobs.[16]

Strike headquarters in a garage at Nineteenth and Chicago became the union's command center as the labor action moved into its first week. Local 574 perfected a new motorized form of picketing as flying squads, roving the streets in their own trucks and cars, prevented strikebreakers from making their deliveries. Demonstrating an effective mastery of 1930s communication technology, Dunne and the union leaders used telephones at strategic locations throughout the city to keep union headquarters in constant touch with the roving unionists. Dunne and his colleagues also understood the importance of internal communication between strike leadership and the union rank and file. Local 574 published its own daily bulletin to keep membership updated on strike developments. At union headquarters and later at the city's parade grounds, the local sponsored mass rallies in an effort to mobilize broadscale union support for the strike.

Business owners, outraged by the strike's effectiveness, called for police action to halt the picketing. Chief Michael Johannes responded by arresting as many picketers as he could find, but there were always more to take their place.

## Blood in the Streets

On May 17, Minnesota governor Floyd Olson intervened, prodding both sides toward a settlement to head off what many feared would be a major, violent confrontation. As a Farmer-Labor governor, Olson's private sympathies lay with the union, but he had to balance those sentiments with what he saw as his public responsibility to maintain order.

Even Olson could not persuade the employers group to negotiate with Local 574, however. Business owners maintained a public posture that they would negotiate with "duly selected and accredited representatives" of their individual company's employees but would not enter into written agreements with any organizations that claimed to represent those workers.

Two days later, police clashed with strikers in the market district for the first time when a group of union sympathizers tried to halt a strikebreaking trucker at First Avenue and Sixth Street. Twelve men were badly beaten, and several were sent to the hospital. The city's regular policemen had done the beating, but their forces were soon augmented by hastily recruited sheriff's deputies, paid five dollars a day to confront the strikers.

A young journalism student named Eric Sevareid observed the week's events from the sidelines. Later a nationally renowned radio commentator, Sevareid recalled those events in his autobiography: "Some of the boys from the Greek fraternities on the campus joined the police and Citizens Alliance forces with baseball bats on their shoulders. Some of my little crowd joined the strikers in noncombative functions. Most of us, be it confessed, were not of the type that is willing to fight for its beliefs with brick, bat or club."[17]

Following Saturday's struggle in the market district, the strikers regrouped at their headquarters on Chicago to prepare for what was certain to be an even larger battle on Monday. On Sunday, the business committee started running the first in a series of full-page ads in the *Minneapolis Tribune* stating that their members would agree to bargain with workers' representatives as long as they did not have to sign a written agreement.

On Monday morning, the police cordoned off the center of the market district as a contingent of workers assembled on its periphery. Then a truck bearing the sign "Spring the trap and rid the city of rats" stopped in the center of the street and broke through police ranks. The signal had been given and the battle began. "The strikers in the truck, armed with clubs, jumped out," the *Minneapolis Tribune* reported. "Other strikers joined in the rush. Swinging clubs, gas pipes and hurling rocks, the strikers charged, and drove the police back by the force of numbers."[18]

The fighting continued through most of morning and then subsided as both sides suffered casualties. More than thirty combatants were taken to the hospital. The strikers, claiming victory, had done what they said they would do: keep trucks from leaving the market district. "In Minneapolis's most brutal taste of class warfare, the huge crowds had jeered the [employers'] army and cheered Local 574. The well-organized ferocity of the union and the sympathetic response of the onlookers portended an ominous future [for the Citizens Alliance]," observed labor historian Millikan.[19]

The next morning, in an atmosphere that some likened to a giant sporting event, twenty thousand onlookers crowded into the market district as KSTP radio announcers prepared to issue play-by-play reports. Now the police stood back as strikers rushed the special deputies, who were considered strikebreakers.

Then, that crate of tomatoes crashed through the warehouse window, and the Battle of Deputies Run began. In less than an hour, the fighting had subsided in the market district as the deputies fled in panic, leaving Arthur Lyman's battered body behind on the pavement. Local 574, now in complete control of the market district, shut down all truck traffic. "The [Citizens Alliance] could no longer rule Minneapolis by brute force. It had fought a civil war and lost," Millikan noted.[20]

That night, Governor Olson met with representatives from Local 574 and the business committee to hammer out a truce that suspended all picketing and all truck transportation by committee members for twenty-four hours.

Over the next few days, the governor, working through the federally designated Regional Labor Board, was able to put together an ambiguous agreement that appeared to give Local 574 bargaining rights on behalf of its members but required each of the trucking firms targeted by the strike to negotiate individual agreements with the union. The agreement was purposely vague about the issue of "inside workers," those employees who worked inside the trucking company warehouses as well as on the docks, loading and unloading goods. The local, in an effort to establish a true industrial union, sought to represent all company workers, not just the men who drove the trucks, but the employers group resisted this arrangement. As a compromise, Governor Olson inserted language stating the agreement would apply to persons "ordinarily engaged in trucking operations." While the employers read their own meaning into this phrase, the governor gave private assurances to the union that the language did, in fact, apply to inside workers.

Olson's compromise did not involve a direct agreement between representatives of the trucking companies' committee and the union. Rather, both sides pledged to abide by a settlement authored by the Regional Labor Board. Thus, the employers could claim they were dealing with the board and not with Local 574.

Once the agreement had been put in place, union leaders needed consent from the rank and file. At the ratification meeting later that week, leaders called for approval of the agreement, even as some of the union's more radical members urged a rejection of the settlement and a return to the streets. "Had the leadership been what the Citizens Alliance had long been publicly protesting, 'irresponsible agitators,' bent on bloodshed and a Russian soviet in Minneapolis, they would have called for an insurrection, and certainly gotten one," Walker observed. "Instead, desiring a trade union and not a revolution, recognizing the need for recoupment and consolidation of actual gains as a basis for future struggle, the leadership urged acceptance."[21]

"There's no question that we could have taken over the city after the Battle of Deputies Run," Local 574 president Bill Brown later recalled. "We controlled it. All that would have been necessary 'to seize power' would have been to urge a few thousand strikers to capture the Court House. They would have done it . . . the union might have made me soviet mayor, huh? That's just what the Citizens Alliance had been screaming for days that we wanted to do, make a Russian soviet in Minneapolis. But we happened to want a truck drivers' union in Minneapolis. And some of our leaders were revolutionists enough to tell the difference between a militant strike and a revolution."[22]

After considerable debate, the membership agreed to a settlement that brought peace to the streets of Minneapolis, at least temporarily. At the ratification meeting, a spy from the Citizens Alliance, disguised in an old raincoat and a slouch hat, watched the proceedings from the sidelines. "There were thousands and thousands of bums and hoodlums and Communists there. Agitators worked the crowd up to the highest pitch of mob fury. They shouted, sang, and yelled. It was really horrible. I felt like slipping away, getting out of Minneapolis onto a farm somewhere, and never coming back."[23]

## The Battle Resumes

The May agreement left unresolved a number of key issues between the employers and the union, but it provided an enormous boost for the local in the eyes of the city's workers. "Local 574 had carried on a successful strike in a city known for the Open Shop, demonstrating to the workers impressive leadership ability and union power," noted Korth. "Legally speaking, the trucking firms may not have recognized Local 574, but the workers certainly recognized that an organization capable of matching the power of the Citizens Alliance had emerged from the strike."[24]

Howard Carlson, a Minneapolis streetcar motorman, later recorded his impressions of the strike: "When this broke out in 1934, this was something new in the labor movement. They had a leadership, that really knew what to do. They took possession . . . Radio was a new thing at that time. They used new electronics. They had microphones and loudspeakers at their headquarters. It wasn't a private affair. Everybody came. Everybody was welcome."[25]

As the summer wore on, the truckers' initial euphoria over the strike settlement soon gave way to frustration, as the union found the individual trucking firms to be intent on violating the spirit of the agreement. The May settlement stipulated that Local 574 needed to negotiate individual contracts with the trucking firms, many of which found ways to subvert the collective bargaining requirement. By the end of June, union leaders realized that the settlement negotiated by Governor Olson had given them little in the way of tangible benefits, and plans were made for another strike.

On July 11, Local 574 authorized the job action, with the strike scheduled to begin the following week. During this period, the Regional Labor Board tried to restart negotiations but garnered little for its efforts. On Tuesday, July 17, as the strike resumed, Local 574 was able to stop virtually all truck movements in the city.

Two days later, in a media event orchestrated by Minneapolis police chief Michael Johannes, a truck bearing the sign "hospital supplies" did start making deliveries, accompanied by a police escort. Ostensibly, the truck was operating under a permit system, sanctioned by the union, which allowed hospital deliveries. That night, Chief Johannes told his men, "we're going to start moving goods. Don't take a beating. You have shotguns and you know how to use them . . . The police department is going to get goods moving. Now get going—and do your duty."[26]

The scene was set for another confrontation in the market district. It occurred the next day, Friday, July 20, on Third Street North in front of the Slocum Bergren Company. Police cordoned off the area as two trucks loaded merchandise at the company's dock and drove out of the district under police escort. The *New York Times* described what happened next:

> Shortly after 2 PM, a third truck moved out from a wholesale house. It was followed by twelve squad cars each carrying four policemen all armed with shotguns. The truck turned on to Third Street North, and another truck loaded with strike pickets cut ahead of it. Police quickly lined the street, but strikers plowed through the cordon and drove directly into the front of the truck. Police rushed from the convoy cars and opened fire with shotguns on the picket's truck. Two pickets fell off wounded, but the truck continued up the street, being fired on from both sides of the street.[27]

Within a half hour, the battle of Bloody Friday, as it came to be known, was over. Sixty-seven strikers had been wounded; two, included a union activist named Henry Ness, later died.

The *Minneapolis Journal* later reported that the police had first fired over the heads of the strikers, warning them to disburse, but union leaders disputed that interpretation of events, pointing to a photo showing a police gunman aiming directly at a striker's back. An investigation ordered by Governor Olson supported the union claim, declaring "police took direct aim at the pickets and fired to kill. Physical safety of police was at no time endangered. No weapons were in the possession of the pickets in the truck. At no time did the pickets attack the police."[28]

In *American City*, Charles Walker commented that the events of Bloody Friday did not greatly affect day-to-day life in Minneapolis—at least not immediately. On the day of the Third Street confrontation, two thousand people took part in the Maple Hill Songfest. Shirley Temple was appearing in *Stand Up and Cheer* at the Boulevard Theater "and James Cagney in *Here Comes the Navy*—A Romantic Comedy-Drama of Uncle Sam's Jacktars— was packing them in at the State. If the atmosphere of Minneapolis was normal on the day of the battle, twenty-four hours later it was not," Walker went on to report. "It was as if a high voltage of electricity had been discharged into the social organism . . . Bloody Friday moved through the minds of Minneapolis citizens, touching pity, fear, hope, class fear and class pride and, above all, the instinct of group preservation."[29]

Very soon, the events of July 20 had created a sharp cleavage in the city's communal life. Prodded by the Citizens Alliance and its allies, civic groups like Rotary Club, the Kiwanis, and the Lions sprang to the defense of the police department and its chief "Bloody Mike" Johannes. But the unions, the Farmer Labor clubs, and organizations like them, with a strong working-class base, condemned the actions of the police and called for the ouster of Chief Johannes: "For each resolution of the Civic and Commerce Association or the Rotary, (Local) 574 acquired 100 new flesh-and-blood pickets for the front."[30]

Henry Ness's funeral on July 24 brought out a huge throng of mourners, who came to pay tribute to the slain union activist. According to the *Minneapolis Labor Review*, as many as 100,000 people lined the route of the funeral procession as it made its way from strike headquarters on Eighth Street, through the market district, and then on to the Crystal Lake Cemetery: "It was a somber throng, a respectful throng, a throng that felt its sorrow deeply and a throng that from this sorrow would bring forth a new and greater determination for victory." Despite these calming words, the *Review* could not hide its anger when it went on to declare that Ness had been shot to death "by the authorities prostituted to the butcher policies of employers."[31]

While it was railing against the "butcher policies" of the trucking companies, the *Review* also noted that Local 574 had agreed to a settlement proposed by two negotiators representing the Regional Labor Board, Father Francis J. Haas and E. H. Dunnigan. The Haas-Dunnigan Plan established uniform pay rates for trucking workers and called for strikers to be rehired, but it was immediately rejected by the employers committee representing the trucking companies. When the employers announced they would start moving trucks again, Governor Olson, provoked by their intransigence, announced he would declare martial law. His move succeeded in angering both sides of the dispute: employers

STRIKERS ACCEPT PEACE PROPOSAL

 **The Minneapolis Labor Review**

TWENTY-SEVENTH YEAR, NO. XXXX    MINNEAPOLIS, MINN., FRIDAY, JULY 27, 1934    PRICE FIVE CENTS

# 100,000 In Tribute To Ness
# Protest Johannes Butchery

**Daily Papers Hiding Facts Of Massacre**

**Truck Strike--U. S. History Parallel**

**C. L. U. Demands Ouster Johannes**

**Workers And Vets Honor Labor Martyr**

**Resolution**

**Strikers Vote To Accept Peace Proposal**

**Resolution**

**F-L Women Picnic Friday, July 27th**

*The militantly pro-union Minneapolis Labor Review used bold headlines to counter the bias shown by the city's daily papers.*

believed a declaration of martial law would perpetuate the strike, while some union leaders feared it would break it.

In fact, the martial law declaration, issued on July 24, created a somewhat muddled outcome. Technically, the strike remained in effect, but the National Guard began issuing permits to allow companies not directly targeted by Local 574 to resume transporting their goods. By July 29, four thousand permits had been issued, infuriating union leaders. Now they believed the man once viewed as their ally had undercut their efforts to achieve their strike goals.

When Local 574 announced it would resume picketing, Olson reacted swiftly by ordering the National Guard to raid union headquarters. During the incursion, which occurred just before noon on August 1, Vince Dunne and his brother Miles were arrested and briefly detained in a stockade at the state fairgrounds. Olson also directed the National Guard to raid the headquarters of the Citizens Alliance two days later, on August 3.

*Vince Dunne, a union leader and key strategist for the strikers, was arrested but soon released by Minnesota National Guard officers operating under orders from Governor Floyd Olson. Olson used the arrest as a gesture to demonstrate he was intent on maintaining law and order in the streets of Minneapolis.*

"The two raids proved more symbolic than concrete steps towards the resolution of the strike," noted Korth. "The raid on the
strike headquarters and on the Citizens Alliance asserted the National Guard's authority over the strikers and employers alike. Olson appeared even handed in his treatment of the two groups."[32]

As the governor pressed for a settlement, the union agreed to
accept the Haas-Dunnigan Plan but the employers group, egged
on by the Citizens Alliance, remained defiant. Then, on August 8,
a new player appeared on the sidelines of this Minnesota drama.
That day, President Franklin Roosevelt came to Rochester for a
ceremony honoring the Mayo brothers. While there, the president
met with Governor Olson, who briefed him on the Minneapolis
strike.

A labor delegation, led by *Labor Review* editor Robley Cramer,
also came to Rochester and met with Roosevelt's chief aide, Louis
Howe. Cramer delivered a letter charging that officials of the
Reconstruction Finance Corporation (RFC) were aiding the Minneapolis employers as they resisted a strike settlement. As representatives of the federal agency that provided credit for banks,
railroads, and other major businesses during the Depression, RFC
officials were in a position to exert substantial influence over Minneapolis business leaders, including those in the Citizens Alliance.
"One word from the President to these [RFC] appointees that they
should use their influence to have employers accept the government [Haas-Dunnigan] settlement proposal would end the
strike," Cramer told Howe.[33]

"Roosevelt's visit to Rochester set in motion forces that ended
the strike," Korth explained. Soon after, the RFC's national head,
Jesse Jones, began making calls to Minnesota industrialists and
financiers who relied on Jones's agency to meet their credit needs.
Jones, a player in the nation's financial circles, lent his considerable
influence to a settlement of the Minneapolis strike, signaling to local business leaders that their relationships with his agency could
be jeopardized if they continued to resist the Haas-Dunnigan
Plan.[34]

After two more weeks of haggling between the union and the
employers group, a settlement was finally reached, giving the union
most of what it wanted. Striking workers would be reinstated by the
employers and a new higher wage rate would be put in place for

As federal labor negotiators, Reverend Francis Haas (center) and
Eugene Dunnigan (right), shown here with Governor Olson,
worked to bring about a settlement of the Teamsters strike.

truckers and their helpers. On August 22, Jones conveyed the news
in a telegram to President Roosevelt: "GLAD TO REPORT THAT
STRIKE IS SETTLED. MEN AT WORK THIS MORNING."[35]

"The end of the strike came with dramatic suddenness," the
*Minneapolis Journal* reported. According to the *Journal*, the settlement had come at a "psychological time," when both sides had
tired of the "long, bitter and costly struggle." The employers' negotiators declined to comment on the settlement, but union representative Grant Dunne expressed relief that the strike was over:
"We did not get all we thought we ought to have, but the union is
recognized, it is now well established . . . If all hands live up to the
spirit of the peace agreement, there will be no more trouble."[36]

Dunne may have been restrained, but the *Minneapolis Labor
Review* was jubilant. "TRUCK DRIVERS TRIUMPH IN STRIKE,"
the *Review*'s headline blared on August 24. "Winning of this strike
marks the greatest victory in the annals of the local trade union
movement. It came when every trick and device that the Citizens

Alliance carries in its arsenal of union smashing was brought out and tried and failed." While the *Review* acknowledged some unionists' concerns about the governor's martial law declaration, the paper praised Olson for his role in helping to bring about the strike settlement: "Organized labor found that the powers of the government in the hands of a battler for the workers and farmers like Governor Olson is something not to be scoffed at." Now, Minneapolis had been transformed from a "scab's paradise" to "a city of hope for those who toil," the *Review* declared triumphantly.[37]

The only sour note during the citywide celebration was sounded by Minneapolis mayor A. G. Bainbridge, who had clearly sided with the employers during the strike. In an obvious reference to the Dunne brothers, Bainbridge said the "settlement of the strike should not be regarded as a victory for the communists." The mayor added, "these men, many of whom injected themselves into the dispute . . . have revealed themselves, as never before as rabid opponents of all law and order . . . I am serving notice here and now that our fight on communism has just begun . . . and I will not be satisfied until all those who foment unrest and hatred of legal authority are driven from our city."[38]

The August settlement put the strikers back to work and gave them a pay raise, but it required Local 574 to conduct company-by-company elections to get bargaining rights for its members. Eventually, the union was able to represent a majority of workers eligible for union membership in the 166 Minneapolis firms that employed truckers. However, workers voted to confer bargaining rights on the Teamsters local in fewer than half of the firms, a fact the employers group played up in a continued effort to undercut the union. Still, Local 574 had achieved a significant victory as a result of its summer-long campaign for recognition. Initially, the union had struck only eleven firms. But summer's end, it represented over seven hundred workers at sixty-two separate businesses.

Most of the trucking employers in Minneapolis wanted to put the months of labor strife behind them and cooperate with the settlement. But some, continuing to fight a rear-guard action, found devious ways to short their workers in their weekly pay envelopes.

Labor strife continued in Minneapolis even after the Truckers

Strike was settled. In 1935, two innocent bystanders caught in the crossfire were shot and killed when a strike at the Iron City Ornamental Iron Company exploded in violence. That same year, a battle between police and picketers at Strutwear Knitting resulted in injuries but no deaths. Both strikes were eventually settled when management essentially yielded to union demands.

In later years, the Citizens Alliance and its successor organization, Associated Industries of Minneapolis, continued working— mainly in the legislative arena—to thwart the aims of organized labor. But increasingly individual businesses charted their own course of action. Business owners would no longer speak with one voice and act with one fist. And at midcentury, with the passage of the federal Taft-Hartley Act, labor would see many of its hard-fought gains starting to erode. But in 1934, the Minneapolis Truckers Strike helped level the city's economic playing field in an important way. The Mill City's labor-management relations would never be the same.[39]

The events of the mid-1930s helped erase a municipal stain that had tarnished Minneapolis's image in the economic sphere, but another blemish remained in the social realm, where divisiveness and discrimination characterized relationships between the city's ethnic and religious groups. Another decade would pass before Minneapolis faced up to this civic shortcoming and took steps to address it.

# The Curious Twin

CAREY MCWILLIAMS may not have set out to shame this city's up-standing citizens, but his 1946 article accomplished that result, just as Lincoln Steffens's "Shame of Minneapolis" had done nearly a half century earlier. In "Minneapolis: The Curious Twin," published in the magazine *Common Ground*, McWilliams uncovered an "iron curtain" of prejudice and discrimination that separated Jews from non-Jews in Minneapolis, making Minnesota's largest city "the capital of anti-Semitism in the United States." McWilliams's title came from his finding that neighboring St. Paul was much more accepting of Jews than its twin city across the river.[1]

The California-based journalist was not the first American writer to discover widespread prejudice against Jews in Minneapolis. Three years earlier, Selden Menefee, writing in *Assignment U.S.A.*, noted, "signs of militant anti-Semitism I found to be almost entirely lacking in the Middle West, as in the South and West—except for Minneapolis." Menefee's observations attracted little local notice when his book was published in the middle of World War II, but the *Common Ground* article received much attention and created more than a little discomfort in the local corridors of power.[2]

The *Minneapolis Star and Journal*'s editors felt they needed to acknowledge McWilliams's accusations, but they did so with some hesitation. They seemed to be squirming in their seats as they reprinted a large section of "The Curious Twin" but went on to cast doubt on the accuracy of the article's findings. In assessing the *Common Ground* article, the *Star* observed that it was merely informing its readers about "what is being said elsewhere in the nation about this city . . . Usually such comment is praise, and is read with pride and satisfaction. But a faithful report of such comment must include the bitter with the sweet." McWilliams's article is "an example of the bitter," the paper noted. The *Star* ended its editorial by maintaining, "perhaps these comments [about anti-Semitism in Minneapolis] can be effectively rebutted at a number of points. The purpose of reprinting them is simply to inform Minneapolitans of what is being said nationally about the community.[3]

Rabbi David Aronson, a leader of the local Jewish community, commended the *Star* for lifting the veil of secrecy about anti-

Semitism in Minneapolis but maintained that the paper did not go far enough in addressing the problem. Writing in *American Jewish World,* Aronson declared, "Now that Minneapolitans know the facts, what are they going to do about it? . . . [The city's community leaders] can no longer plead ignorance of the situation even as an extenuating excuse. Now that the facts are public, silence on their part means consent, and inactivity will be interpreted as acquiescence."[4]

At least one local leader was not willing to acquiesce and remain silent. Minneapolis mayor Hubert Humphrey took McWilliams's findings to heart and used them to promote his ambitious civil rights agenda. Until Humphrey took up the cause, soon after his election in 1945, combating prejudice and discrimination had never been an issue of particular concern for city hall leaders.

## Hate-filled Messages and Ethnic Slurs

During the first half of the twentieth century, before McWilliams's "Curious Twin" appeared in print, Minneapolis's small Jewish community, never more than five percent of the city's population, endured a steady stream of hate-filled messages from a broad range of rabid anti-Semites. Many operated from the city's radical fringe, but some were uncomfortably close to the mainstream.[5]

In the late 1920s, the scandal sheet *Saturday Press* spewed forth a particularly virulent form of anti-Semitism as the paper's editor, Jay Near, crusaded against crime and corruption in Minneapolis. Some Jews, men like Isadore "Kid Cann" Blumenfeld and Mose Barnett, were involved in the city's underworld, a fact Near used to inflame passions and tar the entire Jewish community. "I'm not out to cleanse Israel of the filth that clings to Israel's skirts, I'm out to 'hew to the line, let the chips fly where they may,'" Near declared in October 1929. "I simply state a fact when I say that ninety percent of the crimes committed against society in this city are committed by Jew gangsters . . . It is Jew, Jew, Jew as long as one cares to comb over the records."[6]

Later, Near wrote, "I have withdrawn all allegiance to anything with a hook nose that eats herring. I have adopted the sparrow as my national bird until . . . the [Klu Klux Klan] hammers the eagle's beak out straight." An embittered and embattled journalist,

Near was dismissed as a crank and rabble-rouser by the city's establishment, but another outspoken anti-Semite was able to cloak himself with the respectability of organized religion.[7]

In 1928, a self-styled evangelist named Luke Rader established his River Lake Gospel Tabernacle at the far end of East Lake Street. During his twenty-five-year tenure at the tabernacle, Rader laced his religious messages with the most extreme form of anti-Semitic vitriol. In 1931, he told his mainly middle-class congregation that "Satan's synagogue" controlled much of the country's economy. Later, Rader demeaned Franklin Roosevelt's New Deal, calling it the "Jew Deal." Into the 1940s, he was still raging against the "lying, thieving, cheating, blasphemous Jew."[8]

Rader, an early radio evangelist, attracted a large following and regularly filled the seats of the Lake Street tabernacle on Sunday mornings. In 1939, the rabidly right-wing preacher mobilized his followers to support his foray into local politics. Rader ran a losing race for mayor but garnered a respectable 12 percent of the citywide vote in the mayoral primary. In the Twelfth Ward, where his church was located, Rader pulled in close to 20 percent of the vote.[9]

In 1938, the year before Rader's unsuccessful bid for mayor, anti-Semitism reached into Minnesota's political mainstream when a thirty-two-year-old Republican named Harold Stassen deposed Elmer Benson, the incumbent Farmer-Labor governor, in the gubernatorial election. Benson himself had just come through a bruising primary battle with Hjalmer Petersen. Benson and Petersen, both Farmer-Laborites but bitter enemies, had vied to assume the mantle of the revered Floyd Olson, who died in office in 1935. Petersen helped stoke the flames of anti-Semitism by claiming that Benson had surrounded himself with Jews who were also Communist sympathizers.[10]

Stassen supporters echoed these charges and used them to gain a partisan advantage during the general election campaign in 1938. "The Republicans picked up the antisemitic campaign where the Farmer-Labor opposition left off. What had been largely a whispering campaign and one by innuendo became open, brazen, well-financed and successful," Minnesota historian Hy Berman later wrote.[11]

Taking the high road, Stassen did not directly engage in anti-Semitic appeals himself, leaving the low road to his supporters, who, in the weeks leading up to the November election, circulated a pamphlet entitled "Are they Communists or Cats paw," playing up the Jewishness of Benson's key advisors. At the same time, an inflammatory anti-Semitic cartoon entitled "Three Jehu Riders," showing Benson as a donkey ridden by three men with obvious Jewish features, was widely distributed throughout the state.

*Three men with obvious Jewish features, representing incumbent Farmer-Labor governor Elmer Benson's Jewish advisors, ride a donkey in this anti-Semitic cartoon, which was distributed during the election campaign of 1938.*

On election day 1938, Stassen routed Benson as Republicans rolled over hapless Farmer-Laborites all over the state. "So ended the most successful use of political antisemitism in the United States. Benson might have lost the election without the use of antisemitism as a weapon as an anti–New Deal wave swept the nation, but antisemitism was used and used successfully," noted Berman.[12]

Anti-Jewish attitudes in their more extreme form may have spilled over into religion and politics during the 1930s, but they even appeared, packaged more subtly and respectably, in academic treatises of the period. A sociological study of the Twin Cities commissioned by the Minneapolis Council of Social Agencies in 1936 talked about the "Jewish invasion" of north Minneapolis that had occurred when Jews began moving into previously non-Jewish residential districts during the early years of the twentieth century.

"People became alarmed and frightened at the number of Jews," the study observed. "Many of these families were often very untidy. A fruit man returning from his day's work frequently dumped spoiled fruit in his backyard. A chicken dealer kept crated

*This delicatessen was a Plymouth Avenue landmark in the heart of Minneapolis's heavily Jewish near North Side.*

chickens in his yard. Even the pride and dignity of Highland Avenue finally humbled and succumbed to this affront. In 1912 the first Jewish family moved into the Highland district. To close an estate, one of the large residences was sold to a chicken dealer. From this time on, the whole Oak Lake district was rapidly taken over by Jews."[13]

The more overt forms of anti-Semitism were distressing to the local Jewish community, but the more subtle versions involving ethnic slurs and social ostracism were also deeply hurtful. "People of all groups . . . make the most blatant statements against Jews with the calm assumption that they are merely stating facts with which anyone would agree," Menefee noted in 1943.[14]

McWilliams found that social ostracism of Jews was the norm when he visited Minneapolis in the 1940s. "So far as I know, Minneapolis is the only city in America in which Jews are, as a matter of practice and custom, ineligible for membership in the service clubs. In fact, Jews have never been accepted into membership in the local Kiwanis, Rotary, Lions or Toastmasters organization."[15]

## A More Accepting Twin

Across the Mississippi River in St. Paul, McWilliams found substantially less anti-Semitism. "The Jewish communities, in cities like San Francisco and St. Paul, are relatively free from the odious social restrictions and limitations which exist in Minneapolis," he noted. He explained that St. Paul Jews participated fully in the city's communal life and held leadership roles in organizations such as the Red Cross and the Community Chest. In contrast, Minneapolis Jews were denied such roles in the broader community.[16]

McWilliams speculated that the contrasts between Minneapolis and St. Paul were due, in part, to the differing ethnic and socioeconomic makeup of the two cities. In Minneapolis, a tightly knit Anglo-Saxon Protestant elite with New England roots controlled the local economy and erected informal barriers to participation by outsiders. Members of this privileged group, the city's power brokers, had backed the anti-union Citizens Alliance over the years and faced the wrath of the local labor movement during the Truckers Strike of 1934.

Exclusivity, a defining characteristic of Minneapolis's social order during the early twentieth century, was not as prevalent in St.

Paul—at least not to the same extent. There, the largely German and Irish Catholic community was somewhat more accepting of Jews than the more numerous WASPs and Scandinavians in Minneapolis. In St. Paul, moreover, the Jewish community, with its more acculturated German origins, had a longer history of civic involvement than did its Minneapolis counterpart. "In years past, the Catholics in St. Paul functioned within the framework of a minority psychology, that is, they knew what it was to be singled out as a minority for attack by nativist elements," McWilliams noted. "Also, the Catholics in St. Paul produced some outstanding clerical leaders who are credited with having taken an active part in opposing nativistic movements."[17]

McWilliams went on to explain that Jews from Germany and Czechoslovakia, having accompanied their fellow countrymen to St. Paul, were able to create a bond with non-Jews based on language and customs at a time when St. Paul was still a frontier settlement. Immigration patterns differed markedly in Minneapolis, accounting for a sharp difference in attitudes between the two cities, McWilliams postulated. In contrast to the German and Czech Jews who were part of St. Paul's first wave of settlers, Jews arrived in Minneapolis much later in the nineteenth century, when the city's social patterns were already established. Minneapolis Jews, moreover, came mainly from Eastern Europe and were largely impoverished, unlike the German Jews of St. Paul, many of whom were prosperous merchants. In the late nineteenth century, Scandinavians constituted a major immigrant group in Minneapolis. Unlike the Germans and Czechs of St. Paul, Scandinavians in Minneapolis had virtually no experience with Jews in their native lands, and this lack of familiarity may have provided an environment in which anti-Semitism could take hold.

Despite the prevalence of prejudice and discrimination in St. Paul's "curious twin" in the mid-1940s, McWilliams believed conditions could change: "It is interesting to note that many of the service clubs in Minneapolis which traditionally excluded Jews are affiliated with national organizations which have long boasted that their membership is open to all, regardless of creed. One wonders, therefore, how long it will be before these national organizations begin to exert pressure on the Minneapolis foxholes of anti-Semitism."[18]

*A Campaign to Improve Human Relations*

McWilliams did not study Minneapolis's small African American community and its concerns. If he had, he would have learned that its members faced much of the same prejudice and discrimination experienced by the city's substantially larger and more visible Jewish community. The main form of racial discrimination was economic, noted historian Jennifer Delton: "Employers simply refused to hire black workers, outside a few circumscribed areas. The few jobs open to black Minnesotans in the first half of the twentieth century were in the service industries and on the railroads."[19]

Nellie Stone Johnson, one of the city's early civil rights leaders, recounted the racial slurs she encountered after moving to Minneapolis from the all-white farming community where she had grown up. "You'd see a blond-headed little kid in town here, going along talking about niggers and kikes! The blond kids who were not Jewish talk like that all the time—*nigger* would just roll out of their mouth. I didn't hear it every day, but more than I wanted to. It was kind of like today. You don't hear it, but you know it's just below the surface," Johnson recalled.[20]

Jews and blacks were shut out of jobs by many of the city's largest employers, and both groups found certain residential neighborhoods to be off-limits. But while housing discrimination against Jews was subtle and often unspoken, against blacks it was direct and overt. In neighborhoods throughout the city, real estate deeds, as a matter of course, included covenants making the property unavailable to African Americans. One such agreement, for a home on Forty-first Avenue, prohibited its sale or lease to "any person of the Negro race or to any person married to or living with a person of the Negro race."[21]

When he took office in 1945, mayor Hubert Humphrey was deeply distressed by the city's dismal human rights record. Later, in his autobiography, he commented on the "rampant prejudice" facing blacks, Jews, and American Indians in Minneapolis. The mayor received accolades for his human rights stance from Nell Dodson Russell, an African American writer who interviewed Humphrey soon after his election. "In the matter of inter-race relations, Hubert Humphrey is sincere, frank and determined . . . [He] publicly expressed his opinions on the question of Negro rights long before he ever ran for public office. He is familiar with the problems Negroes face, and he is ready to help solve them if he can get the cooperation he wants," Russell wrote in the *Minneapolis Spokesman,* the city's African American weekly.[22]

In his inaugural address, Humphrey took a strong stand against intolerance, declaring, "government can no longer ignore displays of bigotry, violence and discrimination." Later, he would embellish this theme in his famous civil rights speech to the 1948 Democratic National Convention. Throughout his career, Humphrey used soaring rhetoric to promote practical policies; in his 1945 address, he called for the establishment of a local fair employment practices commission that could help provide equal employment opportunity "to all persons regardless of race, color or creed."[23]

But Humphrey soon found that soaring rhetoric was not enough to get his policies adopted. His initial fair employment practices plan, presented to a city council committee, was rejected by a vote of three to two, showing Humphrey he needed to establish a base of support for civil rights if he was going to make a real difference in city hall. Soon after the council rejection, he started building that base by creating a semi-official advisory group known as the Mayor's Committee on Human Relations.

With political adroitness, the Minneapolis mayor persuaded the noted Lutheran minister Reverend Reuben Youngdahl to head the committee. Youngdahl was pastor of the city's largest Lutheran church and brother to Judge Luther Youngdahl, the Republican who would be elected governor of Minnesota in 1946. With Humphrey's enthusiastic backing, the committee began laying the groundwork for a public response to the issue of racial and religious discrimination in Minneapolis. Humphrey and Reverend Youngdahl were able to attract important local business leaders to this new civic effort aimed at breaking down social

*During his time as mayor in the mid-1940s, Hubert Humphrey pushed for local action to combat ethnic and racial discrimination in Minneapolis.*

barriers. During the prewar era, the need to adjust the social contract would not have been of much concern to the city's social and
economic elite, but now, in the mid-1940s, Humphrey's human
rights initiative marked the beginning of a new, more progressive
outlook by key elements in the city's leadership group.

Soon after it was established, the mayor's committee undertook an ambitious effort to assess the level of racial and religious
discrimination in Minneapolis. Attracting five hundred volunteers, the "self-survey" was revealing. Humphrey's biographer,
Carl Solberg, described the process: "Blacks and Jews walked side
by side with Yankee housewives and Scandinavian farmers' sons
to check out discriminatory practices in specific areas—offices,
factories, schools, and churches." During the two-year-long study,
the committee undertook an extensive analysis of housing conditions affecting Jews, African Americans, and other minorities in
Minneapolis. Professional support for the housing phase of the
study was provided by Charles Johnson and Herman Long from
the Race Relations Department at Fisk University in Nashville,
Tennessee.[24]

As part of their study, Johnson and Long surveyed the local real
estate industry and received responses from seventy-five or about
20 percent of the firms doing business in Minneapolis. One of the
Fisk team's goals was to determine the extent to which racial
covenants affected housing availability for minorities. Participating firms were asked to describe their policies affecting sale and
rental of housing to blacks and Jews. Nearly 80 percent indicated
they would rent or sell to blacks only in those areas already occupied by that racial group. About half the firms recorded they
would rent or sell to Jews only in neighborhoods already considered to be primarily Jewish. About 40 percent of the realtors indicated their new subdivisions contained deeds that sought to ex-
clude nonwhites.

The Fisk researchers also attempted to assess the attitudes of
members of the broader majority community about having blacks
and Jews as neighbors. The researchers surveyed two groups of
Minneapolis residents about this issue. One included current
property owners and renters; the second consisted of people seeking housing in Minneapolis. Both groups were asked whether they
would object to having blacks and Jews as neighbors. Among cur-

rent residents, 32 percent objected to having Jews as neighbors and 63 percent to having blacks as neighbors. Among those seeking housing, negative attitudes were even more pronounced, with 43 percent objecting to Jews and 85 percent to blacks.

While housing was a major focus of the self-survey, the project also examined patterns of minority group participation in the city's civic organizations. In its introduction to this section of the report, the survey noted that "alleged membership restrictions" by these organizations had helped gain Minneapolis the title of anti-Semitic capital of the United States. Despite the subject's sensitivity, the commission was able to amass responses from seventy of the eighty-five organizations contacted to disclose whether they had Jewish, black, or Japanese American members. Over 90 percent of the responding organizations were willing to indicate their level of Japanese or black membership, but less than 80 percent would disclose whether they had Jewish members. Sixteen organizations reported that they had some Jewish members, but ten of them indicated that Jews constituted less than two percent of their total membership. Only seven of the responding organizations indicated they had black members, and only three reported membership of Japanese Americans. The survey concluded its section on civic participation by noting that it was unable to make a general finding of discrimination based on the survey data. It was, however, able to conclude that Jews, blacks, and Japanese Americans were not participating in the city's civic life in proportion to their percentage of the city's overall population.[25]

When the self-survey's full results were released in November 1948, they documented, at least in part, a pattern of minority group exclusion from broad spheres of economic, civic, and social life in Minneapolis. In a front-page story entitled "Better Break Urged for City Minority Groups," the *Minneapolis Morning Tribune* declared, "Human relations in Minneapolis were weighed . . . and found wanting in a number of areas." The *Tribune* also reported on a day-long conference convened by the Mayor's Committee on Human Relations to examine the survey results. The conference concluded by calling for some rather mild corrective actions relying primarily on education. In the field of housing, it proposed some concrete policies, including passage of a statewide fair housing act and elimination of restrictive covenants in any

*The Tribune gave prominent coverage to a 1948 report issued by the Mayor's Committee on Human Relations examining discriminatory practices in Minneapolis.*

proposed subdivisions submitted for review to the city's planning commission.[26]

In a December editorial, *American Jewish World* noted that the survey offered "statistical evidence now for the first time of the degree to which bigotry and prejudice operate among the city's residents. That prejudice exists has long been known: the value of the survey report is that it seeks to define the quantitative degree to which minority elements of the population are subjected to discrimination because of race, religion or national origin. And no one can be proud of the evidence." It went on to note that the committee had also proposed action steps to combat the discrimination its report documented: "The Committee has said in effect: The situation is not good, but it can certainly be improved—if some of these steps are taken."[27]

### Promoting Fair Employment

Even before its report was issued, the Committee on Human Relations achieved a key victory when the Minneapolis City Council approved a fair employment practices ordinance in January 1947.

Adopted by a vote of twenty-one to three, the ordinance banned employment discrimination in Minneapolis and established a five-member commission to investigate discrimination complaints and pursue remedial actions. *American Jewish World* applauded the city's action, noting that it was "the most comprehensive and aggressive measure adopted by any city thus far in the field of human relations. The city which only a few months ago was branded as 'the capital of anti-Semitism' is now officially occupying the most forward position in anti-bias legislation." The *Minneapolis Spokesman* also hailed passage of the ordinance. "Our hats are off to the 21 members of the city council who had the courage and wisdom to take a stand for equal opportunity for all," declared the *Spokesman*.[28]

Several months later, the five members of the Fair Employment Practices Commission (FEPC) were appointed by Humphrey and confirmed by the city council. The appointees, all men, were very much establishment figures. They included two attorneys, one black and the other Jewish. The former, Raymond Cannon, was vice president of the Minneapolis Urban League board, while the latter, Amos Deinard, had founded the firm of Leonard, Street and Deinard and would serve on the commission for nearly twenty years. The other three were Jack Jorgenson, vice president of the Central Labor Union Council, Lawrence Kelly, president of the Minneapolis Junior Chamber of Commerce, and the commission's chair, George Jenson, who had been a leader of the Mayor's Committee on Human Rights. The FEPC got to work in May, hiring Wilfred Leland as its executive director. With Leland as the driving force, the commission began investigating employment discrimination complaints and mediating disputes between job applicants and employers.

One such case involved Jerome Diamond, who lived at 5425 Colfax Avenue South. Diamond reported that he had applied for a job at the Bemis Brothers Bag Company on November 4, 1947, in response to an ad in the *Minneapolis Tribune*. During the course of his job interview, Diamond asked the Bemis representative, Mr. Hopkins, whether being Jewish would make any difference in the company's hiring decision. Hopkins replied that it was company policy not to employ Jews and added that he personally was not against Jews but that he would have to abide by company policy.[29]

FEPC files do not indicate whether Diamond was, in fact, hired at the Bemis Company after filing his complaint, but the commission's records show that Bemis at least changed its job application forms in response to prodding. In June 1950, Leland told J. T. Braxton, Bemis's office manager, that only one more change in the company's job application form was needed to bring it into compliance with the commission's guidelines. "The item on 'Social Groups or Organizations to which you belong' should be modified by adding the words, 'Omit organizations made up of special religious, racial or nationality groups.' I am afraid we failed to point this out to Mr. Bemis when we discussed the form with him and I am extremely sorry for this omission," Leland wrote to Braxton.[30]

During its first three years, the Minneapolis FEPC handled 115 cases. According to its 1950 report, 40 percent of the cases were settled satisfactorily, which means that complainants received the position or were satisfied with the company's commitment to follow a policy of nondiscrimination in the future. About 25 percent of the cases were dismissed because the commission determined that the complainant had not been denied employment. In most of the remaining cases, the commission was unable to either prove or disprove discrimination. Between 1947 and 1950, 60 percent of the cases were brought by African Americans; after 1950, about 80 percent. Initially, Jews were involved in about 20 percent of the commission's cases, but complaints by this minority group tailed off substantially after 1950.

In 1967, as its functions were about to be incorporated into a new city civil rights agency, the Minneapolis FEPC looked back at the previous two decades. In its "Twenty Year Progress Report," the commission noted that while processing complaints remained its key charge, it "soon became aware that compliance on the part of employers was a more effective means of eliminating discrimination. This called for positive affirmative programs on the part of employers themselves taking the initiative." The FEPC explained that this approach yielded positive results when "a major department store" began hiring nonwhite sales clerks and set an example followed by the city's other large retail outlets." The commission also explained that it had persuaded local newspapers to reject biased help-wanted ads and had spearheaded the redesign of job applications to eliminate requests for information about the applicant's race, religion, or nationality. The FEPC also acknowledged that while employment discrimination in Minneapolis based on religion had declined significantly during the commission's twenty-year history, "discrimination against the Negro has been, and still is, a major factor in the fight for equal opportunity."[31]

The commission passed its mantle to a new city agency with broader powers, the Minneapolis Commission on Human Relations, during a year when issues swirling around race would explode with an intensity that Minneapolis and the nation as a whole had never seen before. Despite this turmoil, the commission declared it "goes out of existence with a feeling of much pride in a job well done. The Commission feels that it has helped move the cause of civil rights in a very positive and substantive way in the City of Minneapolis as well as in the State at large."[32]

## A Broader Political Agenda

Hubert Humphrey, the driving force behind the establishment of the Minneapolis FEPC, was motivated by a sincere desire to remedy social injustice. At the same time, he was keenly aware of the political ramifications of civil rights and its usefulness in achieving his political ends.

In the postwar period, as Humphrey struggled to build the newly merged Democratic-Farmer-Labor Party into an effective force, he had to fend off opponents from the left who would defect to Henry Wallace and the Progressives in 1948 and those on the right in the old-line, patronage-based Democratic Party who viewed the crusading young mayor with suspicion. Humphrey had just helped arrange what some called a "shotgun wedding" between the old-line Democrats and Minnesota's faltering Farmer-Labor Party. The young mayor would soon be plunged into a battle to oust the Communist-infiltrated left-wingers from positions of influence in the newly created DFL.

Civil rights gave Humphrey an issue he could use to blunt attacks from Progressives on the left who were suspicious of his anti-Communist slant and his close ties to certain downtown businessmen. It also helped him remake the image of the Democratic Party that had long been closely tied to white supremacists in the South and their supporters in Congress who had blocked civil rights legislation in Washington for decades. Humphrey knew a forthright civil rights agenda would enable the Democratic Party to attract the growing number of blacks in northern states like Illinois, Pennsylvania, and New York with their large electoral votes.

In Minnesota and elsewhere throughout the country, many African Americans still voted a straight Republican ticket, a legacy of emancipation more than a century earlier. Following World War II, some African American leaders were attracted to Wallace because of his staunch support for civil rights during the New Deal era, when he served as Franklin Roosevelt's secretary of agriculture.

Humphrey, who gave his stirring civil rights speech at the 1948 Democratic National Convention, was able to build a national reputation by championing fair employment and fair housing as Minneapolis's mayor. Not coincidentally, that effort helped him bring African Americans into the DFL fold in Minnesota. Humphrey's civil rights initiative also generated substantial support in the Minneapolis Jewish community, which enthusiastically endorsed his senatorial bid in 1948.

"The liberal revival of the national Democratic party was essential to Humphrey's plans for the Democratic-Farmer-Labor Party in Minnesota, as well as his own Senate campaign," Delton noted. "For a majority of Minnesotans, the Democratic Party still signified Catholics, southern Bourbons, and corruption . . . When the national party, then, rallied around the civil rights plank in July 1948, finally standing up to the southerners, it went a long way to convincing Minnesotans that the Democratic Party was finally turning a corner."[33]

## Assessing the Impact

While the campaign to combat prejudice and discrimination in postwar Minneapolis helped propel Humphrey's political career, questions remain about the long-term impact of that campaign, initiated during Humphrey's years as mayor. After the publication of Carey McWilliams's "Curious Twin" in 1946, anti-Semitism, at least in its more overt forms, began to fade away. Clearly, Humphrey and his supporters deserve credit for taking McWilliams's findings to heart and helping change local attitudes about Jews and their role in the community.[34]

But ingrained attitudes and practices dealing with race have proven more intractable. Most observers acknowledge that the Minneapolis FEPC, the local civil rights institution created to deal with these attitudes and practices, did not accomplish all that it had hoped to do. Some critics, pointing to the employment barriers still facing many African Americans, maintain that FEPC ordinances and other legal structures in and of themselves have not addressed the endemic social and economic issues that perpetuate these problems.[35]

But this analysis, valid though it may be, does not fully recognize the significance of Humphrey's human rights initiatives in the context of its time. In 1947, Minneapolis was clearly on the leading edge of what would later become the civil rights movement. At that time, only two other American cities had a fair employment law on the books, and neither of those was as strong as the Minneapolis FEPC. In an important way, the FEPC and the Mayor's Committee on Human Relations helped change the climate of opinion in Minneapolis and, by doing so, established a local foundation on which later state and federal civil rights efforts could be launched.[36]

However, despite the advances achieved by the human rights initiatives of the mid-1940s, Minneapolis was not shielded from pent-up anger in the local black community, which would explode twenty years later at the height of the civil rights movement.

# Plymouth Avenue Is Burning

HARRY DAVIS received the phone call at 2 AM on a July morning in 1967. Minneapolis mayor Art Naftalin was on the line, asking Davis to come down to the North Side's Plymouth Avenue as soon as possible. A group of young people had torched some shops on Plymouth, and now much of the avenue was on fire. Naftalin feared a full-scale riot would break out at any moment. On that hot summer night, the mayor hoped Davis, one of Minneapolis's most respected black leaders, would help the city make some quick decisions that would head off catastrophe.

"I quickly got dressed and drove as fast as I dared to find the mayor," Davis later recalled. "I was distressed by what Naftalin told me but not shocked. I had been worried for weeks about the possibility that one nasty episode would be enough to provoke another eruption. But I was not prepared for the sight of Plymouth Avenue shops burning from Penn Avenue all the way to Humboldt, eight blocks away."[1]

Compared to the full-scale riots that exploded all across America that summer, the Plymouth Avenue disturbance, as it came to be known, was a relatively minor incident during the racially charged decade of the 1960s. In Minneapolis, young blacks hurled rocks and angry words at the police, arson caused some property damage, and random gunshots resulted in some minor personal injuries. But massive destruction and loss of life did not occur there, as it did in places like Detroit and Newark.

On Plymouth Avenue, the property damage was soon repaired, but the psychological scars remained. Jewish-owned shops had been the target of the young blacks' firebombing, and that ethnic divide was deeply unsettling to the North Side's dwindling Jewish community, hastening its exodus out of the city. In the near term, the North Side disturbance also had significant political consequences for the city as a whole. Two years later, in 1969, Charles Stenvig, a Minneapolis police officer who criticized Naftalin's restraint on those hot July nights, was elected mayor after running on a law and order platform.

While the events of July 1967 may have moved Minneapolis's city hall politics to the right, at least in the short term, they also led to some legitimate soul-searching by civic leaders about the causes of racial discord in a city that considered itself a beacon of enlightenment on social issues. In an effort to deal with the underlying causes, local leaders created the Urban Coalition, an important new public-private partnership aimed at addressing a broad range of concerns involving housing, employment, economic development, and police-community relations.

## Hot Nights in July

With the midmonth racial conflict in Newark still front-page news, Minneapolis was tense as it prepared for the Aquatennial's annual torchlight parade on July 19. Rumors of an impending riot had been circulating for several days, but the downtown parade went ahead as planned. As the event wound down, a fight broke out along the parade route between two women, reportedly over a wig. Then, just before midnight, firemen answered a call to extinguish a blaze at Knox Food Market on Plymouth Avenue.

When they arrived on the scene, they were pelted with rocks and stones by young blacks who had gathered in front of the store. The firemen retreated to their trucks just as riot police armed with shotguns began pouring onto Plymouth Avenue. By now, fires had spread up and down Plymouth. Soon the Knox Market was almost

*This Jewish-owned store was badly damaged during the Plymouth Avenue disturbance of 1967.*

completely destroyed. "As far as we're concerned, it's a total loss," the store's owner, Mrs. David Borken, reported. "The insurance on the building couldn't begin to cover [the loss]."[2]

"The scene that night on the street was nightmarish," Davis recalled. "The stench of the smoke was oppressive. The heat was intense enough to break display windows, exposing the stores to looting." A squad of nearly sixty police officers was massed on Plymouth, awaiting orders from police chief Cal Hawkinson. Davis remembers the chief huddling with Naftalin in the mayor's car, discussing the possibility of sending the squad down the street to arrest everyone in sight. Davis and several other black leaders, including Stan King, Gleason Glover, and Josie Johnson, urged Naftalin and Hawkinson not to proceed with mass arrests. "There are too many people on the street, and too many of them are women and children," Davis told the mayor and his police chief. "They live here. They are in the street because their homes are in danger. That isn't a reason to arrest people."[3]

Earlier, neighborhood activists from the Way Community Center, in an effort to ease tensions, had been moving through the crowd, calling on onlookers to remain calm. Davis argued that a police sweep was not likely to snare the people who had actually started the fires and who probably had slipped away from the scene by then. Instead, it would only risk injuring innocent people and provoking a full-scale riot.

Naftalin bought Davis's arguments on the spot and directed Hawkinson not to proceed with a sweep down Plymouth. The decision angered some on the police force who wanted more direct action on that summer night; among their ranks was the head of the police federation, Lieutenant Charles Stenvig. Soon the firemen returned to put out the fires along Plymouth while the police stood guard. A few people were later arrested for looting, but no one was seriously injured. By morning, a relative calm returned to the North Side.

The next night saw some sporadic episodes of rock throwing and fistfights and reports of gunfire. The following day, Naftalin called Minnesota governor Harold LeVander to request a contingent of national guardsmen to help maintain order on Plymouth Avenue. Six hundred guardsmen had arrived on the scene by nightfall, in time to monitor a Friday night dance at the Way Center that proceeded without incident. With that peaceful dance at the Way, the Plymouth Avenue disturbance was over.

In retrospect, Davis felt that Naftalin had called out the National Guard as a way of relieving pressure on the city's police force rather than out of anticipating more street violence. "Art was very smart, and he knew his police force well," Davis recalled. "It was not a contented force. Many cops, including Stenvig and his Police Federation activists, wanted to take a harder line against black militants. Art knew that too much direct contact between cops and black kids was not a good idea just then."[4]

Violence on Plymouth Avenue was not a new phenomenon. A year earlier, in August 1966, skirmishes between young blacks and the police had occurred on that North Side commercial street. But there were important differences between the events of 1966 and 1967. "They (the Negro youngsters) stood up to us this time," said Minneapolis police inspector Donald R. Dwyer. A year earlier, they had scattered when the police arrived, he explained. Moreover, in 1967 the crowd was twice as large as it had been a year earlier.[5]

*Police in riot gear patrolled Plymouth Avenue following the 1967 disturbance.*

Most observers agreed that the events of July 20 and 21 had been propelled, at least in the short term, by young people out looking for excitement. But the angry racial rhetoric of the era had clearly influenced the black youths who roamed Plymouth Avenue on those warm summer nights. "We want Black Power," one youth told a reporter. "Write that down." Another added, "We're tired of white folks completely."[6]

With a headline that declared, "The Minneapolis Riot That Wasn't," the *Minneapolis Tribune* credited the police with preventing a full-scale riot on the North Side. The paper noted that police methods on Plymouth Avenue were "far different from the club-swinging, crowd-inciting tactics that have been used in some other cities at the beginning stages of major riots." On Plymouth Avenue, "the police reaction was levelheaded and professional—despite the provocation of curses, spitting, flying rocks."[7]

While the *Tribune* surmised that the disturbances were largely spontaneous, the paper did call attention to the underlying causes contributing to the anger unleashed on Plymouth Avenue. "How will Minneapolis react to this, its second racial disturbance in two years?" the paper asked. "Will it go into more meetings, come out with more public breast-beating, go back for more studies into cause and effect? Or will it push ahead with even more determination and much more monetary commitment to solve its problems of poverty, discrimination and unemployment?"[8]

The city's afternoon paper, the *Minneapolis Star,* echoed the *Tribune's* views. The North Side incidents "cannot be labeled as race riots. Disturbances with outbreaks of violence, yes, but not riots," the *Star* declared. "Because these were disturbances and not a Newark-type riot, however, the community cannot shrug it off and say 'Forget it,'" the paper observed. "Minneapolis has made some progress in creating opportunities for Negro youths since the similar incidents on the North Side last August, but the program is in constant danger of faltering for lack of funds and community support. Those working with the youths . . . need to spend more time 'on the streets' rather than being forced to solicit funds."[9]

At least one *Star* reader was not ready to focus on corrective actions aimed at black youth. In a letter to the editor, Grady Kinghorn placed the blame for the disturbances on "so-called self-made liberators who excite a crowd into a destructive mob . . . The

Negro leaders believe they are simply making the white population aware of their lack of equal rights. They are making us aware,
however, by turning the American public against the entire race,"
Kinghorn declared.[10]

Davis later said he understood the frustration that provoked
the angry outburst by black youth on Plymouth Avenue, but he
"could not condone the destruction [he] was witnessing . . . This
was organized destruction, and an act of great stupidity too. How
could people be so foolish as to make a point of destroying their
own neighborhood? Would they burn down their own houses to
impress someone?"[11]

Davis's views were shared by the *Minneapolis Spokesman*, often considered the voice of the city's more established black community: "The burning and looting that has gone on is regrettable
and in our opinion will solve no problems and in fact threatens the
lives, property, homes of more than any group our Negro population . . . In Minneapolis and St. Paul there has never been a time in
the past 40 years when officials have not
been approachable to those who wanted
to in orderly fashion present grievances.
Until the peaceful demonstrations prove
fruitless, no citizen should resort to jungle
warfare tactics to gain attention to his demands. It is too costly and dangerous to
our common communities."[12]

While the *Spokesman* was editorializ-
ing about the Plymouth Avenue disturbance in its July 27 issue, the paper also
reported on a mass meeting at Lincoln
Junior High School, where community
leaders called for a Marshall Plan to deal
with social and economic needs of the
North Side. Reflecting the confronta-
tional rhetoric of the late 1960s, the
*Spokesman* noted the "demands" made
by community leaders for more black police officers and improved facilities at
North Side schools.

At the North Side meeting, held a

Prominent local civil rights leader Harry
Davis (foreground) worked with mayor
Art Naftalin (not shown) to help quell urban unrest on the city's near North Side
during the mid-1960s.

week after the July 20 disturbances, Syl Davis, director of the Way Community Center, told the five hundred people packed into the Lincoln Junior High that the causes of the previous week's disturbance could not be eliminated by the black community alone. Davis noted that the North Side lacked major industry that could provide jobs and economic security for the community. "Something is going to have to be done to rebuild what has been destroyed . . . Instead of crash programs to prevent long hot summers there should be educational, training and job opportunities on a year-round basis for residents from 14 years on up," Davis declared.[13]

In 1967, a twenty-one-year-old activist named Harry (Spike) Moss was impatient for progress and not content with crash programs. In contrast with the moderate views of the *Minneapolis Spokesman* and established leaders like Harry Davis, Moss voiced the anger of the young blacks who were on the street during the Plymouth Avenue disturbance. "You back the colored man into a corner and complain when he comes out fighting . . . You tell him rioting is wrong when he doesn't have his freedom," Moss declared.[14]

Forty years later, Moss maintained that not much had changed on the North Side. "We're still fighting for our basic rights in this city, this state and this country. Why? Because we're still denied the equal opportunities—education- and employment-wise—that we have fought, bled, sweat and shed tears over," Moss said in 2007, on the fortieth anniversary of the Plymouth Avenue disturbance.[15]

*The Changing Complexion of the North Side*

Economic and social conditions on the North Side, as Spike Moss perceived them, may not have been transformed over the later decades. The demographics, however, changed markedly after 1967. In 1950, the near North Side was the Jewish center of the Upper Midwest, with a Jewish population of about ten thousand and a thriving commercial district on Plymouth Avenue. Twenty-five years later, that community and its commercial center had disappeared almost entirely.[16]

Harry Davis was particularly distressed that most of the stores vandalized on Plymouth Avenue had been Jewish owned: "Jews and blacks had lived in cooperative proximity in my old neighborhood for more than half a century, but the passions and events of the 1960s were pulling them apart." Ironically, advances on the fair housing front had the unintended consequence of sharpening the divide between the black and Jewish communities. According to Davis, "The end of housing discrimination opened the rest of the city and its suburbs to North Siders, both black and Jewish, with the means to move out. Within the span of a few years, shop owners went from being neighbors to semi-strangers who lived in comfort someplace else."[17]

Following the 1967 disturbances, some Jewish shop owners remained bitter about their loss, maintaining that city officials had been too lax in dealing with the perpetrators. "The Jewish business people who had remained in North Minneapolis, they thought I had run out on them. There was a big feeling that I was soft on crime," recalled Naftalin, who was himself Jewish.[18]

While resentment may have smoldered among those Jews most directly affected by the events of July 20 and 21, the Jewish community's weekly newspaper, *American Jewish World*, took a broader view. "The violence we experienced here is merely one tile in the monstrous mosaic of violence that has stunned and stupefied the nation," *Jewish World* editorialized on August 4, 1967. "It has evoked national anguish, a new and profound proving of causes, an agony of self-appraisal and challenge . . . the time has come to keep the promises, both actual and implicit to deal justly with the Negro community of America."[19]

*Jewish World* noted that the Plymouth Avenue disturbances occurred during the same week that the North Side's Hebrew school building, the Talmud Torah, was sold to the Minneapolis School Board. Because the school board's newly purchased facility would serve "a 'predominantly Negro area' the transfer becomes another meaningful element in the Negro-Jewish relations in Minneapolis," the weekly paper noted.[20]

While *Jewish World* may have viewed the sale of the Talmud Torah building as a positive development in terms of community relations, the sale was an important sign of the North Side Jewish community's decline. Throughout the first half of the twentieth century, in a pattern repeated in many older American cities, the Jewish and black communities had coexisted in close proximity to one another. At the turn of the century, an emerging Jewish neighborhood had been concentrated in a district west of downtown known as Oak Lake, just as a tiny black district was taking shape a few blocks to the east. During the succeeding decades, as the Jewish community moved west toward the city limits at Theodore Wirth Park, a growing black community followed behind.[21]

These demographic shifts were not always perceived in positive terms by the broader community. "The now almost forgotten Oak Lake Addition, on the near North Side of Minneapolis, exemplifies a type of change resulting mainly from the invasion of an exclusive residential community by alien cultural and racial groups of relatively low economic and social status," observed sociologist Calvin Schmid in 1937. Schmid, apparently unaware of his own biases, went on to comment on the property deterioration that accompanied the "influx" of Jews in the district. The former University of Minnesota faculty member explained that African Americans had begun a migration to the North Side about 1910, settling a residential district north and east of Sixth Avenue North formerly occupied by Jews, who had moved west into the Oak Lake Addition.[22]

Soon Jews were moving again, toward Plymouth Avenue and then farther west to the new subdivision of Homewood, which abutted the Minneapolis city limits. "This movement left a considerable number of homes vacant in the now aged Oak Lake Addition, paving the way for the second distinct invasion," according to Schmid, this time by African Americans. By 1920, when the city's black population was just under four thousand, "Oak Lake was almost completely Negro," he reported.[23]

Schmid may have looked at changing demographics on the North Side with barely disguised disapproval, but Davis had more positive memories of those demographics and the interactions they fostered between Jews and blacks in the pre–World War II era. Davis recalled the good relationships between Jewish merchants and their black customers: "A store was not just a store to us but had an owner we knew, from a family we knew, who most often lived close by. Absentee ownership of a business was almost unheard of."[24]

After World War II, attitudes began to change and relationships between blacks and Jews showed some strain. "Some members of the Jewish community were beginning to question whether North Minneapolis was still a place they could call

'home,'" noted Minneapolis historian Rhoda Lewin. "Some of
their children were afraid to go play or ice skating at North Com-
mons park, and there were more and more humiliating and cruel
attacks on Jewish children by both non-Jews and their new
African-American neighbors."[25]

Local Jewish leaders, many of them deeply committed to a national civil rights agenda, did what they could to heal the breach
between their community and the black residents of the North
Side. "Some long-time residents had already decided it was time
to create a working relationship between blacks and their Jewish
neighbors, and began working together in organizations like
MOER [Mobilization of Economic Resources] and TACTICS [Tech-
nical Advisory Committee to Implement Community Services],"
Lewin reported. She noted that the week after the 1967 disturbances, Rabbi Louis Ginsburg and North Side resident Louis
Greene inspected the damage on Plymouth Avenue and later attended a meeting with Jewish leaders at the Beth El Synagogue on
Penn Avenue, just north of Plymouth.[26]

### Searching for Solutions

Minneapolis Jewish leaders were part of the city's broader religious
community that came together following the summer of 1967 to
look for longer-term solutions to the grievances that provoked the
outburst of black anger on Plymouth Avenue. To assess the racial
attitudes of religiously affiliated Twin Cities residents, the Minnesota Council on Race and Religion conducted a survey of 238
churches and synagogues in Hennepin County in April 1968, just
a few weeks after the assassination of Martin Luther King, Jr. In
the words of its sponsors, the survey was intended to "tap the
prevalence of attitudes, opinions and beliefs of white churchgoers
in respect to the questions of race and its influence on the retarda-
tion of progress by black members of our community."[27]

When the survey results were released by the council later in
the year, they showed the 67,000 respondents generally supported
efforts to combat discrimination in housing and employment. But
there were negative undertones to the survey answers, according
to the council's vice chair, Reverend Carl Hanson. "The results . . .
indicate that white church-going people in our community are not
free of racial bias," declared Hanson at a November 16 news con-

ference. Hanson was disturbed by the respondents' attitudes toward interracial marriage. Nearly 50 percent of survey participants said that churches should not work to dispel fears associated with black and white people marrying each other.[28]

Frank Wilderson, a university educational psychologist who helped draft the survey, said it pointed up the need to reeducate whites about the role of black leadership and black self-determination. Wilderson, who was himself black, expressed concern about the negative views of white respondents on this issue. According to Wilderson, more than 40 percent disagreed with the statement: "the black community should be able to decide what kind of help is needed from white people, and when and how it should be given." The psychologist also noted that over 50 percent disagreed with the statement: "Leadership in the cause of black freedom must rest in the hands of black men, as they are in a position to determine what is right at any particular time."[29]

While Hanson and the leaders of the Minnesota Council on Race and Religion were motivated by the best of intentions, their survey may have done more to point up the racial divide in the Twin Cities than to bridge that divide.[30]

Local civic leaders, including those from the religious community, realized Minneapolis needed more than surveys to deal with the aftermath of the Plymouth Avenue disturbances. In August 1967, the groundwork was laid for a new blue-ribbon organization to address urban concerns when a large local delegation accompanied Minneapolis mayor Naftalin to Washington, DC, to meet with John Gardner, Lyndon Johnson's secretary of health, education, and welfare. In response to the "long, hot summer" of 1967, which saw large cities and small towns alike explode in racial violence all across the country, Gardner had convened an emergency conference to deal with a major urban crisis rapidly spinning out of control. He used the conference to launch a new public-private initiative aimed at improving life in urban neighborhoods and tapped Minneapolis's mayor to help direct the effort, which evolved into the National Urban Coalition.

The delegation accompanying Naftalin to Washington included a who's who of the city's political and business establishment. The mayor brought along five city council members: Gladys Brooks, Dan Cohen, Richard Erdall, Robert MacGregor, and Donald Risk. Books, Cohen and Erdall were Republicans, while Mac-Gregor and Risk were DFLers. Delegation members also included business leaders such as John Cowles, Jr., editor of the *Minneapolis Tribune* and the *Minneapolis Star*, and Atherton Bean, board chair of International Milling Company. During an earlier era, these men's predecessors would not have concerned themselves with the issues on the Urban Coalition's agenda. But now, with the city facing a looming social crisis, a new generation of Minneapolis business leaders, motivated in part by enlightened self-interest, realized they needed to do more than focus on immediate bottom-line considerations.

Soon the convention delegation became the planning committee for the new Minneapolis chapter of the Urban Coalition. Naftalin had selected one of the city's most prominent industrialists, Honeywell CEO Stephen Keating, to head the new organization. "Keating was a fortuitous choice," Davis observed. "He was energetic, smart, friendly, and, in my view, an organizational genius.

When he started putting together the coalition's structure, he was in his element. He knew every business in town, it seemed, and was masterful in tapping talent . . . Not only was he committed personally to the ideal of racial equality, he also understood race relations as a matter of his company's self interest. Honeywell's headquarters stood about a mile from my house, in the heart of a racially mixed neighborhood." With staff help from T. Williams, executive director of Phyllis Wheatley House, and Larry Harris, director of urban affairs for the Minneapolis Board of Education, the newly formed Minneapolis Urban Coalition unveiled its ambitious agenda in February 1968.[31]

The coalition was intended to be a catalyst and a resource for other private and public organizations, rather than a direct service provider, explained Davis, who later became its executive director. "[The

*Art Naftalin, a protégé of Hubert Humphrey, served as Minneapolis mayor during an era of urban unrest in the mid-1960s.*

coalition] would provide money, strategic planning, advice, and a platform for constructive dialogue. It would spot needs, propose solutions, and finance their implementation," Davis noted. Soon task forces were at work, preparing the way for initiatives dealing with education, housing, employment and training, economic development, and law and justice. To ensure that the city's top movers and shakers led the organization's work, only corporate officials with a rank of vice president or higher were allowed to chair each of the five task forces. At the top of the coalition's organizational structure, the position of board chair was reserved for someone with the rank of CEO or executive vice president.[32]

Only two months after it was formed, the Urban Coalition faced its first crisis when Martin Luther King, Jr., was assassinated on April 4. "I heard the news on the radio, having just come home for dinner after an Urban Coalition task-force meeting," Davis recalled. "I immediately turned on the television and heard a local newscaster saying, 'It looks like there's going to be another riot in North Minneapolis. Young men are running up and down Olson Highway.' Without waiting to be summoned, I jumped back into my car and headed to my old neighborhood. I knew that was where I needed to be."[33]

Davis spotted a cluster of police cars around the Sumner Library and found that Mayor Naftalin and several Urban Coalition board members were already on the scene. "The streets were also full of distraught and fearful neighborhood residents. I was a bit fearful myself. When you wade into a crowd like that, you never know what is going to happen. But I was reassured to see that there were no police decked out in riot gear and no sign of anyone doing anything obviously criminal," Davis recalled.[34]

Fran Van Konynenburg, an executive with WCCO and a coalition board member, offered to put the resources of his media organization at the coalition's disposal. Davis and the group assembled at the Sumner Library quickly drafted a statement that was broadcast by Van Konynenburg's radio and television stations: "Racism killed Dr. Martin Luther King. In recognition that such racism exists here in Minneapolis, though hopefully in less violent form, the Urban Coalition of Minneapolis will organize immediately an anti-racism program to deal in our area with this basic root of tragic violence in America."[35]

Davis used a loudspeaker to address the people who had assembled in front of the library on Olson Highway. "Let's not make
this look like Los Angeles or Detroit," Davis told the group. "Let's
not tear up our own neighborhood. Dr. Martin Luther King was
shot and killed. Our leader is lost, but this does not end our march
for freedom."[36]

The impromptu rally had a calming effect on the crowd, Davis
later noted. "After a public tragedy, people just want to be together, it seems. They want to hear someone saying something re-
assuring like, 'Look, Martin Luther King is gone, but he would expect us to carry on. What we're doing here in Minneapolis is trying
to get jobs, better housing, better education. We've got the Urban
Coalition . . . We've got a chance to make things better.'" That
night, in the aftermath of King's assassination, there were riots in
towns all across the country, but Minneapolis remained calm.[37]

In its statement of action, the Urban Coalition pledged to work
for "a new level of integration; that is, the integration of public
and private resources in a total, well-planned, and efficiently managed attack on the problems of poverty and race in Minneapolis."
The coalition also declared that it would work "towards a community climate which stresses law and justice over and against
law and order which has a negative implication."[38]

During its early months, the ringing statements issued by the
coalition did not satisfy the more vocal black activists in Minneapolis, who issued their own challenge to the blue-ribbon organization. On April 6, just two days after the King assassination,
the activists, using the rhetoric of militancy, presented the coalition with a series of fourteen demands for action. Represented by
Syl Davis, director of the Way Community Center, the activists
were able to persuade coalition leaders to accept most of their demands after several days of intense negotiations. Included in the
fourteen points, along with calls for increased minority representation on the city's police force and elimination of racism in the ju-
dicial system, was a plea for an end to the war in Vietnam.

While coalition leaders were willing to accommodate Syl Davis
and his followers, at least on rhetorical grounds, black militancy
continued to intrude on the coalition as it began implementing its
ambitious agenda in the late 1960s. At one particularly angry
meeting in September 1969, Matt Eubanks, a fiery organizer, de-

clared that the coalition was "an instrument of slavery." Eubanks vowed that he and his supporters would never return to a coalition meeting: "We'll never come back down here. We're going to do what we have to do. We've got to build our black people. We cannot build our black people, our revolutionary forces, through groups devoted to the status quo." As Eubanks and about fifty of his compatriots marched out of the room, he shouted, "Damn the Urban Coalition. Power to the People."[39]

Through the early and mid-1970s, the coalition continued working to improve living conditions in the city's minority neighborhoods, but the energy surrounding the organization's founding in 1968 gradually began to ebb. Its initial group of high-profile leaders like Keating and Cowles had retired and been replaced by lower-rank business directors. In 1978, the organization's president, Earl Craig, said the coalition's function had changed: "Our role has been to bring together ideas and people to get things started. It's a low key, behind-the-scenes role to get it done."[40]

In 1982, *Minneapolis Tribune* associate editor Leonard Inskip looked back at the previous decade and a half of coalition history. "Gone are the angry rhetoric and confrontations of 1968, when black rage was foremost and when whites worried about the city burning and conflict in the streets. The coalition then was a place where the angry minority could air its grievances against the majority, the system, the establishment—and seek redress. Today, the coalition quietly, but forcefully, lobbies within the establishment for programs that help the poor. And it does so, not on the basis of emotion or angry rhetoric, but the strength of effective information—well-researched information."[41]

By the 1990s, its dramatic, high-profile days behind it, the coalition had become a small local think tank, dedicated to researching issues related to urban poverty. Then, in 2004, with foundation and corporate support all but evaporated, the coalition quietly closed its doors and went out of business.[42]

## Reaction on the Right

While Minneapolis business leaders were addressing minority concerns in the months after the Plymouth Avenue disturbances, their perceived accommodation of militant elements in the local black community was provoking a backlash among the more conservative members of the city's still overwhelmingly white population.

Following the national lead of George Wallace, who mounted a third party "law and order" campaign for the presidency in 1968, Charles Stenvig, the outspoken head of the Minneapolis Police Federation, decided to bring law and order to his hometown. Pledging to "take the handcuffs off the police," Stenvig got himself elected mayor of Minneapolis in 1969, succeeding Art Naftalin, who chose not to run for a fifth two-year term. "Labeled the 'George Wallace of the North,' by his opponents, Charles Stenvig's 1969 mayoral victory marked a decisive shift in Minneapolis's political landscape," noted historians Jeffrey Manuel and Andrew Urban, who mounted an exhibit on Stenvig's life and careers at the University of Minnesota in 2007. Stenvig went on to win a second term in 1971, decisively defeating Harry Davis, Minneapolis's first black candidate for mayor. The former police detective lost his re-election bid to DFLer Al Hofstede in 1973 but staged a comeback by defeating Hofstede in a close race two years later. Stenvig's political career came to an end in 1977 when he lost to Hofstede in a rematch.[43]

As head of the Minneapolis Police Federation, Stenvig had chafed under what he saw as the overly permissive stance of the Naftalin administration. In a 1969 interview, Stenvig recalled that a fellow officer had been on the scene in 1967 when the disturbance began on Plymouth Avenue: "He gauged the situation, decided he had the men he needed to stop things before they got worse—by use of a flying wedge . . . He radioed in for permission to move and was given orders to do nothing. He was told to stand and wait. The next thing he knew three men firebombed two buildings. But he had orders from higher up not to do anything, so the stores burned."[44]

In 1969, while still a police detective, Stenvig launched his mayoral bid as an independent without ties to either of the city's two major parties. His campaign, with its dominant law and order theme, was organized around his pledge "to protect the lives and property of the responsible, law-abiding citizens from hoodlums and criminal elements that are so evident in our city today."After running a low-key campaign relying mainly on personal appearances around town and support from an army of volunteers, Stenvig surprised political pundits by running first in the April 29 primary, outdistancing his Republican opponent, city council president Dan Cohen, and eliminating his DFL opponent, alderman Gerald Hegstrom, who had pledged to continue the policies of the Naftalin administration. Following the primary, *Minneapolis Tribune* reporter Bob Lundegaard maintained that Stenvig was referring to black militants when he vowed to protect local residents from "hoodlums and criminal elements" and that Stenvig's victory was a possible indication of a "backlash" by the city's predominantly white electorate.[45]

Just days before the June 10 general election, the *Minneapolis Tribune*, with more than a hint of condescension, noted, "Detective Stenvig often has conceded candidly his lack of knowledge about many important city problems and programs—except mainly in the area of police works where he has avoided being very

*In 1976, Charles Stenvig's second inauguration took place in front of the Father of Waters statue in the city hall rotunda. Shown here with Stenvig (left to right) are aldermen Walter Rockenstein, Alice Rainville, Dennis Schulstad, Lou DeMars, and Charlee Hoyt.*

specific . . . Although this is a complex society and although the problems of an urban community are difficult, Stenvig has argued, in effect, that any citizen is qualified to be mayor."[46]

The *Tribune* had supported Cohen, but at least one reader challenged the endorsement. In a June 9 letter to the editor, Leonard Peterson predicted that Stenvig would defeat Cohen. Acknowledging that Stenvig may not have been the better candidate with the more impressive credentials, Peterson maintained that the police detective would get elected, in any case, "because voters are sick and tired of endless endorsements and other tactics used by the establishment." Peterson was right. The next day, Stenvig overwhelmed Cohen in the general election, winning 62 percent of the vote and carrying eleven of the city's thirteen wards.[47]

Apparently aware of his perceived lack of qualifications, the victorious candidate sounded a defensive note that very night. "I'm not stupid, I'm not irrational, and I'm not goofy," Stenvig told a *Tribune* reporter. "I'm going to be talking with a lot of people, including Arthur Naftalin, and I'm going to think about a lot of things before I make any statements. And then you can see how goofy I am."[48]

Soon conservative-leaning editorial writers throughout the state were weighing in on the election. Harry Davey, editor of the *International Falls Journal,* declared the mayor-elect's landslide victory "a reaction by the dominant, white middle class against militancy . . . and permissiveness." Donald Olson, editor of the *Marshall Messenger,* noted that "the small amount of disapproval" expressed by Minneapolis voters "was just disapproval with the lenient permissive attitudes that many feel are a threat to normal family life. While intellectuals and liberals will laugh at this attitude, it is there for everyone to see, and it is the most powerful force in America today."[49]

Stenvig himself sounded a firm but reasonable note as his inauguration drew closer. The mayor-elect indicated he would be willing to talk with militant civil rights leaders provided that "we act like ladies and gentlemen when we meet and . . . we don't break laws and ordinances." But Stenvig went on to state, "If we get down to the point where, after all deliberation and reasoning, they're going to have a confrontation and break laws, they're going to go to jail."[50]

At his inauguration on July 7, the newly elected mayor used moderate language in an effort to reassure his opponents that he was not an extremist. On the issue of law enforcement, Stenvig described his position as "not threatening or complicated. Simply speaking, as mayor, I will back the police department in their efforts to provide you with strong, fair, impartial law enforcement for everyone. I will not knuckle under to pressure from hoodlum elements. I am a firm believer in the American right to petition for redress of grievances and also in lawful demonstrations . . . However, I will not condone the actions of the few who would use the excuse of having alleged grievances to disrupt the orderly flow of government by using violence and coercion."[51]

Sensitive to negative perceptions about his stance on minority rights, Stenvig also declared that he was "a firm believer in equal rights for all people. Nothing troubled me more during the campaign than the charges and inferences that I am not sensitive to the problems of the minorities—that my sole solution would be a . . . 'get tough policy.' Nothing could be farther from the truth. My philosophy is simple. Color should not be a cause for harassment, nor a shield for wrongdoing. As your mayor, I will not tolerate biased treatment towards any individual or group."[52]

A year into his first term, Stenvig received attention from the national media that was not particularly flattering. "Not only did Stenvig exhibit little grasp of complicated urban problems such as housing decay, pollution and unemployment, but as a hard-line law and order man, he seem[s] to consider his lack of understanding a prime qualification for office," noted *Newsweek*. The national news magazine stated further that Stenvig connected with "the city's poor whites," who were "more the victims of change than its beneficiaries" of "some of the most imaginative urban schemes in the country" promoted by the city's former mayors, Arthur Naftalin and Hubert Humphrey. According to *Newsweek*, Stenvig "by turning thumbs down on such schemes . . . has made shrewd political capital within the conservative whites' disgruntled ranks."[53]

Writing nearly forty years later, Manuel and Urban echoed the *Newsweek* view of Stenvig, but in more academic terms. The two historians noted that Naftalin, Stenvig's predecessor, had "established a progressive legacy that imagined government as the technocratic manager of the people, organizations and resources that comprised society. Stenvig rejected this ideology of governance, consistently emphasizing liberals' seeming disdain for the knowledge and concerns of the average citizens." The two historians continued, "Stenvig presented himself to the voters as a politician with the first hand experience necessary to deal with crime, precisely the type of on-the-ground knowledge that liberals supposedly lacked." Stenvig claimed to "know the crime problem—and have the ability to solve it—not through the abstractions of sociology or criminology, but through his personal knowledge of criminals gained from years of working a beat."[54]

In 1971, as he mounted a reelection campaign, Stenvig could not point to "imaginative urban schemes" that he had championed as mayor. But the police detective, on leave from his post in the Minneapolis Police Department, was able to play up his role in maintaining law and order. Under a photo of Stenvig with his wife and four children, the mayor's reelection brochure noted that, during his first term in office, Minneapolis had "not had a repeat of 1966–67 when burning and looting took place on Plymouth Avenue and police officers were told to stand by and watch."[55]

In 1971, Stenvig garnered more than 70 percent of the vote in a lopsided race against civil rights leader Harry Davis. On election night, a young girl with tearstained cheeks approached Davis after his crushing defeat and told him how sorry she was that he could not be mayor. Davis was philosophical. "When you try, you have to accept the disappointment of losing," he told her. "Who knows? This may be the part of your life that sets the stage for you. Who knows? Someday you may be mayor."[56]

Eventually, the wounds caused by the Plymouth Avenue disturbance would heal and the backlash to those events would dissipate. Davis's 1971 prediction would come true: twenty-two years later, the young girl with tearstained cheeks—Sharon Sayles-Belton— became the first woman and the first African American elected mayor of Minneapolis. As relations between the city's white and minority communities stabilized in the 1990s, Sayles-Belton looked beyond race to a broader civic agenda. As mayor, she would help lead an impressive effort to rediscover and reclaim the city's birthplace on the downtown riverfront.

# Reimagining the Riverfront

JONATHAN RABAN was not at all impressed with the downtown riverfront. In 1979, the British author had used Minneapolis as the starting point for his trip down the Mississippi on a sixteen-foot motorboat. Later, he would write about the trip in his book *Old Glory: A Voyage Down the Mississippi:*

> I had crossed and recrossed the Mississippi. There were eighteen bridges over it in as many miles, and it seemed that already I had been on most of them. Yet I was having almost as much trouble as DeSoto or La Salle in actually reaching the riverbank . . . The Twin Cities went about their business as if the river didn't exist. No road that I could see led down to it. From a gloomy little bar on First Street, I could smell the Mississippi, but didn't know how to reach it. Feeling foolish, I called the bartender over.
>
> "How exactly do I get down to the Mississippi?"
>
> "The river, she is on the far side of the tracks."
>
> The wrong side of the tracks.[1]

Raban could not have known it at the time, but the downtown riverfront was about to undergo a dramatic transformation, creating a vibrant new urban district in what was then a rubble-strewn no-man's-land. The makeover was spurred by a group of urban pioneers who looked beyond the rubble and imagined what the riverfront could become. Over a period of three decades at the end of the twentieth century, they were aided in their work by some farsighted city bureaucrats who used the tools of city planning to help propel a major riverfront revival.

## Origins of the City

In the beginning, the place had several names. The Ojibwe people called it *Kakabikah* (severed rock), while the Dakota knew it as *Minirara* (curling water) or *Owahmenah* (falling water), but the name that would endure was provided by a Franciscan priest named Father Louis Hennepin. In 1680, Hennepin, one of the first white men to explore the upper Mississippi, discovered the swirling cataract on the river and named it for his patron saint, St. Anthony of Padua. From then on, the only true waterfall on the entire length of the Mississippi was known as the Falls of St. Anthony.

For the next 140 years, the falls remained undisturbed in its natural state. But then, in the 1820s, as the first white settlements intruded into the region, the newcomers sought to harness the power of the falls for their own purposes. Over a two-year period from 1821 to 1823, soldiers from Fort Snelling built a sawmill and gristmill at the site. Through 1837, land on the west bank of the falls was part of the Fort Snelling military reservation, while land on the east bank remained under the control of the nearby Ojibwe and Dakota tribes. That year, a treaty with the federal government forced the natives to give up their rights to the east bank, and a land rush began.

One of the first to stake his claim at a prime riverfront site was a young civilian named Franklin Steele, who ran a store at Fort Snelling. Steele eventually built sawmills at the falls and laid out the east bank town of St. Anthony. Later, in the 1850s, the tiny settlement of Minneapolis, on the west bank of the Mississippi, took shape. By 1855, a narrow suspension bridge spanned the river, connecting the two frontier communities. Following the Civil War, Minneapolis overtook its older riverfront neighbor in size and prominence, aided by a construction boom on its side of the falls. Then, in 1872, St. Anthony lost its separate civic identity when it was swallowed up by Minneapolis through a new municipal charter established by the Minnesota Legislature.

Initially, St. Anthony Falls powered a small group of sawmills, but soon flour rather than lumber was the primary commodity produced there. The riverfront had become "the flour-dusted industrial heart of Minneapolis, a densely built environment of mills and factories powered by a subterranean maze of racing waterways," according to architectural historian Larry Millett. On the west bank, the Washburn Crosby Company built its substantial mill, which was destroyed by a spectacular explosion in 1878 but quickly rebuilt. Across the river, on the east bank, the Pillsbury Company built what was then the world's largest flour-producing facility, the mammoth A mill. By 1880, Minneapolis had become the flour milling capital of the country, its twenty-seven mills producing two million barrels of flour annually. The nation's milling center retained its title for fifty years, until 1930.[2]

## Losing the Title

In 1904, the Minneapolis-based Washburn Crosby Company built a small flour mill in Buffalo, New York, on the shores of Lake Erie.

That obscure development, just after the turn of the last century, helped launch a set of economic forces that shook the Minneapolis milling industry's foundation to its very core. Within a few decades, as Buffalo achieved a substantial competitive advantage over its midwestern rival, Minneapolis's milling industry began a slow decline toward oblivion.

Several factors accounted for Buffalo's emerging dominance. To begin with, the New York city was substantially closer to the huge eastern markets than Minneapolis. Shipping costs were lower there, and rates were skewed in Buffalo's favor. By 1917, Buffalo enjoyed a fifteen-cent differential over Minneapolis, and by 1931 that gap had risen to over thirty cents. Buffalo could also take advantage of an arrangement known as "milling in bond," which enabled that city to import Canadian wheat duty free, mill it, and ship it back to Canada, only a few miles away.[3]

During the early years of the twentieth century, the forces set in play by construction of the first Buffalo mill were not yet evident. Annual milling production increased steadily in Minneapolis during the years leading up to World War I, reaching a high point of more than eighteen million barrels in 1916. But then production leveled off and began to decline. In 1930, Buffalo was crowned the new milling capital of the country when it produced more flour than Minneapolis for the first time ever. By 1960, the Minneapolis milling industry had declined to a production rate of only about 50 percent of its output a half century earlier. Riverfront historian Lucile Kane described the impact of this decline on the city's milling district: "Gradually stillness enveloped the once busy area. Some mills were abandoned, while historic structures . . . were razed . . . and the industry vanished from the west side."[4]

While the city's milling industry was slowly fading away, local community leaders were about to realize a long-held civic dream to extend navigation on the Mississippi above the falls. After years of planning and politicking by the city's congressional delegation, the U.S. Army Corps of Engineers finally completed the Upper Harbor Project and its locks, enabling river navigators to bypass the falls. At opening-day ceremonies on September 21, 1963, Fifth District congressman Walter Judd, a key Upper Harbor booster, was effusive in his praise of the project. "I don't know of any public works appropriation that I voted for that will bring as many benefits as this one in 50 or 100 years," Judd declared.[5]

Over the next half century, Judd's hopes for the Upper Harbor were never fully realized. The project's benefits were only minimal, but its impact on the riverfront was substantial. Much of the milling industry's remaining infrastructure was destroyed to make room for the navigation project. The engineers also obliterated a small rocky formation known as Spirit Island, which had been a sacred site for the area's native people before the era of white settlement. Spirit Island was gone, but nearby Nicollet Island remained. An upscale residential district during the late Victorian era, the island had fallen on hard times, and its once elegant homes were little more than moldering wrecks by the time the first barges began to move through the new Upper Harbor locks.

With the exception of the Upper Harbor, the city had turned its back on the river during the decades following the milling industry's collapse. "It's been ignored so long people have forgotten it's there," *Minneapolis Tribune* reporter Howard Erickson declared in 1971. But this lack of regard would soon change.[6]

### The New Pioneers

In 1962, a Japanese immigrant named Reiko Weston was looking for a new site for her popular downtown restaurant when she hap-

The downtown riverfront had not yet been revitalized
in this mid-twentieth-century photo.

pened on St. Anthony Falls. "I saw this spot . . . and I was so sure, this is the place," she later recalled. It was the site of the former Columbia flour mill, and the farsighted entrepreneur used the remnants of the mill as the foundation for her Fuji-Ya Restaurant, which opened six years later, in 1968. "With the exception of the upper-lock facilities, the Fuji-Ya was the first new structure to appear for many years among the desolate west side's parking lots, gravel piles, and aged buildings used for storage," noted Kane.[7]

A year after Fuji-Ya opened at its new riverfront location, a young architect and avid preservationist named Peter Nelson Hall purchased one of the aging storefront buildings across the river on Main Street. The building, known as the Pracna, had been constructed as a saloon in 1890. Later it had been used as a machine shop and warehouse. Hall faced a substantial amount of skepticism from his family and friends when he started taking about buying the Pracna. "Everybody thought I was crazy. Even my mother," Hall later recalled. The young architect borrowed five hundred dollars from a friend to exercise his option on the property, but he kept encountering roadblocks when he sought the ten thousand dollars needed to complete the purchase. "I went to every bank in town and they all turned me down." Hall reported.[8]

Eventually, the aspiring developer got the financing he needed from a well-to-do transportation company owner named Louis Zelle. Zelle, like Hall, had a vision of what the riverfront could become. The older man helped his young colleague redevelop the 1890s building as the site for a bar and restaurant known as Pracna on Main. Soon Pracna was attracting throngs of patrons to what had been a barren stretch of Main Street facing the Mississippi.

Weston and Hall had both taken a chance on the riverfront when most deep-pockets developers saw only blight and decay there. But neither of these two pioneers had the financial means to undertake a more wide-ranging and ambitious redevelopment effort. That task fell to Zelle, whose family had extensive real estate holdings in the area.

With his interest in riverfront restoration whetted by Hall's project, the Minneapolis business owner had started making plans in the early 1970s to redevelop a two-block stretch of Main Street extending down to the massive Pillsbury A Mill. Zelle's firm already owned much of the property along this route, which included the historic Upton Block and the Salisbury and Satterlee mattress factory. Soon he would control other property on the site.

In 1974, Zelle announced that he was developing a mixed-use project on Main Street modeled after Boston's Faneuil Hall Marketplace. Designed by Benjamin Thompson, Faneuil Hall was an eighteenth-century building, originally a farmers market, adapted for use as a modern shopping complex. The project introduced the concept of the festive marketplace, which used historic ambience as a magnet to attract visitors and shoppers.

Zelle, a board member for the St. Paul Academy, had met Thompson when the Harvard architect designed a new building for the private St. Paul school. Soon Zelle engaged Thompson to produce Minneapolis's very own festive marketplace on the downtown riverfront. Originally known as St. Anthony Main Street, the project's name was later shortened to St. Anthony Main.

When he unveiled his ambitious redevelopment project in April 1974, Zelle said he intended to preserve the best of the old and add some new buildings, "so people of the city can relate to their past without retreating into it." *Minneapolis Star* writer Barbara Flanagan hailed the project: "Zelle's charming and comfortable ideas for the two-block-square redevelopment overlooking the Mississippi River on SE Main St. is the best news I've had all week."9

*Minneapolis developer Louis Zelle (left) stands in the
shell of the building that would become St. Anthony Main.*

The $20 million development opened in phases, starting in 1977, when the first building, part of the Salisbury mattress complex, was renovated as the home for two popular restaurants, Gaudalaharry's and the Wharf. Later, the English-themed eatery Winfield Potter became a big draw at the complex. By 1981, when St. Anthony Main's Salisbury Market opened, the east bank riverfront revival was already generating an active street life. "I'll bet that St. Anthony Main on a summery Friday night is just as downtown Hennepin Avenue must have been 40 years ago—packed with relaxed and happy people," noted Flanagan. "No one I saw last Friday looked at all anxious about the environment. They were just out to walk, sip, talk, eat, window-shop . . . enjoy the view of the cityscape and look at crowds of other people doing the same."[10]

In its early years, St. Anthony Main received widespread praise from community leaders and the general public, but critical voices began to be heard after 1979, when Zelle unveiled plans for his second project, a luxury condominium to be built above the riverfront at the corner of Central Avenue and Second Street. Known as Winslow House, after the Victorian-era hotel that once occupied the site, the twelve-story, $10 million building would contain fifty-seven units selling for between $120,000 and $300,000. Winslow House began marketing its units in the early 1980s, when record mortgage interest rates were causing a serious real estate slump. To help offset those high rates, Zelle's development team sought assistance from the City of Minneapolis in the form of mortgage bond financing to lower rates for Winslow House buyers. The mortgages backed by the tax-exempt city bonds would carry a rate of 11.5 percent, an attractive alternative to the market's 15 percent.

But some in city hall, including mayor Donald Fraser, questioned whether the city's mortgage bond program, then targeted at low-income and first-time home buyers, should be used to subsidize high-end luxury condominiums. Fraser was concerned that the Winslow House bonds could restrict the city's ability to assist lower-income home buyers because of the overall cap on the total amount of mortgage bonds it could issue in any given year. Proponents of the Winslow House bonds, including a majority of city council members, countered that city assistance was needed to spur the continued redevelopment of the riverfront district and to attract middle- and upper-income home buyers to the city's urban core. While the council briefly delayed final approval of the bond issue at the mayor's request, it eventually agreed to issue the tax-exempt bonds.

By the mid-1980s, Zelle and his partners, following Hall's lead, had injected a new vitality into the once moribund east bank. But St. Anthony Main's glory days were short-lived. Soon, it languished in the shadows of a new, more ambitious riverfront development.

## Planning the Riverfront Rebirth

While entrepreneurs like Weston, Hall, and Zelle were putting their capital at risk, city hall officials were developing a series of often overlapping plans intended to guide the rebirth of the riverfront. This planning effort occurred within an elaborate governmental system that at various points during the decades-long process involved as many as a dozen separate municipal agencies. According to riverfront historian Kane, the development structure in city hall was so complex "that it was compared to Henry VIII's family tree." Yet even with the multifaceted structure and a crazy quilt of various plans, the entire planning process worked remarkably well. Many observers attribute this success to the efforts of Ann Calvert, a quietly efficient city official who worked on riverfront development behind the scenes for decades. In one of her rare public interviews, Calvert acknowledged her role as the unofficial "riverfront point person" who "gather[s] information, answer[s] questions and stand[s] back to look at if this is all working as a package."[11]

Well before Calvert's era, the city embarked on planning efforts that touched on the riverfront. As early as the 1880s, landscape architect Horace W. S. Cleveland, who designed the "grand round" of city parkways, called for extension of the system into the central riverfront. But by then it was too late: the area had already filled with mills and factories.

Early city plans during the first two decades of the twentieth century called for opening up the riverfront but had little practical impact at the time they were prepared. But one plan was implemented during this era for an area known as Bridge Square, just a few blocks up from the river. By 1900, Bridge Square, the city's earliest retail center, located at the intersection of Nicollet

and Hennepin, had fallen on hard times. As retailing moved farther up Nicollet Avenue, the square became filled with seedy tav-
erns and squalid flophouses. To combat this early urban blight, in
1908 the city built Gateway Park in the middle of the district. But
the park, with its ornate fountain and classical pavilion, did little
to uplift the surrounding area. Gateway would remain the city's
skid row well into the middle of the twentieth century.

In the 1950s, as community leaders faced the prospect of a de-
clining downtown core, city hall planners embarked on an ambitious effort to eliminate blight surrounding Gateway in an area
known as the Lower Loop, adjacent to the fading milling district.
Using the new tools of urban renewal and the stream of federal
funds it provided, the city, working through its housing and redevelopment authority, created the Gateway Urban Renewal project, which cleared a huge swath of land in the Lower Loop. Later
criticized by historic preservationists, who decried the destruction
of much of the city's early architectural history, the project accomplished what it set out to do: clean up the Lower Loop. Gateway reached only as far as Washington Avenue, however, and did
not extend into the downtown riverfront, which continued to
molder as bulldozers were at work just a few blocks away.

In 1970, as the empty Gateway blocks started to fill in with new
commercial buildings, city planners unveiled a comprehensive
downtown plan known as "City Center 1985." This influential document would guide development in the downtown core for the
next thirty years. Several of downtown's most significant future
projects were initially proposed in the 1970 plan, including a system of peripheral parking ramps at downtown's west end, a governmental center around the courthouse, and a community college campus at Loring Park. Most significantly for the riverfront,
"City Center 1985" called for converting the decaying milling district into a new, high-density residential neighborhood. In 1972,
planners followed up on this proposal with a document that directed the city's attention toward the riverfront in an important
new way. Known as "Minneapolis, Mississippi," the plan made a
convincing case for a major effort to revitalize the east and west
banks of the Mississippi as it flowed through the city's center.

In its introductory section, the plan declared, "a natural
amenity with greater potential than the Mississippi River does not

exist. Only an asset such as the river and its environs can offer the juxtaposition with nature that people so often find lacking in other places. It can serve as an anchor offering an advantageous surrogate to the suburban life style." The plan went on to state, "the river can provide . . . needed open space . . . And this in-city alternative to present growth patterns can be provided in a location that does not carry with it the stress of long commuting time nor the blatant monotony of many of the outer areas. Minneapolis is on the doorstep to providing the kind of complete environment that has been lacking in American cities for several decades. There is no other part of the City that can better serve to fulfill this long awaited renaissance than the river area."[12]

Later plans issued by a variety of local agencies built on the foundation established by "Minneapolis, Mississippi," but no single document provided a comprehensive blueprint for developers and architects to unroll on their drafting tables. As plans proliferated, various official and quasi-official groups were established to bring to the same table representatives from the maze of local private and governmental entities that each laid claim to some aspect of riverfront development. The most significant of these coordinated groups was the St. Anthony Falls Heritage Board, created by the state legislature in 1988 to oversee development along a broad swath of the riverfront between Plymouth Avenue on the north and the I-35W corridor on the south.

### The Island War

The heritage board appeared on the scene several years after a bruising battle between two powerful local agencies over a key piece of riverfront real estate was finally settled. For years, the Minneapolis Park Board and the Minneapolis Housing and Redevelopment Authority had butted heads over the future of Nicollet Island. The park board, which controlled much of the land on the island, had long sought to convert it to a regional park, but the HRA thought the forty-eight-acre mid-river site was a candidate for urban renewal and should be redeveloped as a high-density downtown residential district. Tempers flared as the spat continued into the 1980s. At one point, the two sides became so incensed that they began throwing things at each across the negotiating table. "It was a war," one observer recalled.[13]

Mayor Don Fraser inherited the controversy when he took office in 1980. A year later, his deputy, Ed Dirkswager, was searching for a way to break the impasse between the two agencies. When he asked for some recommendations from the city's planning department, he received the following response: "We think the greatest contribution the Mayor . . . could make would be to gain consensus on a theme for Nicollet Island. Once there is agreement, by whatever means achieved (cajolery, fiat, reason, purchase, superior power or exhaustion—and all have been tried at some point) on the theme, then everything else readily falls into place."[14]

As the battle raged between the HRA and the park board, a small group of Nicollet Island residents were caught in the middle. Determined to preserve their unique lifestyle out of the economic mainstream, the residents did not like being pushed around by either side. "The island has been a rundown, overgrown haven for artisans, musicians, carpenters and free souls, people who have created a tightly knit, pleasant community, who didn't mind living in houses with marginal plumbing and lights that flickered off and on," *Minneapolis Star and Tribune* writer Martha Allen observed. "But it's smack-dab in the middle of the city on one of the best pieces of real estate in the city—a patch of green surrounded by the costliest land in the city's historic heart."[15]

Doris Parks was one of the free souls who wanted to stay on the island with her donkey named Sheba, her chickens, and her bantam rooster. Parks and her neighbors were unified in their resolve to fight the plan to turn the island into a regional park. "We are going to fight [the park plan] until the last drop, and don't you forget it," declared Doris Armbrust, a thirty-one-year resident. "Living on the island is more like living in a small town than it is like living anywhere else," added a nearby neighbor, John Chaffee. "If you live in a neighborhood that's geographically isolated like this one is, you feel closer to your neighbors. If you live in a neighborhood that goes on and on, you tend not to feel connected."[16]

Parks, Armbrust, Chaffee, and their neighbors kept pushing for the right to stay on the island. "They organized and went to precinct caucuses," noted Allen. "They voted time and time again for then–Council President Lou DeMars, and he repaid them—

*Neighborhood activist John Chaffee helped lead the effort
to preserve Nicollet Island's historic character.*

promising that they and the houses could stay. They got the heritage preservation people interested in the houses . . . they so-
licited help of the Catholic Brothers who teach at the DeLaSalle
High School and live on the Island."[17]

Finally, in 1983, with prodding from the residents, a compromise was reached between the HRA and park board that seemed to be a win for all sides. The residents got to stay on the island while their ramshackle houses were renovated. Later, several historic houses from other parts of town were relocated to create a picturesque Victorian village on the island's north end. In the middle of the island, DeLaSalle High School retained the campus it had occupied since 1900, while on the south end the park board redeveloped a site as a public park, retaining two historic structures, which were adapted for new, more modern uses. But not everything remained as it was: the park board, which still owned the land under the private homes, wanted the island to look spiffier than it had in the past, so residents had to take down their clotheslines, fence in their gardens, and cart away their junk cars. Sheba and the chickens had to leave.

As the dispute between the park board and the HRA was being resolved, two developments were under way that would help define the character of the soon-to-be restored Nicollet Island. In 1982, a local developer named John Kerwin rebuilt the once elegant Grove Street Flats that had become an abandoned wreck. Kerwin snatched the building out from under the wrecking ball when he rushed his purchase agreement down to the city council just as it was about to approve a demolition permit for the flats. Across Hennepin Avenue, on the south end of the island, another abandoned structure, originally built for the Island Sash and Door Company, was rebuilt as the upscale Nicollet Island Inn. Next to the inn, the park board converted the former Durkee Atwood Building into a park pavilion.[18]

## High-rises on the River

While the battle over Nicollet Island was playing out, another fight was taking shape on the river's east bank. This time, preservationists and other community activists were lined up against a big-time developer who wanted to rebuild a large swath of the riverfront using the deep pockets of his Japanese partners.

In 1978, Robert Boisclair, whose past projects included a highrise condominium overlooking Lake Calhoun, unveiled plans for a massive mixed-use development spanning East Hennepin Avenue on the east bank. Boisclair's project, with its mix of apartments, condominiums, offices, and shops, would extend for three blocks along Main Street, surrounding the historic Our Lady of Lourdes Church. His initial plan showed the project anchored by two tall residential towers, each more than thirty stories high. The new development was hailed by HRA head Richard Brustad, who, noting that the city had been working for ten years to revitalize the riverfront, declared, "This development is exactly what we hoped would occur." But Boisclair's project was not quite ready to move forward at that point, even with support from Brustad's agency. A large obstacle would not be easily moved. Most but not all of the three-block site was owned by the City of Minneapolis. The city was willing to work with Boisclair by leasing its property to him, but a strategically placed warehouse in the middle of the site was owned by a real estate investor who refused to cooperate with the developer. Sol Kronick was the holdout, even going so far as to place major legal roadblocks in Boisclair's path.[19]

In July 1978, Boisclair approached the city with a request to help him gain control of the three-block site through the use of tax increment financing. HRA director Brustad was supportive, noting that a $4 million contribution by his agency would generate about $850,000 a year in property taxes. "I've been stewing over here, wondering where opposition to this could come from," said Brustad at the time. "We've talked to Father Moss with Lourdes Church and the area businessmen and residents. I can't see what about [this development] might be controversial." Brustad's optimistic assessment was premature. The project, known as Riverplace, soon stirred up a storm of protest that, short of scuttling it, succeeded in delaying its final approval for nearly two years.[20]

The main source of opposition came from a group of community activists who maintained that the project's height and scale would overpower the riverfront's historic ambience. Opponents organized themselves as the Historic Riverfront Development Coalition and enlisted the support of allies like state representative Phyllis Kahn, Minnesota Historical Society director Russell Fridley, and *Minneapolis Star* columnist Barbara Flanagan.

As the battle heated up, Flanagan used her column to blast Boisclair's development. Under a headline that shouted, "C'mon, let's stop that riverfront eyesore," Flanagan contrasted Riverplace with the earlier St. Anthony Main, developed by Louis Zelle: "As I've said before, apartment towers belong anywhere but on the historic east bank of the Mississippi River alongside our Lady of Lourdes Catholic Church. Developer Louis Zelle understands that. With his award-winning architect, Benjamin Thompson, Zelle has carefully integrated new condominiums with an old factory he recycled as the St. Anthony Main shopping center. The buildings are in scale with the heritage of the area." Representative Kahn, soon to be a Nicollet Island resident, based her opposition on the use of city-funded tax increment financing to support the project. "I also consider it appalling to use the public subsidy of tax-increment financing for development in an area that is a prime site for private development," she declared. "If this proposal goes through, I hope that every public official who supports it will feel the righteous wrath of a taxpayers' revolt."[21]

Despite opposition from the coalition, Boisclair had the support of city council president DeMars and mayor Al Hofstede, who were both in office when the project was first proposed. All three men had a common tie: they were graduates of DeLaSalle High School, which overlooked the Riverplace site from Nicollet Island. Throughout a three-year period, a majority of city council members voted consistently in support of the project, although several, including the Second Ward's Judy Corraro and the Eighth's Mark Kaplan, were outspoken opponents.[22]

In a concession to his opponents, Boisclair modified the project. One of his residential towers was originally scheduled to be thirty-eight stories tall and the second thirty-four stories. Both were shortened to twenty-seven stories, set back from the river, and spaced father apart to open up a view of Our Lady of Lourdes Church. But Boisclair's alterations did little to mollify the riverfront coalition, which pressed ahead with its campaign to block the project.

In December 1979, the coalition filed a suit in district court to block the sale of city bonds for the development but quickly backed off when it learned that a $7 million bond was required to follow through with the legal action. Finally, on March 26, 1981, Boisclair's project cleared its final legal hurdles when district judge Michael O'Rourke dismissed Kronick's suit to block condemnation of his warehouse, which straddled the Riverplace site. That same day, the Minnesota Housing Finance Agency (MHFA) considered whether to stop the City of Minneapolis from issuing

tax-exempt revenue bonds to provide below-market-rate mortgages for Riverplace buyers. Earlier in the year, MHSF had scolded
the city for issuing bonds to provide lower-rate mortgages for
Zelle's upscale Winslow House. State auditor and MHFA board
member Arne Carlson was uneasy about the Riverplace bonds.
"How do I justify a tax subsidy for higher-income families when
I'm told to sit on a board [that has] lower-income policies?" he
asked. The board's chair, Robert Worthington, was even more outspoken. "If I had the power, I would tell the city I don't want any
more applications back here [until they contain housing for the
poor]," Worthington declared. In the end, the board voted to take
no action, thereby allowing the bond sale to go forward.[23]

Finally, in October 1981, construction was ready to begin. Boisclair brought local dignitaries to the ground-breaking site in
horse-drawn carriages. In 1984, as the first occupants moved into
the three-block-long complex, Boisclair's marketers were effusive
in their praise for the project. "In Paris, it's the Champs-Élysées.
In New Orleans, it's the French Quarter. In San Francisco, it's Ghirardelli Square. And in Minneapolis, it's Riverplace" declared one
of the project's promotional brochures. Boisclair may have hoped
to create another Ghirardelli Square on the Minneapolis riverfront, but his project was never able to achieve that ambitious
goal. Soon, Riverplace faced serious financial problems as the retail section of the development began to fail. Eventually, the project took a huge personal toll on Boisclair himself, as he was forced
to declare bankruptcy, his wife divorced him, and he suffered a
nervous breakdown.[24]

Riverplace also claimed another victim: nearby St. Anthony
Main, which had opened only a few years before Boisclair's larger,
more ambitious development. By 1987, festive retailing along the
riverfront seemed to have run its course, and Zelle's project also
began to fail. Real estate consultant James McComb believed
Riverplace had caused St. Anthony Main to lose its identity.
"When St. Anthony Main was there alone, everyone knew St. Anthony Main was on the river . . . Today, people at St. Anthony Main
think they are at Riverplace . . . There is a real blurred consumer
image of those projects. So if people say something negative about
Riverplace, that reflects on St. Anthony Main."[25]

In August 1987, Zelle's son, Charles, watched as the Hennepin

County sheriff began foreclosure actions on a section of St. Anthony Main. "It's a bittersweet ending," said the younger Zelle, whose family had lost $5 million on the riverfront project. "In some ways, it's a relief. I feel confident St. Anthony Main is going to be there. Our family is proud of that. We are just going to go home and cry and wake up the next day and start our next interest."[26]

By 1990, the bright promise of an east bank revival had dimmed considerably. But the financial setbacks facing Zelle and Boisclair provided an opening for a new small development firm to make its mark on the riverfront. Known as Brighton Development, the firm was established by Dick Brustad, the city's former development director, who had struck out on his own with the help of two partners, Linda Donaldson and Peggy Lucas. Embracing the concepts of historic preservation, the trio helped spur a revival of East Hennepin Avenue by undertaking successful small projects in the shadow of Riverplace. Then, the three turned their sights across the river to the west bank.

## Stirrings on the West Bank

In the mid-1980s, while all the glitz and glamour swirled around the east bank, development was just beginning on the other side of the river, where early efforts proved to be something of a false start for downtown riverfront revitalization. In 1988, a complex of milling-era buildings at the foot of the Stone Arch Bridge was rebuilt and renamed the Whitney Mill Quarter. The complex included the Standard Mill, converted to the luxurious Whitney Hotel; the Ceresota, best known for the large advertisement-inspired mural painted across its windowless south front; and the Crown Roller Mill, gutted by fire in 1983, a totally new building constructed within the remains of its historic facade.

The Mill Quarter became a victim of the downtown office glut of the early 1990s, surviving only through an economic rescue by the Minneapolis Community Development Agency, which moved its offices there in 1991. "Hopes that the Whitney block would soon form the cornerstone in a $250 million riverfront facelift have been swept away by an austere economy and a flood of office space in downtown Minneapolis," wrote *Tribune* reporter Allen Short in 1993. "For the next five to 10 years at least, the Mill Quarter is likely to stand alone on the river's downtown west bank, a struggling if tasteful monument to bad timing, overdevelopment and a civic zeal for historic preservation." The year the Mill Quarter opened, ground was broken for the adjacent twenty-three-story RiverWest Apartments. The bulky, graceless building, which blocked a view of the riverfront, was soon considered one of downtown's least favorite new developments.[27]

Just to the east of the Mill Quarter stood a collection of empty mills and grain elevators extending down Second Street South from Portland to Twelfth avenues. For years, a stretch of empty land filled with rubble stood between the decaying structures and the river. More than a hundred years earlier, landscape architect Horace Cleveland had called for the creation of a parkway there, along what was then prime riverfront real estate. Starting in the mid-1970s, park board planners took on the task of realizing Cleveland's dream. Led by planning director Al Wittman, the board worked diligently to extend the existing West River Parkway north into downtown. By packaging a variety of federal and state funding sources, Wittman and his team were able to inch the parkway along, building it in increments through the 1980s and '90s. Finally, in 1998 they completed the final twelve hundred feet of roadway, filling in the gap under Highway 35W as it crossed over the river

That final segment proved a real challenge for Wittman and his group. In order to complete the parkway construction, they had to relocate a sand and gravel company, resolve some complicated environmental issues, and respond to historic preservationists' concerns. "If there was something that was an obstacle, it pretty much raised its ugly head," noted one observer. The parkway, extending along the river between Minnehaha Park and West Broadway, passed just below the opulent new Federal Reserve Bank, which opened in 1997 on the downtown side of the Hennepin Avenue Bridge.[28]

By the late 1990s, progress was occurring on another front, as officials at the Minneapolis Community Development Agency finally found a credible developer to rework the abandoned Milwaukee Depot. For years, a parade of wheeler-dealers had tried but failed to revitalize the historic depot at the corner of Washington and Third avenues. Finally, Gary Holmes, president of csm Corporation, appeared on the scene, and mayor Sharon Sayles-

Belton quickly gravitated toward his potential. Holmes had built shopping centers throughout the metro area, but he had not yet done an inner-city, adaptive reuse project on the order of the depot. "Sharon really put the screws to Holmes," recalled architectural historian Linda Mack. "She kept calling Gary and telling him: 'You can do this.' Finally, he agreed."[29]

With the help of the MCDA staff, Holmes was able to maneuver through the maze of local approval processes and overcome some serious obstacles, including a labor dispute that threatened to derail the project. Meeting stringent historic preservation guidelines, Holmes saved the Victorian-era depot and renovated it for use as the lobby for a brand-new adjacent hotel. Behind the depot, the graceful train shed became an ice rink.[30]

Earlier in the decade, just a few blocks away, another historic landmark barely escaped the wrecking ball after burning nearly to the ground. The spectacular 1991 fire at the Washburn Crosby mill created important consequences for the riverfront well into the twenty-first century. More than a century earlier, the mill had been the site of an explosion that killed eighteen workers. After

*The Washburn Crosby mill stood as a shell of its former self after a 1991 fire badly damaged the historic riverfront structure.*

the 1991 fire, a plaque commemorating their death remained in
the wreckage of the newer mill built on the same site.

The twentieth-century fire, which destroyed most of the mill's
equipment, was a huge loss to local preservationists. "I feel like a
friend of mine died," said archaeologist Scott Anfinson at the time.
"There is no more significant structure in the state of Minnesota,
and I include Fort Snelling in that." But preservationists did more
than lament the destruction caused by the fire. Almost immediately, the Minnesota Historical Society's Nina Archabal got on the
phone to Sayles-Belton, then city council president, and urged her

The Mill City Museum was built into the ruins of the Washburn Crosby mill.

to tell the city's firefighters to pull their hoses off the building. "Sharon called the fire chief and told him to do just that," riverfront developer Peggy Lucas remembered. "If she hadn't made that call, the entire building would have collapsed." More than a decade later, Lucas and her firm assisted Archabal and the historical society in creating a dramatic new museum within the ruins of the Washburn Crosby mill.[31]

## Lofts on the River

As the 1990s drew to a close, Lucas and her partners at Brighton Development played a key role in revitalizing the west bank and helping ignite a major real estate boom there. Brighton had begun its work in the early 1980s, focusing on small neighborhood-based projects. "From the beginning our niche had been the development opportunities in the central city to build both affordable housing and market rate housing," recalled the firm's founder, Dick Brustad. "Back in 1981 there were not a lot of people willing to take on that challenge. Most of the development focus then was in the suburbs."[32]

Brighton began partnering with community groups and won high marks for its small residential projects that fit comfortably into surrounding neighborhoods. When Boisclair's real estate empire collapsed in the late 1980s, Brighton was able to pick up the development rights to a piece of property next to Riverplace called the Coke site (after the soft drink bottling plant once located there). Brustad's firm built a low-rise but upscale townhouse development known as Lourdes Square. The look of the brick-clad townhouses was both contemporary and evocative of an earlier era. Unlike the massive Riverplace, which turned its back on the adjacent St. Anthony neighborhood, the Brighton development seemed very much a part of its surroundings. Lourdes Square was a great success almost from the beginning, attracting some of the city's movers and shakers, including Joe Dowling of the Guthrie Theater and Peter Gillette, head of the state's economic development agency.

Brighton went on to develop the adjacent Marquette Block on East Hennepin, a collection of historic but dilapidated commercial buildings. "We wanted to save the buildings, but many of the nearby businesses wanted to tear them down," recalled Lucas. "I remember going through the buildings with Lucy Thompson from the Historical Preservation Commission and we were sure the buildings were going to fall down around us." Eventually, Brighton was able to save and renovate the buildings, in the process creating affordable apartments over their commercial storefronts. The firm's experience with the Marquette Block gave it the confidence it needed to take on even more substantial renovation challenges as it began working across the river on the west bank. At Sayles-Belton's urging, in the mid-1990s Brighton began eyeing the empty North Star Woolen Mill, across from the Whitney Hotel. "North Star was structurally unsound like the Marquette block had been," said Lucas. "By now, we knew something about adaptive reuse, and we decided that we could apply the lessons we learned on East Hennepin at the North Star."[33]

Knowing of the loft movement under way in Chicago, Lucas and her partners traveled there to take a look for themselves. They

quickly realized that the Chicago loft style, with its exposed brick walls, high ceilings, and open floor plans, would be a good fit for the North Star. As they assembled the project, the three developers found that local banks were not lining up to provide needed financing. "Back then the lenders hated condos," Lucas recalled. "But we had a track record with U.S. Bank from earlier projects. Eventually, we were able to put a financing package together with them." To make the numbers work, Brighton secured tax increment financing from the city, just as Boisclair had done for River-

*Sharon Sayles-Belton, who served as mayor* place more than a decade earlier. Gar-
*from 1994 through 2001, worked effectively* nering strong support from Mayor
*behind the scenes to promote revitalization* Sayles-Belton and city council leaders,
*of the downtown riverfront.* Brighton did not face the same push
back that Boisclair encountered for his ill-fated project.[34]

Even with a financing commitment in hand, Brighton

needed to market the loft units to prospective buyers. Unsure about the nature of the market, Lucas and her partners took a leap of faith that buyers for a new style of housing in an unfamiliar setting would appear. "The area looked terrible. It felt like a wasteland. The Sheehy gravel pit was still there. There was a lot of broken glass and dead pigeons and graffiti," recalled Lucas. But Brighton soon attracted a steady stream of buyers who were able to look past the rubble to imagine what the riverfront could become, much as Reiko Weston and Peter Hall had nearly thirty years earlier.[35]

In fact, a new amenity provided a marketing boost for what would become North Star Lofts. In 1994, the historic Stone Arch Bridge, built by James J. Hill in 1883, was converted to a river crossing for pedestrians and cyclists. Described by Larry Millett as the "most poetic of all Twin Cities bridges and a spectacular feat of Victorian engineering," the gently curving brick structure became a huge riverfront attraction. "Now you could loop around the riverfront like you could around Lake of the Isles," noted Mack. "It made a walk or a bike ride along the riverfront a much more enjoyable experience." Later, the innovative Mills Ruins Park was developed just under the downtown end of the bridge, creating a permanent archeological site on the riverfront.[36]

By early 1999, as the first buyers prepared to move in to the rebuilt mill, all but one of the units in the building had sold, and potential buyers were lining up, ready to sign on for the next phase of Brighton's riverfront vision. North Star may have been the most visible of the new developments as the decade of the 1990s came to an end, but it was not the only new housing to be built along the river during that period. On the north riverfront, behind the Federal Reserve Bank, several new projects were taking shape, including Hunt Gregory's Heritage Landing, Sherman Associates' the Landings, and Rottlund Homes' Renaissance on the River. Clearly, a riverfront real estate boom was under way, and with it housing prices rose rapidly. Initially, advertising signs for the Rottlund project priced its units "from the $230s"; within a few months, those signs had been painted over to read "from the $270s"; and only weeks later the new message was "from the $290s." Rising prices meant that certain of the projects, once touted for their affordability, were now out of average Minneapolitans' reach.[37]

## Turning Toward the River

The riverfront developments may have been more upscale than some preferred, but their revitalization impact was undeniable. Projects like Brighton's North Star Lofts, by taking advantage of an upswing in the real estate cycle, had an important catalytic effect, while the much larger Riverplace development across the river had the bad luck to open during a downswing in the cycle. At the same time, the newer projects were able to tap into a new appreciation of historic preservation and a warmer urban ambience than the earlier ones could. Because of public improvements like the Stone Arch Bridge and the West River Parkway, the riverfront—particularly on its downtown side—was a much more appealing place than it had been during an earlier era.

A new century would bring even more amenities to the west bank, as it became home to a new Guthrie Theater and a new MacPhail Center for Music, even as another downward turn in the real estate cycle caused at least a temporary pause in the riverfront's transformation. But twenty years after Jonathan Raban came searching for the river, the city no longer showed its back to the Mississippi. Instead, it had turned to embrace one of its most cherished assets. Elements of this asset were preserved and enhanced while city leaders continued working, just a few blocks away, to revive another prime piece of urban real estate that, like the riverfront, faced physical and economic obsolescence at the midpoint of the twentieth century.

# Downtown Revival

"SOUTHDALE HAS TO BE SEEN TO BE BELIEVED," the *Minneapolis Tribune* gushed in October 1956 when the country's first fully enclosed shopping center opened at France Avenue and Sixty-sixth Street in Edina. The center "is an astonishing combination of modern retailing and the traditional town square in an always summertime atmosphere," the paper declared. The project's architect, Victor Gruen, echoed the *Tribune* in even more grandiose terms: "I hope it becomes the crystallizing force for this sprawling suburban area . . . This is the town square that has been lost since the coming of the automobile. It should become the center of this civilization."[1]

The businessman who made it all possible avoided Gruen's hyperbole when commenting on the $20 million project. "An economic survey made before the project even was announced indicated the Southdale site . . . offered the most suitable location for a center of its regional nature," noted Donald Dayton matter-of-factly. Southdale was the first in a network of suburban shopping centers, all identified as "dales," developed by Dayton and his brothers, who ran the company established by their grandfather, George Draper Dayton, a half century earlier.[2]

When it opened in 1956, Southdale was anchored by the Dayton Company's first suburban store, but the Edina center also housed Dayton's chief competitor, Donaldson's. In downtown Minneapolis, Dayton's and Donaldson's shared the Seventh and Nicollet intersection, facing each other diagonally across that corner. In Southdale, the two stores occupied opposite ends of the sprawling enclosed mall. The *Minneapolis Tribune,* eager for advertising revenue from Southdale's new retailers, prepared a thirty-six-page supplement to accompany the center's opening in early October. But the insert neglected to mention that many of the retailers, including Dayton's and Donaldson's, still had stores in downtown Minneapolis.

With all the hoopla surrounding the development of the nation's first climate-controlled, indoor shopping center, Minneapolis leaders could only wonder what impact the suburban project would have on the city's historic central business district, located adjacent to the riverfront. Dayton's, Donaldson's, and many other Southdale merchants had substantial ties to their downtown real estate, but those ties could fray if suburbia's allure began to overwhelm an aging, congested central city. Already General Mills, one of Minneapolis's premier companies, had left downtown in 1955 and built a shiny new campus for its eight hundred employees in Golden Valley.

All across the country during the last half of the twentieth century, suburban attraction proved overpowering to much of urban America. In Minneapolis in 1956, downtown's future was very much in doubt. Could it survive and flourish even as the "dales" began to pop up with increasing frequency on the Twin Cities' periphery, or would it go the way of other U.S. cities that stood by and watched their central cores shrivel and die? During the succeeding decades, local leaders, operating through a network of public-private partnerships, worked with great determination to keep Minneapolis on the first path. By the end of the century, they had by and large succeeded.

## Rebuilding the Gateway

In 1956, the threat to downtown was located nearly ten miles away, in what was once a suburban cornfield. Earlier in the century, the city's retail core faced a threat from within as urban decay enveloped the city's Gateway District near the downtown riverfront, the site of Minneapolis's original commercial center.

After the Civil War, the retail core began to move up Nicollet Avenue and away from the river, leaving behind a skid row of seedy bars, flophouses, and pawn shops. In 1908, to combat the district's blight the city created Gateway Park, its first urban renewal project, at the intersection of Hennepin and Nicollet avenues. The park, with its classical pavilion and landscaped grounds, did little to improve the immediate area during the early decades of the twentieth century. Soon the park became an open-air living room for the impoverished, aging, and often alcoholic men who rented sleeping cells in the area's flophouses. Even the upscale Nicollet Hotel, built across the park on Washington Avenue in 1923, did little to stem the decay.

Despite occasional calls for renewal by reformers and newspaper editors, the Lower Loop, as it was known, continued to fester up through World War II. In the postwar era, local leaders, impatient to create a new image for Minneapolis, agitated for a fresh effort to clean up the district that still functioned as the city's gateway. In their 1989 book on urban renewal in the Twin Cities, Judith Martin and Antony Goddard noted that a shabby, decaying Gateway impeded dreams of modernizing Minneapolis and repositioning it as a major financial and communications center. "Creating a corporate city required new modern buildings to serve the needs of financial institutions and the merging information industries," they wrote. "Planners argued that if downtown Minneapolis . . . had to be completely rebuilt to accommodate those new functions, then that is what would be done."[3]

The movement for Lower Loop redevelopment gained momentum in 1955 with creation of the Downtown Council, organized to promote the interests of the central core's retailers and businesses, just as construction of the Southdale Shopping Center was getting under way. Downtown's major retail anchors, Dayton's and Donaldson's, became active members of the council, but the two commercial powerhouses had to straddle the divide between central city and suburbia. "The very fact that Dayton's and Donaldson's had found it necessary to enter into vigorous competition with themselves . . . dramatized the force of the suburban surge," noted University of Chicago political scientist Alan Altshuler in 1962.[4]

In the mid-1950s, the city agencies charged with overseeing local planning and development were reinvigorated by a change of leadership. In 1958, Lawrence Irvin became the city's planning director, following a successful stint with a Columbus, Ohio, redevelopment agency. Two years earlier, Robert Jorvig had been appointed head of the Minneapolis Housing and Redevelopment Authority (HRA). Irvin and Jorvig teamed with the Downtown Council's leaders to fashion an ambitious redevelopment agenda for central Minneapolis.

In 1957, Jorvig was able to secure a federal planning grant to convert the city's decaying Lower Loop into a modern Gateway Center. Initially, federal officials were skeptical that the city could accomplish its ambitious goal to rebuild a third of the downtown. But Jorvig, with the backing of Minneapolis mayor P. Kenneth Peterson and a delegation of downtown business leaders, was able to persuade the bureaucrats that Minneapolis could meet the plan's expectations. Eventually, the federal Urban Renewal Administration agreed to pay three-fourths of the $18 million cost of the downtown project.[5]

Federal approval for Gateway, soon to be the largest downtown urban renewal effort in the country, enabled the HRA to start buying property in the seventy-acre project area, which generally ran from First Avenue North to Third Avenue South and from First to Fourth Streets. Over a twenty-year period, bulldozers moved through the district, clearing Minneapolis's skid row and, with it, much of the city's early commercial history. *Minneapolis Star* columnist Bob Murphy later reflected on Gateway's "wide open space" that was so unfamiliar to him. "It used to be that I never had to look at a street sign down there. There were always plenty of landmarks. The landmarks are practically all gone now, though, and I find myself gaping at street signs to figure out just exactly where I am," Murphy observed.[6]

The HRA kicked off the Gateway project on February 20, 1959, when it purchased a two-story brick building on Washington Avenue that housed the Acme Box Lunch. Within weeks, it began moving aggressively to buy up the remaining 220 parcels in the project area. Not all property owners wanted to sell. Soon the agency became embroiled in a series of bitter condemnation battles with owners determined to resist urban renewal or at least to hold out for a higher price than originally offered. Probably the HRA's most difficult fight occurred at its front door in the Metropolitan Building, where the agency was housed after outgrowing its initial office space in city hall. The twelve-story landmark at Third Street and Second Avenue, known originally as the Guaranty Loan Building, was the tallest office structure between Chicago and the West Coast when it was built in 1890. Romanesque Revival in style with ornate arched entrances, the Metropolitan was best known for its dramatic open court extending from the second floor to the roof. The building's offices, including those of the HRA, were housed on cantilevered balconies overlooking the open court.[7]

The Gateway renewal plan called for demolition of the Metropolitan Building as part of the overall development strategy, but local preservationists, led by the Hennepin County Historical Society, rallied to save the building. In June 1959, the society presented to the HRA a resolution calling for the building's protection because of its historical and architectural value. Ray Ewald, a member of the society's board of directors, reacted with angry frustration when the preservationists' pleas were rebuffed. The

*The Gateway Urban Renewal project cleared a large swath of Minneapolis's Lower Loop.*

*Minneapolis Star* reported, "[Ewald] said it was 'obvious that the authority has made up its mind' to condemn the building. 'If they don't give us a better chance, there may be another Boston Tea Party.'" Jorvig defended his agency's action, explaining that the building needed substantial rehabilitation that would cost at least half a million dollars. "We asked the owners to come forward with a plan for rehabilitation and financing, probably with help from a government subsidy, but so far they have not presented one," Jorvig reported.[8]

After a protracted legal battle that reached the Minnesota Supreme Court, the HRA finally won the right to acquire the building. Second Ward alderman Robert MacGregor made a last-ditch effort to save the Metropolitan by converting it to a city use, but his idea was rejected by his colleagues on a nine-to-four vote. In December 1961, with no more weapons at their disposal,

*The Metropolitan Building, one of the city's most prominent architectural icons, was demolished as part of the Gateway project; its loss inspired the emerging historical preservation movement.*

preservationists had to stand by and watch bulldozers attack one of the city's most significant architectural landmarks. The Metropolitan Building was lost, but it became a martyr to the cause, spurring creation of new legal tools to protect the city's other historic structures.[9]

During the early years of the Gateway project, the HRA was able to move swiftly to clear much of the area, but it took awhile for new buildings to replace those that were destroyed. Initially, a group of public buildings including a new library, a federal district courts building, and the city's public health facility were built on the periphery of the project area, but the task of private development fell to the Knutson Construction Company, which had signed a master development agreement with the redevelopment authority. Over a decade, Knutson found buyers for most of the thirty-seven acres available for private development. By 1971, construction had started or been completed for a series of showcase projects, including an $11 million Sheraton Hotel and a headquarters for the Northwestern National Life Insurance Company.[10]

With the exception of the elegant Northwestern National Life Building with its graceful front columns and the dramatic cable-slung Federal Reserve Building, Gateway's new buildings reflected the bland, conventional architectural styles of the 1960s and early 1970s. One of the district's most significant projects was notable for its use rather than for its architecture. In 1964, the five-hundred-unit Towers Apartments brought the first major development of middle- and upper-income housing to downtown Minneapolis, launching a housing boom that continued well into the twenty-first century.

Before urban renewal, the Lower Loop had been a housing center only for the poor and infirm. The district was home to nearly three thousand people, most of whom were male and elderly and lived in the notorious cage hotels lining Washington Avenue. These hotels rented small sleeping cubicles for fifty cents a night. "The walls did not reach to the ceiling; they were topped by chicken wire," recalled Greg Bownik, who worked as a rehab inspector for the HRA in the 1960s. "The stench was incredible. It was hard to imagine that people could live in such conditions." The HRA had considered building public housing on the fringes of downtown for former Gateway residents, but the plan was scrapped after it met stiff resistance at city hall. Most of the former residents melted away into the nearby neighborhoods of East Hennepin, Seven Corners, and upper Nicollet Avenue, which still had a supply of low-rent housing.[11]

### Connecting the Buildings

While bulldozers moved through the Gateway, a dynamic local businessman was hard at work promoting his own urban development scheme. Leslie Park wanted to connect downtown buildings at the second-story level through a network of covered walkways. Park's plan was motivated by enlightened self-interest: his Baker Properties owned a large chunk of downtown real estate threatened by the suburban exodus. "From the day Southdale Shopping Center opened its doors (with free parking), Park knew the Central Business District was in deep trouble," noted newspaper publisher Sam Kaufman. "Les was an imaginative, farseeing guy," added his partner, Ed Baker. "He knew the Downtown had better compete with the suburbs . . . or go down the tube."[12]

As a way of revitalizing downtown, Park began promoting his idea for the covered walkways in the mid-1950s but encountered skepticism from other business owners, who feared his plan would cut into street-level retail activity. In 1959, the developer was able to test his idea when Baker Properties designed the Northstar Center, a multi-use project at Seventh and Marquette that included an office building, retail shops, a hotel, and a parking ramp. Park included a pedestrian bridge spanning Marquette Avenue and linking the Northstar Center to the Northwestern National Bank Building across the street. Park's creation, later known as a skyway, soon proved a great success. "Pedestrians found the new structure irresistible as they swarmed over it, comfortable and protected from the August heat and the bustling street traffic," observed Kaufman. "No one in Downtown Minneapolis needed convincing after Les Park's first Skyway opened," recalled Baker. "It drew traffic; it had immense business potential. It was finally—tangible."[13]

Slowly the skyway system began to grow as additional links were added in the blocks surrounding Northstar Center. In 1962, when Park inaugurated the system, neither the *Minneapolis Star* nor the *Minneapolis Tribune* considered the event significant enough to warrant even an article. Growing in popularity, the skyways later received extensive coverage as each new link was opened. Because the adjoining building owners covered the construction cost, each bridge was unique: some were rather pedestrian, but others were architecturally significant. "Depending on the perspective, Minneapolis' Skyways look like a hodgepodge of designs or an exciting display of pedestrian traffic solutions," observed Kaufman.[14]

By 1972, seven skyways were in place in the downtown core, but they were not yet interconnected. The next year, the towering IDS Center on Nicollet Avenue became the first major downtown development with bridges on all four sides. Its strategic location connected skyways in the Marquette office district with those serving retail stores along Nicollet. When the city's eighth skyway opened in November 1972, the *Tribune* noted that Minneapolis was gaining a national reputation as a "second-story city." "The

*Downtown developer Leslie Park and other civic leaders cut the ribbon celebrating the pedestrian bridge spanning Marquette Avenue, the city's first skyway.*

skyways are more than bridges to a network of second-story corridors, for many corridors have small stores, snack shops and bank-teller windows geared directly to the heavy foot traffic," the paper observed. "Second-floor rents have zoomed to nearly double in some instances, often equaling ground-floor rents." By mid-1974, with all four IDS skyways in place, the system connected eight downtown blocks from Fifth to Ninth streets and from Nicollet to Second Avenue South. The *Minneapolis Star* noted that the skyway system, "born of winter, may prove to be the main contribution of Minneapolis to urban architecture."[15]

Building on Park's successful 1962 experiment, the system grew like a giant octopus, reaching its tentacles ever deeper into downtown Minneapolis. Nearly fifty years after Park linked his Northstar Center with the Northwestern National Bank across the street, Minneapolis had created the world's largest skyway system, connecting eighty blocks through a sometimes confusing but always climate-controlled maze of walkways extending over eight miles.

## A Downtown Mall

Park's skyway attracted little public attention when it opened in 1962, but the project he championed five years later was a major media event. In 1956, while trying to drum up interest in his skyways, Park begin promoting a plan to create an enclosed, climate-controlled shopping mall on Nicollet Avenue by covering a four-block stretch of the downtown roadway between Fifth and Ninth streets. The real estate mogul's plan never got off the ground, but Park had planted the seeds of an idea to update and reconfigure downtown's premier retail district. "The shopping centers were coming in," noted downtown business leader O. D. Gay. "Southdale had just been built, and there were many others on the boards. We knew we'd better plan something now, rather than act later in panic."[16]

Park's seeds took root when the Downtown Council created a task force to devise a plan for Nicollet Avenue that would retain and build on its existing customer base. The task force hired the Evanston, Illinois, planning firm Barton-Aschman Associates to prepare some options. The consultants determined that a large percentage of Nicollet Avenue shoppers used the local bus system to get to and from the downtown stores, but most of the buses ran down Hennepin, Marquette, and Second Avenue, not Nicollet. To entice more people to shop downtown, Barton-Aschman proposed creating a transit way on Nicollet that would be used by buses but not other motorized vehicles. The transit way, enhanced by a heavy dose of aesthetics, would not run along a straight line, as did other downtown streets; instead it would become a gently curving roadway embellished by landscaping, public art, and broad pedestrian sidewalks.

The Barton-Aschman plan, unveiled in February 1962, generated enthusiasm from downtown retailers, who saw its commercial potential. Behind the scenes, it also won support from Minneapolis city planners, who recognized that the transit way could breathe new life into the city's aging central business district. Soon the Downtown Council hired San Francisco landscape architect Lawrence Halprin to fill in the specifics. Two years later, Halprin unveiled a model of what would later become the Nicollet Mall. It showed a serpentine transit way stretching from Washington Avenue to Tenth Street, with trees, flower beds, artwork, and bus shelters lining the eight-block roadway. "What's being done on Nicollet Ave. is being done as a business stimulant, but the results at the same time will produce the beauty we think a downtown should have," Halprin told the council members. "We want to make it the kind of an environment to which people will want to come—even if to do no more than sit—a place of trees and fountains and sculpture."[17]

Almost immediately, downtown business leaders began working with their city hall counterparts to make Halprin's plan a reality. Park's skyways were private endeavors, involving partnerships between neighboring business owners, but Nicollet Avenue was a public street, and the proposed mall would require substantial public involvement. About 70 percent of the project's $3.8 million cost was covered by special assessments levied by the City of Minneapolis on property owners within a block of the mall. The remaining 30 percent was funded mainly by federal grants for beautification and transit improvements.

The Nicollet Mall opened on November 20, 1967, to rave reviews by city leaders and downtown retailers, but the project's long-term economic impact remained an open question. William Burns, an executive with Apache Corporation, which managed a suburban shopping center and downtown's landmark Foshay Tower, was skeptical: "Visitors will praise Minneapolis, but what kind of business improvement it's going to bring, I don't know; I'm very dubious." Harmon Ogdahl, executive vice president of the Downtown Council, was cautious on opening day. "It's premature to make any economic guesses" about the mall and its impact, he declared. As it turned out, Ogdahl was more cautious than he needed to be: Nicollet Avenue merchants reported increased sales after the mall's opening. And, starting in 1970, Minneapolis's downtown shopping street received weekly exposure on network television with the premier of the *Mary Tyler Moore Show*. The opening credits for the popular series showed the leading character, Mary Richards, tossing her cap in the air on the mall in front of the IDS Tower.[18]

By the early 1970s, the mall's initial success encouraged downtown business leaders and city planners to propose its extension three blocks south to Grant Street, connecting it with the new Loring Greenway. The extension was not implemented until 1982,

*Minneapolis received national acclaim for its innovative downtown transit mall, shown here in 1968.*

and by then the mall, nearly fifteen years old, was beginning to show some wear and tear. As those signs became more pronounced, the Minneapolis City Council created the Nicollet Mall Implementation Board in 1987 to oversee the mall's renovation. The public-private body, composed of retailers, city officials, and downtown residents, found it difficult to reach consensus. "Life would be a hell of a lot more simple if this was a private company where you have a board of directors and a CEO and you were making decisions," declared board chair Jack Hodnett in 1989. Eventually, the board agreed on a makeover plan that replaced the worn and cracked sidewalks, installed new all-glass bus shelters, and reconfigured Halprin's serpentine roadway with more pronounced C-shaped curves.[19]

When the $22 million renovation project was completed in 1991, it did not garner positive reviews. "Bland and boring," wrote *Star Tribune* columnist Barbara Flanagan. "There was nothing wrong with the old Nicollet Mall that sensitive renovation and meticulous maintenance couldn't have cured. It's the new Mall that needs to be redesigned," architecture critic Linda Mack would later write. Despite the critics' complaints, the mall endures as a major Minneapolis landmark. Through the 1990s, annual Holi-dazzle Parades brought throngs of people to the Nicollet retail district during the frigid winter holiday season, and a weekly farmers' market on the mall did the same during the summer, when balmy temperatures pulled shoppers and office workers out of the climate-controlled skyways and on to the streets.[20]

## Reimagining the City's Center

The skyways and Nicollet Mall both put Minneapolis on the national urban development map in the 1960s. Delegations from all over the country came for a firsthand view of the two innovative projects and their apparent success in protecting the central business district from the suburban onslaught so devastating to downtown retailing in many American cities. While local business leaders basked in this national acclaim, city planners were at work preparing a long-range blueprint for downtown. Unveiled in 1970, the plan, known as "Metro Center '85," imagined what downtown would look like fifteen years later. Unlike many planning studies gathering dust on the back shelves of obscure city offices, "Metro Center '85" had a major impact on downtown development over the course of thirty years. With amazing accuracy, the 1970 plan anticipated development needs and trends during the final decades of the twentieth century.

The plan envisioned a downtown filled with skyscrapers that would add 4 million square feet of office space and bring 43,000 new jobs, a 50 percent increase over 1970 figures. Most significantly, it predicted a future with fifty thousand people living in and around downtown. "Metro Center '85" proposed major high-density residential development on the downtown riverfront, a new civic center around city hall, an expanded community college at Loring Park, a cultural center near the Milwaukee Depot, and large multilevel parking ramps at the west end of the loop connected to the downtown core through skyway extensions. In one form or another, these developments would all occur, but over a somewhat longer time frame than envisioned by the city plan.[21]

In 1970, "Metro Center '85" was not much more than words on paper. Another plan five years later helped jump-start the development process it envisioned. By 1975, the era of federal urban renewal had come to an end. Moving forward, city leaders knew they could no longer rely on federal funding, similar to the Gateway, to propel downtown development. The alternative to urban renewal became a locally controlled source known as tax increment financing, or TIF, which captured increased property tax revenues generated by a development project, using them over a multiyear period to cover public costs associated with the project.

TIF proved an intensely controversial development tool up through the early years of the twenty-first century. Opponents maintained that development would have occurred on TIF sites without government intervention and that tax increment financing merely siphoned property tax revenues away from the city's general fund and into projects that mainly benefited well-heeled developers. Supporters argued that blight would continue to fester without TIF and that development projects had a positive impact on the city's tax base by increasing the value of nearby properties.

In the mid-1970s, city officials, led by city coordinator Thomas Thompson, had targeted a site in need of redevelopment centered on the block immediately to the north of Dayton's, bounded by Sixth and Seventh streets and Nicollet and Hennepin avenues. Thompson and his planners proposed to redevelop that block and several adjoining ones through a project that came to be known as City Center. Back then, the site was a jumble of aging commercial buildings occupying more than twenty separate parcels in the heart of downtown. A decade earlier, Nicollet Mall and the skyways had helped rejuvenate downtown. By 1975, however, local leaders feared downtown would start losing ground unless it could eliminate the economic obsolescence that characterized the City Center site.

"There was a general impression that downtown was on the decline," noted former city council member Keith Ford. "Dayton's was still a family-run business, and the Dayton brothers were supportive of what we were trying to do, but they didn't want to be downtown by themselves. Across from Dayton's, the block between Sixth and Seventh was filled with blight, and it was right in the heart of the city's retail district. It abutted on the 100 percent corner at Seventh and Nicollet," said Ford, who helped lead the city hall effort to promote the City Center project. With an estimated public price tag of $37 million, the plan won approval from the council, at least in concept, in 1975. But members were skittish about moving ahead with a tax increment project on the site. Earlier TIF projects at Nicollet and Lake and at Loring Park were not going well. The city had initiated both projects without firm development commitments in hand, and work had not yet begun by early 1975.[22]

In the case of City Center, council leaders decided to select a developer before implementing a tax increment project. After inviting proposals, it selected Oxford Properties to rebuild the downtown site. The Canada-based developer already had real estate interests in Minneapolis and a track record of similar projects in other U.S. cities. Oxford spent the next two years putting together a plan for City Center that called for a fifty-story office tower, a hotel, a parking ramp, and a new facility for Donaldson's Department Store, then located on the east side of Nicollet Mall between Sixth and Seventh. In mid-1977, the Edmonton developer presented its plan to a city council that had some misgivings. Oxford pitched the project to the council by promising to reimburse the city for the full cost of acquiring the downtown block. As a sweetener, the developer also offered to pay the property taxes while the site was off the tax rolls. First, though, the city would have to acquire the site using its powers of condemnation, bulldoze the existing building, and prepare the site for construction.

Oxford's offer helped persuade a majority of the council to support the plan. "The assurance was what aldermen, gun-shy from criticism about lagging progress in two other development districts, were looking for—minimal risks," noted the *Minneapolis Star*. First Ward alderman Walt Dziedzic was won over: "Either this is the greatest revitalization gift for a city in North America, or we're all dreaming . . . The question we should be asking is: What happens to downtown Minneapolis if we don't go ahead with City Center? Will Donaldson's close? Will Minneapolis become another St. Paul or Newark?"[23]

Dziedzic was a forceful advocate for City Center, but certain of his council colleagues were skeptical. "The opponents, and they included Lee Munich and Tom Johnson, thought the project was a boondoggle—that it wouldn't work," recalled Ford, who chaired the council's ways and means committee. "As we got ready for the final arguments, Lee wheeled out a blackboard and began to fill it with all sorts of numbers to bolster his case that the project was a mistake. I thought he was wrong, but he was making very persuasive arguments. Finally, I got up, went over to the blackboard, and erased all of Lee's numbers, and we voted to approve it."[24]

The council action occurred in the summer of 1977, but court challenges delayed the start of construction for two more years. Finally, in December 1979, ground was broken for the massive downtown project. Because the site was paved over, local officials, led by city council president Lou DeMars, dug their shovels into a large box filled with sand. According to onlookers, DeMars celebrated the project's start by throwing his shovelful of sand higher into the air than any of his colleagues. City Center was completed in phases, starting in August 1982, when a new Donaldson's opened across Nicollet Avenue from its original location. Later that year, the Northwestern National Bank Building, adjacent to the old Donaldson's, was destroyed in a Thanksgiving Day fire. That block would later become the site of the upscale Gaviidae Center and a dramatic new office tower for Northwestern Bank, designed by Cesar Pelli. In 1983, other phases of City Center were completed, including an office tower for International Multifoods Company, an Amfac hotel, and an interior retail mall containing more than ninety shops.[25]

From an economic standpoint, City Center proved a success, generating a substantial cash flow that was used to seed other city development initiatives, including Minneapolis's ambitious Neighborhood Revitalization Program. However, its bland design was a disappointment to the city's architectural enthusiasts. "City Center may not have lived up to all its expectations, but it was a critical intervention at a time when the economic future of downtown was clearly in doubt. It accomplished what it set out to do, and that was to boost downtown retail," noted Ford.[26]

### Theater Lights on Hennepin Avenue

After City Center, Minneapolis officials looked farther up the Nicollet Mall, to Tenth Street, where a French development firm, La Societe Generale Immobiliere, had proposed a fanciful and ultimately unfeasible plan to build a dome over the intersection. When the LSGI project failed, the city turned its attention to the rapidly fading entertainment district along Hennepin Avenue.[27]

In the 1930s, Hennepin Avenue had been Minneapolis's Great White Way, with ten theaters lined up between Sixth and Ninth streets. But World War II brought massive social, cultural, and economic changes that eventually doomed the downtown theaters. Television offered people the entertainment they craved without having to leave home; when they did go out, their cars freed them from reliance on the streetcars that used to funnel everyone into the city's downtown core. In the 1960s, the faded movie palaces got at least a temporary lease on life when several theaters, including the Orpheum, the Pantages, and the World, were purchased by entertainment mogul Ted Mann, who had started his business career in Minnesota. For Minneapolis, Mann's acquisition was both good and bad news, according to former city development official Phil Handy. "The good news was that Mann brought much-needed capital to the theaters. The bad news was that he ripped out many of the theaters' historic features and replaced them with a 1960s-era modern décor," said Handy, who helped oversee redevelopment of the downtown theaters as a project coordinator at the Minneapolis Community Development Agency.[28]

But even Mann could not withstand the negative economic forces impinging on the theaters. Through the late sixties and into the seventies, the Great White Way gradually went dark as downtown movie palaces either closed or were converted to venues for adult entertainment. As Hennepin Avenue declined into a seedy pornography district, city officials became increasingly concerned that the formerly popular entertainment center was now casting a blighting shadow on the rest of downtown. But behind their shabby facades, the theaters provided an important hidden resource for the city, Handy explained. "Retail was losing ground to the outlying shopping malls, and a housing boom was drawing people out to the suburbs, but downtown still had the theaters, and many of them retained their historic features even with the Mann modernization," he said. "By the 1980s, historic preservation was gaining new importance. Cities were looking for ways to link preservation with the promotion of culture and entertainment, so the development of the theaters was just waiting to happen."[29]

Minneapolis's first foray into the theater business came at

Ninth and Hennepin, the site of the aging and barely functioning Orpheum. In 1984, the theater was purchased by a former Minnesotan named Bob Dylan. The famous pop star and American legend turned over the operation of the theater to his brother, who struggled to book acts in the crumbling venue. "Dylan may have had deep pockets, but he wasn't willing to put in the massive amounts of cash needed to renovate the theater," Handy recalled. "It was in need of major overhaul. Dressing rooms stacked up on each wing of the stage house. The plumbing stacks ran through them, and they were leaking raw sewage. No wonder it was hard to book acts with conditions like that."[30]

Minneapolis officials knew Dylan wanted to sell the Orpheum. Concerned that the theater might get snapped up by local porn king Ferris Alexander, the Minneapolis Community Development Agency (MCDA) began to explore the option of a city purchase. "At city level, we didn't know anything about operating theaters, but there were people in town that did, and we were lucky enough to connect with them," Handy explained.[31]

Handy and his colleagues at MCDA teamed up with Fred Krohn, a local theater promoter, Lee Lynch, head of Carmichael Lynch Advertising, and James Binger, a Minnesota business leader who owned a string of Broadway theaters. The Krohn-Lynch-Binger partnership established a management company that offered to operate the Orpheum for the city. Krohn would oversee day-to-day operations, and Binger would use his wide-ranging contacts to bring touring Broadway shows to the Hennepin Avenue theater. With an operating entity in place, the MCDA moved ahead to purchase the Orpheum and fund some minimal repairs needed to keep it functioning. "Initially, the Orpheum purchase was intended to be a holding action. We expected to keep the theater only long enough until we could find a nonprofit group to buy it from us, but that didn't happen," Handy explained.[32]

After the Orpheum purchase, the city turned its attention to the block diagonally across the street. That block, bounded by Hennepin and LaSalle avenues and Eighth and Ninth streets, contained the Minneapolis YMCA, a longtime downtown institution that wanted to construct a new facility next to its existing building. The youth-serving agency did not have the financial capacity to redevelop its site, so it eventually connected with a local

developer, the Bloomington-based Frauenshuh Company. Frauenshuh would build a new facility for the Y and develop a major
office tower on the rest of the block. The ambitious project, later
known as LaSalle Plaza, soon encountered a major complication:
the block contained the State Theatre, targeted for demolition to
make way for the new office tower.

City officials had a different view of the State, considering it a
valuable cultural resource that needed to be preserved, and they
pushed Frauenshuh to retain the theater within the larger project.
Despite initial resistance, an agreement was eventually reached
calling for the city to own the theater and cover restoration costs
through the use of tax increment financing. The negotiations were
protracted, recalled MCDA project coordinator Tom Hoch. "Forc-
ing a theater on a developer created bad development dynamics.
Once we resolved that the city would own the theater, everything
moved forward," said Hoch, later head of the Hennepin Theatre
Trust, which manages the city's historic downtown theaters. City
council president Sharon Sayles-Belton, a preservation enthusiast, provided the political muscle needed to win support for the
restoration plan in city hall, according to Linda Mack. The city's
future mayor "tussled with the tough issues of development vs.

*A refurbished State Theatre, renovated as part of the
LaSalle Plaza project in the early 1990s, brought
1920s elegance back to Hennepin Avenue.*

preservation and the city's financial bottom line vs. its physical and social fabric," Mack wrote.[33]

The State, restored to its 1920-era elegance, opened to rave reviews in November 1991 even though an early blizzard bombarded theatergoers attending the newly renovated theater's first production, the musical *Carousel*. "The restoration of the State Theatre was a smash hit," recalled Handy. "It was wildly popular with the public. Because the public was enthusiastic, that helped generate the momentum needed to restore the Orpheum."[34]

But city officials encountered a major financial problem when they began working on an Orpheum plan. Funds to renovate the State had come from TIF related to the LaSalle Plaza project, which surrounded the theater; however, no full-block development to generate tax increment funds was possible on the Orpheum site. As an alternative to TIF, development officials at MCDA hatched a plan to establish a one-dollar surcharge on theater tickets, yielding a yearly cash flow the city would use to pay off bonds issued to finance the Orpheum restoration. Handy remembers that he and his colleagues had to do some selling to encourage council members to support the Orpheum's funding plan: "One day, we brought the city council up on scaffolding to see the amazing terra-cotta ornamentation that had been uncovered as we were preparing a restoration plan. A month later, we had the money we needed to complete the renovation."[35]

Reconstruction of the Orpheum began in January 1993. A year later, the $10 million project was completed in time for the opening of the Broadway hit musical *Miss Saigon*. Restored to its original ornate splendor, the theater generated positive notices, just as the State had three years earlier. With the Orpheum, the city had taken "another giant step toward reviving Minneapolis' principal entertainment street. The streetscape is livelier and friendlier with its glamorous restoration," enthused *Star Tribune* columnist Flanagan.[36]

By the mid-1990s, Minneapolis had brought back its Great White Way. Throngs of theatergoers converged on Hennepin Avenue, providing a much-needed boost to the downtown economy. Over the next ten years, the city acquired two more historic theaters, the Shubert and the Pantages. The Pantages joined the Orpheum and the State as a trio of historic theaters operated by the

Hennepin Theatre Trust. But the Shubert took a different path. Abandoned and badly deteriorated, the former vaudeville house was sold to the nonprofit developer Artspace. In 1999, the six-million-pound theater was lifted off its foundation and moved to a new site two blocks away to make room for the controversial Block E project. Well into the twenty-first century, the Schubert remained vacant while Artspace sought the funds needed to rebuild the historic theater.[37]

*A Look Back at Downtown Development*

In 1956, the opening of Southdale, the nation's first fully enclosed shopping mall, threatened to sap the economic vitality of Minneapolis's retail core. Thirty-six years later, an even more ominous threat to downtown loomed as the Mall of America opened in Bloomington in August 1992. Again city leaders wrung their hands in alarm, fearing the massive suburban mall would sound the death knell for downtown Minneapolis. At least through the end of the century, those fears proved unfounded. In August 1993, Downtown Council president John Labowsky reported that the mall's effect on the city's retail core had been "neutral, if not better." In fact, the Bloomington center had boosted downtown restaurant and hotel business by attracting tourists, thereby prompting a greater sense of urgency about renewal efforts.[38]

During the previous decade, a huge development boom had boosted downtown's share of the city's total tax base from 21 percent in 1980 to 34 percent in 1987, with a further increase to 50 percent projected by 2000, according to Jim Moore, the MCDA's director of downtown and riverfront development. In the early 1990s, the continuing boom enabled city council leaders to siphon property tax revenues from City Center and other nearby tax increment projects to support an ambitious multiyear neighborhood development initiative. "We're saying downtown has had plenty of resources and we need to start redirecting it," declared council member Tony Scallon as city leaders established the framework for what would later become the Neighborhood Revitalization Program (NRP). "[I'll] introduce a resolution at today's council meeting to redistribute the money to neighborhood projects."[39]

Through the nineties, downtown development efforts continued, including the city's ill-fated acquisition of the Target Center

arena, which would later suck up a steady stream of public resources. By the end of the decade, city hall was embroiled in two
high-profile development controversies involving the notorious
Block E on Hennepin Avenue and a proposed Target store on
Nicollet Mall. Proponents of the two programs maintained that
city assistance was required to move the downtown revitalization
agenda forward; opponents objected to the level of public funding
sought by the projects' private developers. Both disputes spilled
over into the new century.

One of the central figures in the controversies, council president Jackie Cherryhomes, was an unapologetic supporter of city-
assisted development: "It is government's role to prime the pump
and prime it enough so that the private sector can take over. That
is what we did in downtown Minneapolis, and it worked." At the
end of the decade, as the Sayles-Belton and Cherryhomes era
drew to a close, both city hall leaders could reflect on a period of
steady economic growth for a downtown that had withstood the
challenges of Southdale and the Mall of America. In 2000, the annual state of the city report, prepared by the city planning department, declared, "Downtown continues to be a magnet for growth
in the region," with a workforce of over 160,000 and a residential
population of 25,000.[40]

"State of the City 2000" marked forty years of sustained development activity in Minneapolis's downtown core, beginning with
the Gateway project in 1959. Four decades of energetic public-
private partnerships had given Minneapolis a vital, economically
healthy downtown, envied by most other midsize American
cities. A new century brought a new set of city leaders who faced
great challenges as they worked to perpetuate the gains achieved
during an earlier era—a period that might later be viewed as
downtown Minneapolis's golden age. That prosperous time ex-
tended at least into the early years of the twenty-first century,
when a new modern mass transit system using fixed rails, like the
area's earlier streetcar network, helped preserve downtown's central role in the region's commercial life.

# Roads and Tracks

KEN FLETCHER'S HAND-DRAWN MAP shows a gently curving line interrupted by a series of black dots. An amateur transit enthusiast, Fletcher produced his map in 1976, at a time when transportation in Minnesota meant highways. Back then, few people had heard of the system Fletcher called "Light Rail Transit." The simple map, unembellished by colorful graphics, portrayed a transportation mode now known as LRT. Fletcher's arc delineated a route along Hiawatha Avenue that connected downtown Minneapolis with a Bloomington site later occupied by the Mall of America. His black dots identified stations along the route, at the Veterans Hospital, Minnehaha Park, Thirty-eighth Street, and Lake Street.

Fletcher's diagram was remarkably farsighted. Twenty-five years later, transit planners would incorporate most of his ideas in

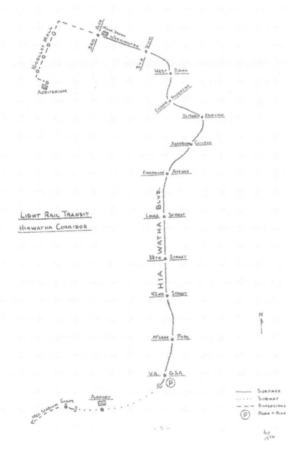

This map, hand-drawn by transit enthusiast Ken Fletcher in 1976, helped establish the route for Hiawatha LRT.

the state's Hiawatha LRT line, named for the corridor it serves. His early plan, decades ahead of its time, was intended to help ease escalating congestion on Twin Cities highways and combat the urban sprawl enveloping so much of the metropolitan region.[1]

Fletcher produced his map and its accompanying background paper for a group of south Minneapolis residents who wanted transportation to mean more than highways in Minnesota. Over a period spanning several decades, these residents and others like them worked diligently and effectively to reshape Highway 55, one of the state's most contentious roadway projects. In the end, they laid the groundwork for a new form of transit that redefined transportation in the sprawling Twin Cities metropolitan region during the first decade of the twenty-first century.

During the early battles over Highway 55 (a final one erupted in the late 1990s), activists found they were lined up against a powerful group of opponents, including the Minneapolis Central Labor Union, the *Minneapolis Star and Tribune*, and the city's influential local think tank, the Citizens League. Organized labor was generally more pro-freeway than anti-LRT, defining the issue in terms of construction jobs for union members. The league took a more policy wonkish approach. Eventually, the self-appointed "good government" group reversed course and supported LRT, but in the early years, led by executive director Ted Kolderie, it maintained that rail transit did not constitute a cost-effective approach to meeting the region's overall transportation needs. In place of light rail transit, Kolderie and his followers called for increased use of car pools, commuter vans, and bus ways as the prescription for combating the metro area's transportation ills.

## The Contending Forces

The origins of the Highway 55 controversy extend back to the early 1960s, when the Minneapolis City Council approved a plan to rebuild the historic roadway that connected downtown with the Sixty-second Street Crosstown. For much of its route, Highway 55 followed Hiawatha Avenue through south Minneapolis. Hiawatha's origins stretched to the early nineteenth century, when it was a trail connecting Fort Snelling with St. Anthony Falls on the Mississippi River. These many decades later, the plan was to convert the city street to a full-fledged, limited-access freeway.

In 1963, the city council jump-started the project with an ini-

This mid-twentieth-century photo shows Hiawatha Avenue before it was rebuilt into a four-lane parkway as part of the Highway 55 project.

tial $10 million so the state highway department could start acquiring rights-of-way, even though final construction plans had not yet been put in place. Soon residents and business owners along Hiawatha Avenue found notices in their mailboxes informing them they were about to be bought out. The department's preliminary plan called for six lanes of concrete north of Forty-sixth Street and four lanes south to the Crosstown. That the plan ripped up a corner of Minnehaha Park did not seem to concern the Minneapolis Park Board—at least not initially. At a February 1965 public hearing, no one spoke up in opposition to the plan.

But 1966 marked a change of leadership at the park board and a new, more critical view of the Highway 55 plan. Under its new superintendent, Robert Ruhe, the board decided it did not want to sell a piece of Minnehaha Park to the highway department after all. In response to the board's tougher stand, highway planners proposed to reroute the freeway away from the park. But this new configuration meant that additional homes—nearly three hundred in all—and more than a dozen commercial buildings would need to be acquired. Area residents started to complain about the project that threatened to disrupt their neighborhoods. Soon planners discovered that Highway 55 had become something of a hot potato. Over a two-year period, from 1969 to 1971, in response to growing pressures the highway department prepared several alternative plans, one of which—known as Plan D—included a tunnel through Minnehaha Park under Minnehaha Creek.

Through the early 1970s, opposition to the various Highway 55 plans continued to build. By then, skeptics were able to draw on the new federal Environmental Impact Statement (EIS) process for support. In the spring of 1971, the state department submitted its Highway 55 EIS to the highway administration in Washington, DC, but it was rejected by the federal agency because the plan did not adequately satisfy requirements for noise abatement and air quality.

The EIS rejection provided fresh encouragement to an ad hoc group of community activists who called themselves the Highway 55 Task Force. An offshoot of the broader Southside Coalition, the task force had came together to plot strategy. Its leaders included Jim Tennessen, Judy Winzig, and Wally Bratt, all of whom lived in the neighborhoods adjacent to the proposed roadway project. By mid-1974, task force members thought momentum for the Highway 55 project had been blunted when the Minneapolis City Council, responding to increased pressures, voted to rescind all previous approvals for the roadway reconstruction.

"Then, out of the blue, we discovered this federal amendment that breathed new life into the whole project," recalled Tennessen. The amendment was quietly inserted in the 1974 Highway Bill by Minnesota's Eighth District congressman, John Blatnik. Blatnik, who chaired the powerful House public works committee, represented Duluth and the Iron Range. Because he was retiring from Congress at the end of 1974, Blatnik had no personal political stake in the Highway 55 controversy. His amendment authorized $53 million for a "high density urban highway intermodal transportation connection between Franklin Avenue and Fifty-ninth Street South in Minneapolis, Minnesota."[2]

Furious about the amendment, task force members turned on their own congressman, Don Fraser, whom they had considered an ally in their effort to delay construction of Highway 55. More than two hundred south Minneapolis residents confronted Fraser outside his downtown office on a chilly January night in 1975, irate about his vote in support of the highway bill, which contained the amendment. Community activist Bill Milbrath spoke for the group, declaring that Fraser "speaks out for mass transit and against more freeways, and then votes $53 million for a freeway on Hiawatha Avenue. We want to know why the deception and the contradiction." The Minneapolis congressman replied that he based his vote on what he thought was the wish of the Minneapolis City Council and, therefore, the wish of Minneapolis residents. When Fraser said he did not want to see more freeways built in the city, a woman in the crowd yelled back, "Not if you want to get back into office, you don't," and the crowd cheered. The impromptu session ended on a more positive note when Fraser said he would explore whether federal guidelines would permit the appropriation to be used for an upgraded roadway including a bikeway and mass transit rather than a six- or eight-lane freeway.[3]

Following the angry January meeting, Fraser huddled with Minneapolis mayor Al Hofstede and urged him to appoint a formal citizens advisory committee that could help defuse what was becoming an increasing contentious local issue. The Hiawatha Avenue Design Advisory Group was established in early 1975 with fourteen members appointed by Hofstede, the city council, and house and senate members from the affected state legislative districts. Members included Tennessen and Bratt from the Highway 55 Task Force as well as Archie Shand from the Central Labor Union Council and Kolderie from the Citizens League.

Tennessen and Bratt worked together to represent the interests of the citizens-based task force. "We had a good cop–bad cop routine," Bratt recalled. "Jim came on strong. He had all those embarrassing statistics that put everyone on edge. I could be a little more moderate. I was the good cop." They made sure they had done their homework when highway department officials met with the advisory committee to make the case for a freeway along Highway 55. "We got statistics from the Met Council and the highway department, and we would study those reports. When the highway department people came to our meetings and presented their reports, they didn't know what the numbers represented. Wally and I would have the numbers down to the fourth decimal point. We would start asking questions, and they would have no idea how to respond. We were able to win allies on the committee because we had the numbers. The highway guys were just talking in generalities," Tennessen said.[4]

While the advisory committee was getting organized, the citizen-led Highway 55 Task Force continued to work on its own proposals.

Early on, Tennessen, a key player in both groups, recognized that mass transit should be an integral part of any highway reconstruction plan. The young community activist had recently returned to the United States from a three-year stint as an air force captain stationed in Germany. "When I was over there, I saw at firsthand what LRT could do," Tennessen recalled. "We used it all the time. Back then, Americans were complaining about paying a dollar for a gallon of gas. Europeans were paying two to three dollars. They thought we were crybabies. 'Why don't you Americans start using mass transit,' they kept asking. 'That way you won't have to pay such high gas bills.'"[5]

"We kept saying 'no' to a freeway," recalled Kathy Mackdanz, a Tennessen ally who would chair a Highway 55 citizens advisory committee in the early 1980s. "But we kept being asked what our alternative was, so we decided that we had to get serious about an alternative." Mackdanz, Tennessen, and others realized the language of the Blatnik amendment gave them an opening. "The amendment called for an 'intermodal' transportation connection," Mackdanz remembered. "No one was quite sure what *intermodal* meant. Why couldn't *intermodal* include light rail transit, we decided, so that is what we pushed for."[6]

The south Minneapolis activists sought technical expertise to ensure that they would be taken seriously, bringing in two local LRT enthusiasts, George Isaacs and Ken Fletcher, to advise them. Isaacs and Fletcher provided arguments for LRT and numbers to support their position. Fletcher prepared a well-documented, seventeen-page report for the Highway 55 Task Force entitled "Light Rail Transit in the Hiawatha Corridor." In the report Fletcher explained, "light rail is a rather ambiguous term that was given to us by the aerospace industry. The term has nothing to do with the size or the weight of the rail. It is defined as an intermediate capacity system, using modern vehicles, capable of moving 2,000 to 24,000 passengers, per hour, in one direction on private or semi-private rights of way. Because light rail vehicles are propelled by electricity, they do not need imported fuel to operate. Also, because their source of power is electric, the vehicles do not pollute the air we breathe."[7]

Eventually, the task force included the Fletcher proposal in an overall plan calling for an at-grade, thirty-five-mile-an-hour park-

# Boulevard Yes — Freeway No!

A NEWSLETTER OF THE HIGHWAY 55 TASK FORCE

October 1976

In the past couple of months, a number of questions have been raised concerning the future of Highway 55. Especially disturbing are the statements made by a number of politicians on the South Side--statements which we feel are misleading or do not tell the whole story on Hiawatha Avenue. Therefore, this edition of the newsletter attempts to answer those questions and issues which have been raised.

## 1. How wide is the Kolderie Freeway plan?

The plan proposed by Ted Kolderie of the Citizens League (which was passed by the City Council in March, then studied by the City Engineer, and is still pending before the Council, having failed to obtain approval last June) calls for a normal width of 262 feet for most of its length. This makes it wider than the original six-lane freeway plan. As if that were'nt enough, at 46th Street the Kolderie plan broadens into a huge interchange some 400 feet wide!

## 2. Is the Kolderie Freeway really a 10-lane freeway?

Judge for yourself: the Kolderie plan calls for the following: a four-lane depressed express-type roadway (two travel lanes and two shoulder lanes, plus buffer zones, a Jersey concrete median, and slopes or walls), a two-lane service road for trucks (including 10-foot parking bays), and a four-lane boulevard. The sum total is ten lanes wide. The term "depressed express-type roadway" is not ours, but is Clayton Sorenson's official description of the road to the Metropolitan Council. In addition, the Kolderie Freeway falls within the boundaries of the freeway moratorium law, since it includes expressway standards, is wider than six lanes, and requires the taking of more homes.

## 3. Is the Kolderie Freeway a "compromise" concept for Hiawatha?

No. It was proposed by Ted Kolderie as a minority report of the Citizens Advisory Committee, and was rejected by the majority of that committee. It is a pro-highway plan which has the support of specific interest groups such as the Central Labor Union and the construction trades unions.

## 4. Is there ANY compromise plan for Hiawatha?

Yes, the plan calling for the combination of a four-lane boulevard with a light rail transit line. The Citizens Advisory Committee endorsed the boulevard idea, and urged consideration of light rail.

*South Minneapolis activists published a newsletter opposing construction of a full-scale freeway along Hiawatha Avenue but supporting the use of transit in the corridor.*

way along Highway 55 rather than a depressed freeway. Tennessen and his allies used Fletcher's report to build support for LRT. As the controversy over Highway 55 continued to simmer, Bratt, a pro-transit member of the design advisory group, wrote, "we have studied the available options, heavy rail, Personal Rapid Transit, busways, light rail. For Hiawatha Avenue, light rail makes the most sense. It is not heavy or as costly as the subway or the automated rail systems. It is not technologically futuristic, as in Personal Rapid Transit. Unlike the depressed express busway, it would serve the community without dividing it, and it could traverse Minnehaha Park without the enormous cost of being enclosed and submerged in a tunnel."[8]

Parting company with the *Minneapolis Star* editorial writers who opposed LRT, at least one local journalist agreed with Bratt. Outspoken columnist Barbara Flanagan wrote in 1976, "I don't want a freeway on Hiawatha, even if the lanes for busses and trucks are depressed into a kind of ditch. It's an out-of-date idea that would only add more air and noise pollution to our already over-polluted town . . . The solution to Hiawatha, I think, is a light rail line from downtown to the airport. At least one stop on the route would be at the historic Minnehaha depot alongside Minnehaha Park. What a tourist attraction that rail line would be."[9]

Despite support from public figures like Flanagan, LRT advocates faced intense pressure from opponents, some of whom saw transit undercutting the case for a full-scale freeway in the Highway 55 corridor. Tennessen remembers being pressured by a member of his own family, his brother, Bob, a DFL state senator: "One day Bob pulled me aside and told me that I should not be supporting LRT because the legislature was against it. Today, Bob is supporting LRT like everyone else in Minneapolis. He has probably forgotten about our little chat back then."[10]

DFLers at the state capitol and in city hall responded to intense pressure from organized labor, whose leaders lobbied hard for the new freeway. It was left to one of the city council's two Republicans, Eleventh Ward alderman Walter Rockenstein, to make the case for LRT. At a May 1976 press conference, Rockenstein declared, "the time has come for the Minneapolis City Council to move forward in providing our citizens with a modern rapid transit system." Rail transit would bring improved access to downtown Minneapolis; improved transit between the airport, the university, and downtown; and park-and-ride facilities for Dakota County commuters.[11]

Rockenstein's press conference came while the city council faced a vote on Highway 55. On the city's advisory committee, pro-freeway forces had coalesced around a proposal by the Citizen League's Kolderie. His plan called for four lanes at grade along Highway 55, with two additional below-grade lanes reserved for multi-occupancy vehicles such as buses, commuter vans, and car pools. "We called that plan 'Kolderie's ditch,'" Tennessen recalled derisively.[12]

On the fourteen-member committee, Kolderie and his allies were able to muster only six votes when the time came to act. An eight-member majority, including Bratt and Tennessen, called for a four-lane boulevard roadway along Highway 55 but sidestepped the contentious issue of a tunnel through Minnehaha Park. Unable to earn strong endorsement of LRT from the majority, Bratt and Tennessen settled for a recommendation to reserve space along the highway for "a future transit addition." Almost immediately, the *Minneapolis Star* condemned the majority report, calling it "disappointing and essentially inconclusive. To treat Hiawatha mainly as a local street is to miss the entire point of the issue that has bedeviled Minneapolis for 15 years," the *Star* declared on October 14. "We much prefer the [Kolderie] alternative plan."[13]

The city council, caught in the cross fire between freeway supporters and opponents, dithered for more than six months before considering the advisory committee report. Finally, on June 10, 1976, the council's DFL caucus reluctantly agreed to support the advisory committee's majority report. But the next day, after heavy arm-twisting by labor leaders Dan Gustafson and Virgil Moline, four DFLers reversed themselves in the full council and voted to oppose the plan, dooming it to defeat on a vote of nine to three.

Just as the Friday council meeting was starting, Tenth Ward alderman Keith Ford confronted Gustafson, declaring angrily, "You guys are jacking us around on this."

Gustafson replied defiantly, "You're jacking us around."

An unidentified alderman told a *Minneapolis Tribune* reporter, "I am just psyching myself up. I am trying to get sick so I won't have to vote. Did you ever do that in school—try to get sent to the nurse's office so you wouldn't have to take the test?"[14]

In the end, the council ducked the political brickbats, voting merely to refer the Highway 55 plan to other government agencies without taking a stand on it. By doing so, the council forfeited the opportunity to access the Blatnik amendment's $53 million for an "urban highway intermodal transportation connection." The *Minneapolis Star* was right in at least one regard: the advisory committee's report was inconclusive. The controversy over Highway 55 was no closer to being resolved than it had been several years earlier. Tennessen, Bratt, and their allies had helped raise LRT's profile, but rail transit in the Hiawatha corridor was still not official public policy.

Eventually, labor's opposition to LRT began to melt away, helping move the issue forward. Tennessen credits Doug Kelm with bringing labor around. Kelm served as chief of staff to Rudy Perpich, a transit supporter who was elected governor in 1976. "Doug helped show the labor guys that transit could mean permanent jobs, not just construction jobs, and that made a big difference," Tennessen said.[15]

Initially, the highway department had planned to tunnel the freeway under Minnehaha Creek. But that plan raised a red flag for Bratt, a member of the Hiawatha Avenue Design Advisory Group and a professional geologist. "I knew that the tunnel would require a lot of digging and blasting, and that would affect the falls," Bratt recalled. He kept prodding the highway department to provide a construction plan for the tunnel. Finally, the massive 150-page plan arrived at his home on Forty-seventh Avenue. "I remember that the house smelled like an ammonia factory from all those blueprints," Bratt said. "Once I started reading through the plans, I knew right off the dangers posed by the tunnel. They would be digging down thirty feet into bedrock and coming within four or five hundred feet of the falls. All the blasting into the bedrock would have been very threatening to the falls. [The highway department report] gave me the ammunition I needed to fight the plan for the tunnel."[16]

With Bratt leading the fight to scuttle the tunnel and consensus proving elusive, the advisory committee disbanded without resolving the Highway 55 controversy. After a brief cooling-off period, a new committee was established, this time with twenty-eight members, chaired by southside resident Kathy Mackdanz. This committee devised a new way for the proposed roadway to traverse Minnehaha Park, a problem whose solution had confounded the earlier group. Instead of tunneling under Minnehaha Creek, the committee called for a covering or berm over Highway 55 that would connect the falls area with the lagoon at the west end of the park. The berm helped build consensus for a revised roadway plan that was eventually adopted by the Minneapolis City Council. Gone was the Kolderie ditch. In its place, the Mackdanz committee proposed a four-lane, at-grade parkway in its March 1982 report. For the first time, light rail transit was to be an integral feature of the revised roadway plan.

With a plan for a covered roadway at Minnehaha Park in place, south Minneapolis residents thought the Highway 55 battles were over—but they were wrong. In 1996, a group of environmental activists discovered that a section of the new highway between Fifty-second Street and the Crosstown would be rerouted through a stretch of state-owned property that included Camp Coldwater Springs, considered a sacred site by some Native Americans. The Highway 55 reroute would also eliminate a small group of houses on Riverview Road that were already owned and rented out by the highway department.

While the highway protests in the 1970s and '80s were led by middle-class residents who considered themselves "good government" advocates, the new protests in the mid-1990s attracted radical environmental activists who relished a confrontation with public authorities overseeing Highway 55's reconstruction. In her sympathetic account of the reroute protest, Mary Losure recognized the protest leaders' shortcomings: "They could be strident and irrational. They could be naïve and impractical. Some stretched the truth. Others seemed to do everything possible to alienate the ordinary citizens they hoped so fervently would join their cause . . . But the better I came to know them, the more I had respect for what they were trying to do."[17]

When legal and political action by the protesters did not halt the reroute, the group's most radical members took matters into their own hands, occupying the site for several months as squatters in the empty houses owned by the highway department. The

*Reroute protestors were ultimately unsuccessful in their efforts to block construction of the final phase of the Highway 55 project.*

occupation ended violently in the early morning of December 20, 1998, when a force of six hundred state and local officers stormed the site and forcibly removed the remaining protesters. Though believing in their noble cause, in the end the protesters were not able to win the fight. The reroute proceeded as planned, and with it LRT moved one step closer to reality. The battle had occurred in the streets and fields around Highway 55, but other more genteel disputes over transportation and its funding needs in the metropolitan region had been under way for decades prior to the climatic raid at the reroute site in 1998.

## False Starts for LRT

Jeff Spartz was optimistic: "If everything goes according to plan, LRT construction could begin in about two years, and the system could be operating about three years after that." Back in 1988, when he made that prediction, Hennepin County commissioner Spartz could not have known that LRT was still more than fifteen years away. Everything did not go according to plan in the 1980s and through much of the 1990s, as LRT became involved in complex political battles that caused one delay after another.[18]

Starting in about 1980, LRT began to emerge as a top priority for the Hennepin County Board, which saw itself as a driving force for rail transit in the Twin Cities. Led by the hard-charging John Derus, Spartz's colleague on the seven-member board, Hennepin County began planning for an ambitious system of rail lines that would reach out into the west metro suburbs from downtown Minneapolis. Derus served on the county board for more than twenty years, until his defeat in 1992. "It's arguable that no other public official did more in the long run to put urban rail transit on the radar of policymakers and the populace," *Star Tribune* reporter Steve Brandt wrote in 2001. "Walk into his office during the heyday of the county's light rail planning, and he'd peddle it like a kid beseeching Santa for an electric train. If there was a map handy, he'd extemporize routes through the metro area and beyond, with trains linking Duluth and Mankato or St. Cloud and Rochester."[19]

Peter McLaughlin, Spartz's successor, credits Derus with pushing the board to acquire right-of-way for the Hiawatha line. "He got us to purchase the site for what is now the LRT shops and yards near Franklin Avenue. That might never have happened without him," McLaughlin said. "The irony is that Derus won the war even though he lost his biggest battle," Brandt wrote. "Light-rail transit is getting built. But counties are no longer in the driver's seat."[20]

Derus, McLaughlin, and others promoted a regional approach to transit through a multicounty alliance which proved tenuous and eventually fractured as the region's other urban county, Ramsey, chafed under Hennepin's dominant role. At that same time, the Minnesota Legislature began to eye the counties and their transit ambitions warily. Eventually, the legislature stripped the counties of their transit planning responsibilities, shifting those duties to the state-controlled Metropolitan Council. While Hennepin County no longer held a direct line into planning and operating a rail transit system, McLaughlin, who inherited Derus's advocacy mantle after 1992, continued to play an important behind-the-scenes role in pushing forward an LRT agenda in St. Paul and Washington, DC.

## A Federal Funding Spigot

While local politicians were squabbling over LRT in Minnesota, transit advocates made note of a favorable environment for transit funding in Congress. "We had terrific opportunities in Washington because we had House members who were so strategically placed," McLaughlin explained, referring to Minnesota's Eighth District congressman Jim Oberstar, chair of the powerful House public works committee, and Fifth District congressman Martin Sabo, who served on the House appropriation subcommittee that controlled federal transportation funding.[21]

The taciturn Sabo, who succeeded Fraser in the House in 1979, played a key role by earmarking funds for LRT and other Minnesota projects in federal spending bills year after year. While Sabo's office would occasionally churn out a press release announcing the federal appropriations, the low-key Minneapolis congressman tended to shy away from the spotlight. "Martin is one of those rare people who always under-promises and over-performs," McLaughlin observed.[22]

Sabo was willing to direct the federal funding spigot toward Minnesota, but he was not willing to arbitrate disputes over LRT back home. A strong mass transit advocate, Sabo helped provide operating funds for the Twin Cities bus system but was somewhat skeptical about rail transit—at least initially. "I wanted to make sure that whatever was proposed for the Hiawatha corridor made sense and had broad support," Sabo later said. "During my first few years in Washington, there were competing plans and little in the way of consensus. After that changed and we had a workable plan, I did what I could to help move the plan along in Washington." Sabo was sensitive to charges that his House subcommittee was merely engaged in pork barrel politics. "If you take a bite out of a bus and it tastes like pork, then I guess it's pork," Sabo told the *Star Tribune* in 2001. "But when I see a new bus, it looks like a good transportation investment to me."[23]

Up through the 1980s and into the early 1990s, the state legislature had shown little inclination to fund light rail transit in the Twin Cities, but advocates hoped they could jump-start the funding process with a large federal allocation. "Light-rail transit might be here sooner than any of us dared hope," Hennepin County commissioner Mark Andrew reported in April 1991, restating Spartz's optimistic prediction of three years earlier. Minnesota stood a good chance of getting a congressional committee to approve $60 million for LRT during the following six months and $190 million in the two years beyond. Oberstar was the "key person making all this happen," Andrew explained. Under the two-step Congressional approval process, Oberstar's public works committee authorized federal transportation projects while Sabo's committee funded these projects in the yearly appropriations bill.[24]

According to Andrew, the state's first LRT was not scheduled to go along Hiawatha Avenue. Instead, it was to follow a northwestern route from downtown Minneapolis up into Brooklyn Park, conveniently close to Oberstar's Eighth Congressional District, which reached into the northern end of the metro area.

Andrew's optimism was short-lived. Almost immediately, Ramsey County commissioners attacked the northwest corridor proposal, saying it eliminated a link to St. Paul that had been included in an earlier plan approved by the seven-county regional transportation board. On April 16, fewer than two weeks after Andrew made his optimistic prediction, the Ramsey County board adopted a sharply worded resolution accusing Hennepin County of making a power grab to gain the $250 million in federal funds. Hennepin-Ramsey battles arose in later years as the two urban counties continued to arm wrestle over LRT.

Andrew reacted quickly to the attack from his neighboring board. "Until a small, parochial group of people in Ramsey County began to subterfuge this effort, we were in a good position to obtain federal funds for this project," he declared angrily. But Oberstar and Sabo backed off, saying they did not intend to obtain congressional funding for an LRT system in the Twin Cities until the metro area had a consensus, a plan, and matching funds.[25]

In 1991, consensus was clearly lacking. Earlier in the year, the influential Citizens League had restated its decades-long opposition to LRT, claiming it would be an expensive mistake because it would not do enough to relieve traffic congestion or air pollution. As in the past, the league called for improved bus service and more incentives for car pools as an alternative to LRT. League spokesman Peter Vanderpoel dismissed the transit advocates' claims that LRT would become cost effective over the long term. "Why should we believe in magic?" he asked derisively. "What would [LRT] grow? Their thesis is that if it's there, somehow, people will ride it. You have to compete with the car. You have to think about service, not about hardware, and what [the advocates] do is they start with the hardware."[26]

Vanderpoel's critique was received sympathetically in the state legislature, which declined to approve a new one-cent metropolitan area sales tax to fund LRT. Governor Arne Carlson, doubting LRT would ever be built, proposed setting a deadline two years later, in 1993, on the transit debate. If proponents had not made their case by then, the idea should be dropped, Carlson said.

In 1994, Ramsey and Hennepin county officials healed their breach, at least temporarily. Hennepin County's McLaughlin and Ramsey County's Richard Wedell appeared together before a congressional subcommittee in Washington to plead for planning funds for an LRT line that would connect the two downtowns. But the Fifth District's Sabo was cautious: LRT wouldn't move forward until the state did its part by providing matching funds, he warned. "With lackluster support in the Minnesota legislature and opposition from some neighborhood groups, the project [LRT] has barely inched closer to implementation in the 30 years it has been talked about," *Star Tribune* reporter Jean Christensen observed following testimony by McLaughlin and Wedell in Washington.[27]

The next year, LRT received another setback when an ambitious $2 billion plan to rebuild Interstate 35W imploded. The plan, put forward by the Minneapolis Department of Transportation (MNDOT), would have run an LRT line down the middle of the reconfigured urban freeway. By 1996, MNDOT commissioner James Denn, a relatively recent convert to the transit cause, was not at all optimistic about the future of LRT in the Twin Cities. "I don't sense the enthusiasm or confidence today in LRT anywhere near what it was three or four years ago," Denn observed.[28]

## A New Approach

After the I-35W plan was scuttled, McLaughlin decided the time had come to stop talking about LRT only as a transportation issue. "We needed to realize that development was equally important," McLaughlin said. "LRT was a way to preserve the core of Minneapolis as the core of the metro area. Were we going to go the way of Chicago with a strong core, or the way of Phoenix which lacked one." McLaughlin promoted LRT as a way of strengthening Minneapolis's downtown, already clogged with buses. "The Mall of America was a new element in the mix," McLaughlin explained. "Initially, downtown interests had opposed the mall, but once it was there, they began to see it as an opportunity, and they wanted a link to it."[29]

McLaughlin helped arrange a meeting between Sam Grabarski, the Downtown Council's president, and John Wheeler, the mall's general manager. "Before that meeting, they had never met," McLaughlin recalled. Grabarski and Wheeler recognized that a transit connection between the region's two major retail centers would be mutually beneficial. This understanding helped revive the original Hiawatha LRT route, hand drawn by Ken Fletcher in 1975.[30]

After the plans for other routes floundered, transit advocates realized the Hiawatha corridor had a lot going for it. LRT had already been written into the plan to rebuild Highway 55, much of the right-of-way was already publicly owned, and a downtown-to-the-mall connection was possible with a stop at the airport. From a procedural standpoint, an environmental impact statement had already been completed, which would speed up the federal approval process. As a sop to rail opponents, McLaughlin and the transit planners hedged their bets by calling for a "transitway" in the Hiawatha corridor that could be used for exclusive bus lanes or for LRT. McLaughlin recalled,

> The business interests were attracted to LRT, but they were skeptical. They remembered the earlier false starts. They thought that a Hiawatha LRT would go the way of other failed efforts . . . I kept telling the skeptics that we had strong support in Washington. We had Oberstar and Sabo, who were key on transportation, so why dissipate our efforts on relatively small projects like bus lanes? Let's go for broke, I told them. If we

can't get LRT, then our fallback will be a bus way. But if we fall back to buses, we will do them forever. We will never get LRT.[31]

Sabo was waiting in the wings, ready to deliver, but he kept reminding McLaughlin and other transit advocates about a local match requirement. In other parts of the country, transit agencies were able to rely on a regional tax to generate the local match, but that revenue source was not available in the Twin Cities. "We had to get our match from the state legislature, and we had to crawl over cut glass to do so," McLaughlin said.[32]

At the capitol, the heavy political lifting fell to Carol Flynn, the south Minneapolis legislator who had been a transit advocate on the Metropolitan Council prior to her election to the state senate in 1990. "I had always felt that transit was important, and I wanted LRT to happen. In the beginning, I didn't think it would necessarily happen in my own district," Flynn recalled. "When that looked like a real possibility, I was pleased, but then I had to absorb all the slings and arrows from the transit opponents." By 1998, Flynn was chair of the senate transportation committee and a key player on transit issues at the capitol. She worked hard to forge an alliance with rural legislators: "They needed roads and we needed transit, so we could come together, but our real problems were with the suburbanites—particularly the suburban Republicans."[33]

Arne Carlson, a transit skeptic, was still governor, but his appointee as Met Council chair, Curt Johnson, lent his support to the cause. A fierce foe of LRT in his previous job as head of the anti-rail Citizens League, Johnson had experienced a change of heart. His conversion was prompted, at least in part, by increased population pressures, an overburdened transportation system, and the ineffectiveness of measures such as carpooling and exclusive bus lanes in easing traffic pressures. "Seeing all of this, Johnson said: 'I've come to believe that we are going to experience—by Minnesota standards at least—unspeakable congestion,'" reported the *Tribune* in January 1998.[34]

His support provided a pipeline to Carlson, who seven years earlier had predicted that LRT would never be built. By 1998, as his term drew to a close, the Republican governor was ready to deal.

In an end-of-session bargain, engineered in part by Flynn, Carlson agreed, albeit reluctantly, to a $40 million bonding allocation for LRT in exchange for a $60 million loan for a St. Paul hockey arena. "He agreed to the $40 million only because it was part of a package deal," Flynn recalled. "Arne and [St. Paul mayor] Norm Coleman wanted the hockey arena. That was their highest priority. I went along with it because it helped us move transit forward."[35]

After Carlson signed the bonding bill, MNDOT's local manager, Richard Stehr, was anxious to move ahead. "We certainly have enough money in the bonding bill to get us off to a real fast start," he announced in April. "We would proceed with planning and design while we wait for things to work out at the federal level." Federal approvals were still required for the project.[36]

LRT was not a done deal, even in 1998. The $40 million was only a start. An additional $200 million was needed from the federal treasury, along with $60 million from the state and $70 mil-

This cartoon from the 1980s highlights skeptics' concerns that light rail transit did not represent a cost-effective approach to meeting the region's transit needs.

lion from local governments including Hennepin County and the City of Minneapolis. MNDOT and the Metropolitan Council divided up responsibilities for the project, which was approaching $400 million in costs. The state agency would build the line, while the regional council would own and operate it.

Policy makers and the technicians who worked for them still had to make some critical decisions about the route and station locations. The middle section of the Hiawatha line, in the right-of-way for Highway 55, had pretty much been determined, but the route at the beginning of the line in downtown Minneapolis and at the end of the line in Bloomington was not yet established. Expensive options needed to be explored for the crossovers at Lake Street and Highway 62 and the tunnel under the Minneapolis–St. Paul airport. Transit advocates relied on Sabo to move a federal appropriation for the Hiawatha LRT, but Sabo couldn't deliver a check to Minnesota on his own. The Minnesota project had to vie with 180 rail transit proposals from all over the country in a competition overseen by bureaucrats at the Federal Transit Administration (FTA) in Washington.

Transit planners at MNDOT and the Met Council knew they faced a tight deadline in order to compete in the FTA's next funding round. "We only have about six to seven months to tie up loose ends," the council's transportation planning director, Natalio Diaz, announced in May 1998. By July, the general location of fourteen stations along the twelve-mile route had been determined by the interagency policy group overseeing LRT planning. Question marks were placed around a fifteenth station at Fiftieth Street to serve Minnehaha Park. Later that year, the Minneapolis City Council approved a route through downtown along Fifth Street— and almost immediately became embroiled in controversy with Xcel Energy over relocating utility lines that ran under the street. Eventually the debate was resolved when a federal judge ordered Xcel to move the lines.[37]

The year 1999 brought a new governor, the flamboyant Jesse Ventura. While Carlson had acquiesced to the initial $40 million only as part of an end-of-session agreement, Ventura was an enthusiastic LRT booster who earmarked $60 million for the project in his first biennial budget. Newly appointed Met Council chair Ted Mondale told an interagency transit planning group, Ventura "sees that light rail has been in the planning stage and he wants to be the governor who implements it."[38]

Ventura had been introduced to the possibilities of LRT during a trip to Atlanta for a meeting with Ted Turner at the Cable News Network (CNN). According to McLaughlin, "Jesse was ready to take a cab in from the airport to Turner's office in downtown Atlanta when the man next to him told him about Atlanta's light rail line. The two of them got on the LRT, and it deposited Jesse right in front of the CNN building. 'That was just great,' Jesse later told me. 'With the money I saved on cab fare, I could fill up both of my jet skis with gas all weekend long.'"[39]

Ventura didn't directly buttonhole legislators, but his administration hired a well-connected lobbyist, Joe Bagnoli, to promote LRT in the house and senate. "Bagnoli was very effective," according to Flynn. "He knew how to push all the right buttons." Ventura's bonding recommendation was applauded by transit advocates, but almost immediately the proposal was attacked by east metro politicians, including St. Paul mayor Norm Coleman and state senator Randy Kelly, who later succeeded Coleman as mayor.[40]

As plans for Hiawatha LRT took shape, additional rail lines were being proposed for the Northstar line up to St. Cloud and for a Riverview line that would link downtown St. Paul to the airport. Coleman was irate that St. Paul had been left out of the bonding bill. "To invest in light rail simply in the west metro area will hurt the economic vitality of the entire region and I won't support that," he declared angrily. "Unless we're treated much more fairly, we are not going to acquiesce to a proposal that is western oriented," Kelly added. Met Council chair Mondale felt more than a little threatened by Coleman's and Kelly's efforts to torpedo the $60 million for Hiawatha LRT. In early April, he said he was nervous about prospects for winning federal construction funding in light of the intra-regional squabbling. "'We need to get our act together' in the next month or two, he said, because competition from the other 180 cities is fierce," reported the *Tribune*.[41]

Coleman and Kelly were eventually mollified when Ramsey County transit projects were included on MNDOT's priority list, but attacks from another power center could not be so easily quelled. Opposition in the Republican-dominated house was hardening, and LRT opponents such as Phil Krinkie and Carol Molnau led a

bitter fight to derail the Hiawatha line. Krinkie and Tim Work-
man, backed by house majority leader Tim Pawlenty, continued
working to defund LRT even after Ventura's $60 million request
was approved by a house-senate conference committee. Rail transit opponents latched on to the issue of operating costs, and even
proponents acknowledged that fares would cover only about a
third of annual operating costs, leaving a deficit of $6 million. Pro-
jected operating deficits continued to hang over LRT like a dark
cloud for the next four years.

## Dodging the Bullets

With a $100 million state match wrapped up, transit planners
rushed to complete the state's massive grant proposal to the Federal Transit Administration in Washington. "It's a red-letter day
for the Twin Cities," *Star Tribune* reporter Laurie Blake announced on September 28, 1999. ". . . 37 pounds of paper carrying
the final pitch for construction of the Hiawatha Avenue light rail
line will be mailed overnight to land Wednesday on the desks of
the Federal Transit Administration officials."[42]

But the celebration was cut short by immediate charges from a
group of house Republicans that the Ventura administration had
withheld information from the legislature that pushed the price
tag for Hiawatha LRT up to $548 million. Krinkie announced that
he would write to federal transit officials, urging them not to approve the Minnesota project until a study was done of options that
could cut costs. If charges of cost overruns killed the project,
"that'll make one guy happy," Krinkie declared. Only a few days
earlier, the Hiawatha line had dodged another potentially fatal
bullet when the Bloomington City Council approved a route to the
Mall of America by a vote of four to three. A switch of one vote
would have killed the project.[43]

Even as the federal approval process was moving forward,
Krinkie and his band of LRT opponents stepped up their attacks.
Saying he was willing to go to "quite extreme lengths" to stop construction of the transit project, the Shoreview representative,
along with nine other Republicans legislators, filed suit in state
court in December to block it. Five months later, Ramsey County
district judge A. James Dickinson threw out the suit, saying he
was not willing to referee "a political dispute" between the governor and the legislators.[44]

## A Done Deal

Turned back in state court, Krinkie and his allies also made little headway at the Federal Transit Agency. Even though Hiawatha LRT was not ranked in the "highest priority" category by the federal agency, the Minnesota project earned passing marks and the green light to receive the federal construction dollars Sabo had squirreled away in the federal budget. When the required sixty-day congressional review posed no further roadblocks, *Star Tribune* reporter Blake was able to announce on January 14, 2001, "light rail in the Twin Cities is a done deal." Met Council chair Mondale breathed a sigh of relief. "We were on a critical path timeline for a year and a half," Mondale reported. "We came within a day of being killed a number of times."[45]

Three days later, Governor Ventura told a cheering crowd at a hastily arranged ground-breaking ceremony, "The Hiawatha light-rail line is happening today because the people demanded more transportation choices." The January 2001 event was one of the few opportunities Ventura had to celebrate a major achievement of his embattled administration. By the time the Hiawatha LRT opened for business three and half years later, Ventura was no longer in office.[46]

Even through LRT was officially a "done deal," Krinkie and his allies continued to fight a rear guard action to block the project. In October, the Krinkie team used the September 11 terrorist attacks

*Fifth District congressman Martin Sabo and Hennepin County commissioner Peter McLaughlin were key players in the successful effort to develop the region's first light rail transit line.*

as a reason to halt construction of the LRT tunnel under the Twin Cities airport. Krinkie urged the Metropolitan Airports Commission to mothball the tunnel in light of sagging revenues. One of his allies, Representative Tim Wilkin, maintained that a tunnel would make the airport more vulnerable to terrorist attacks. Despite these and other political shots, construction of the tunnel and the rest of the twelve-mile line continued on schedule. A few minor flare-ups occurred over routes and station locations, but the three-and-a-half-year construction period was remarkably uneventful—particularly in comparison to the years of controversy that preceded it.

In 2003, when LRT legislative foe Tim Pawlenty became governor, transit advocates were apprehensive that the new Republican administration, with Carol Molnau as MNDOT head, would try to sabotage the project. Their fears were eased somewhat when Pawlenty came out in support of the Northstar commuter rail line, which waited in the wings for funding. Pawlenty and his Met Council chair, Peter Bell, came in for new criticism when in March a bitter transit workers strike forced a delay in the scheduled April opening date for the Hiawatha line. Some union supporters maintained that Bell was using LRT as a bargaining chip in the dispute, a charge he denied. By mid-April the strike was settled, paving the way for the Met Council to move ahead with plans to open the new LRT line later that spring.

On a sunny weekend at the end of June, trains were filled with eager riders who took advantage of the free fares to inaugurate the Hiawatha LRT. On Monday morning, commuters lined up at the ticket kiosks to pay for their first ride. During that week, 93,000 paying passengers boarded the trains, surpassing Metro Transit estimates by nearly 70 percent. Bell was cautiously optimistic. He was pleased with the numbers but wanted to wait for more of them. "At this time next year, we'll know if we have a successful system," he said.[47]

A year later, as ridership continued to exceed all predictions, Bell had the numbers he wanted. Even many of its former critics conceded that the Hiawatha light rail line was a great success. Soon planning was under way for new transit spokes radiating from the Hiawatha line that could create a metro-wide system for the Twin Cities. A goal established by transit advocates like Ken Fletcher more than twenty-five years earlier was finally in sight.

# Epilogue

THE POLLS OPENED in Minneapolis at 7 AM on Tuesday, September 11, 2001. That day, in elections throughout the state, voters would narrow the field of candidates for local public offices. Just as polling was getting under way, word of the terrorist attack on the World Trade Center in New York City arrived. In the resulting turmoil, as people all around the country remained glued to their television sets, some called for Minnesota's primary elections to be cancelled. But that afternoon, Governor Jesse Ventura appeared on the steps of the state capitol and announced that the elections would go on as usual. "Now, more than ever, is the time to show the power of democracy," he declared.[1]

In some ways, the twentieth century ended for Minneapolis in the fall of 2001. The expansive 1990s had passed, and the post–9/11 era would bring new limits and new challenges for Minnesota's largest city. For city hall, that year's municipal elections represented a changing of the guard, as mayor Sharon Sayles-Belton was denied a third term by Minneapolis voters. While Sayles-Belton survived the four-person mayoral primary on September 11, she ran considerably behind her chief challenger, R. T. Rybak. In the general election two months later, the incumbent mayor suffered a stinging defeat, garnering only 35 percent of the vote in the two-person race.

The ebullient, outgoing Rybak, who took office on January 2, 2002, presented a marked contrast to his two self-effacing predecessors, Sayles-Belton and Donald Fraser. Between them, the DFLers had occupied the mayor's office for more than twenty years. A tireless and effective cheerleader for his hometown, the city's new twenty-first-century mayor was always on the go. When he wasn't at city hall, Rybak was leading a cross-country ski race through south Minneapolis, bicycling the neighborhoods to promote the latest green technology, or cultivating a hip, techno-savvy image by becoming the first U.S. mayor to use Twitter. But Rybak's upbeat enthusiasm soon collided with the bleak realities that descended on Minneapolis as the century's first recession rolled through Minnesota. A deteriorating economy pumped up demand for state social services just as revenues were plummeting. The result was a massive state deficit that needed to be erased to meet the constitutional requirement for a balanced budget.

In 2003, Minnesota's newly elected Republican governor, Tim

Pawlenty, was determined to balance the budget by relying almost exclusively on cuts. Over DFL legislative leaders' objections, Pawlenty pushed through a budget that slashed spending for a broad range of programs, including the state's funding for cities, known as Local Government Aid (LGA). Minneapolis absorbed a cut of $26 million from its LGA funds, which translated into a 7 percent reduction in the city's 2003 operating budget. Initially, city officials anticipated trimming as many as seventy firefighters and one hundred police officers to offset the cuts, but early retirements and some funding shifts reduced the number of layoffs.

The city's libraries were hit particularly hard by the loss of LGA funds. An elected board, normally independent, oversaw operation of the city's libraries but lacked authority to levy taxes to cover those costs. Unlike other city departments, where funding shifts could help cushion the LGA cuts, the library board lacked options. As a result, it was forced to cut its operating budget by one-third, sharply reduce library hours, and close three neighborhood branches. The budget reductions arrived just as Minneapolis was ready to break ground for a dramatic new $125 million central library designed by the internationally renowned Cesar Pelli. City leaders considered delaying construction of the new facility but decided to move ahead because bonding was already in place for the project thanks to a referendum approved by Minneapolis voters in 2000. Those voters were understandably perplexed by the decision to spend heavily for what some considered an overly ambitious new facility at the same time that library services in Minneapolis were being slashed. Library officials' explanation that their capital and operating budgets moved on separate tracks often fell on deaf ears.

The turmoil over library funding led to a key structural change in Minneapolis city government during the first decade of the twenty-first century. In 2007, city and county officials agreed to abolish the city's independent library board and unite the Minneapolis libraries with the Hennepin County library system. The merger, which provided a broader, countywide funding base for the Minneapolis libraries, enabled the Hennepin County board to reopen the three closed branch libraries in 2008.

Despite the budget pressures facing Minneapolis in the early 2000s, the city moved ahead with a major publicly financed development. Soon after taking office in 2002, Rybak created a new agency known as Community Planning and Economic Development (CPED), which brought together the city's planning activities and its development functions into one department. In partnership with a private developer, the Ryan Company, CPED renovated the long-vacant Sears complex on East Lake Street, converting the sprawling former warehouse and department store to a mixed-use development anchored by Allina Hospital and Clinics, which moved its corporate headquarters to the site. Renamed the Midtown Exchange, the former Sears property also housed an innovative retail center known as Midtown Global Market, whose impetus came from a group of Latino business owners who had wanted to open a grocery in the retail space. This plan evolved into a multi-ethnic market developed by the nonprofit Neighborhood Development Center and its partners, the Latino Economic Development Center (LEDC) and the African Development Center (ADC).

As the city's Latino and African populations mushroomed during the early 2000s, LEDC and ADC helped promote the entrepreneurial spirit of their ethnic communities. In south Minneapolis, along a two-mile stretch of East Lake Street between I-35W and Hiawatha Avenue, more than two hundred Latino businesses helped revitalize what had been a deteriorating inner-city commercial district. However, by the end of the decade the East Lake Latino boom slowed as a deepening recession combined with a crackdown on undocumented workers drove many immigrants back to their home countries. While LEDC was assisting Latino businesses on Lake Street, ADC was working with East African entrepreneurs at two large Somali malls in south Minneapolis, considered by some to be the largest markets of their kind outside of Mogadishu in Somalia.

While the city helped promote the development of East Lake and the Midtown Exchange, major cultural institutions embarked on their own ambitious expansion plans. In 2005 and 2006, one organization after another cut ribbons for new high-profile developments, each built by a celebrity architect. The Guthrie drew the most attention, opening its massive riverfront theater, designed by Jean Nouvel, in the summer of 2006. That same year, the Minneapolis Institute of Arts completed work on its tasteful and relatively modest new wing built by Michael Graves. A year earlier Graves had completed an addition for the Children's Theatre adjoining the institute. Also in 2005, the Walker Art Center captured the architectural spotlight with an aggressively modern addition built by the Swiss firm Herzog and de Meuron. In all, the four institutions spent nearly $300 million on their real estate projects, funded in large part by wealthy donors who had benefitted from the economic boom of an earlier era. Later in the decade, these premier organizations were forced to cut their operating budgets when the boom ended and a market crash decimated their endowment funds.

Minneapolis, like much of the rest of the country, rode the real estate bubble that inflated property values all across town during the early and mid-2000s but which thousands of pinpricks deflated as predatory lending wrought havoc in the city's older, inner-tier neighborhoods. As early as 2000, warning signs of an impending housing crisis began to appear in the local papers. In March, the *Star Tribune*'s Steve Brandt reported on the high level of predatory loans in Minneapolis's low-income and minority neighborhoods. At a time when the housing crisis was not yet front-page news, Brandt needed to define the term *subprime* for his readers. He explained: "subprime loans are made to people with poorer credit standing, usually at higher interest rates and fees than conventional loans. HUD [Housing and Urban Development] officials said that most mortgage fraud—and predatory activities such as excessive fees or prepayment penalties—occur in the subprime market."[2]

"Only a few years ago, it seemed like everyone could buy a home regardless of their financial circumstances," noted Rony Davis, a longtime north Minneapolis housing advocate, writing in 2008. "There were mortgage brokers marketing at churches, ethnic and social organizations and, it seemed, on every corner. And, unfortunately, many people were preyed upon by people they knew and trusted. There simply was so much money to be made in the system. The problem was compounded by the fact that there was virtually no regulation of the mortgage broker industry." The bubble burst early in north Minneapolis. By 2005, foreclosures, provoked in large part by predatory loans, had ravaged the community. Decades of improvement efforts washed away as one block after another sat pockmarked with vacant, abandoned houses. "I don't think there is any way to explain adequately how devastating one or more vacant houses on a block is to a community," noted North Side community activist Roberta England.[3]

The wave of foreclosures in north Minneapolis and other inner-city neighborhoods caused property values to plunge as mortgage lenders worked feverishly to unload homes they were forced to repossess. During the first quarter of 2009, foreclosed properties on the North Side were selling, on average, for about $40,000—less than a quarter of what they might have earned only a few years earlier. Yet these plunging values planted the seeds of rebirth, as newly affordable housing, coupled with city incentives and federal support, brought throngs of first-time homebuyers to the city's North Side neighborhoods.

What began as an inner-city phenomenon soon spread to the broader economy, as Minneapolis, like most of the rest of the country, became caught up in the national foreclosure crisis. By 2008, the worst economic slump since the Great Depression stalled the region's economic expansion and pushed the Twin Cities' unemployment rate up toward 10 percent. In Minneapolis, the recession slowed but did not halt development along the riverfront as several proposed residential projects were cancelled but others moved forward. The slumping economy cast a chill over downtown when Target Corporation, one of the area's largest employers, announced in January 2009 it was trimming its workforce by 7 percent. The recession only exacerbated the troubled Block E project on Hennepin Avenue, initially touted as downtown's premier entertainment center. Despite the project's ballooning vacancy rates, Block E's developers remained hopeful that the nearby Minnesota Twins ballpark, scheduled to open in 2010, would help resuscitate their project. Transit would help: on opening day, Twins fans could reach the new ballpark via an extension of the Hiawatha LRT line, connected to the new Northstar Commuter Rail Line through the northwest suburbs.

In the summer of 2009, city leaders were preparing for $30 million in LGA cuts over two years. The cuts would take effect as Minneapolis moved into its 2009 municipal election cycle. In November, voters used a new instant-runoff system, ranking electoral choices for local offices in their preferred order. Minneapolis voters, like those at the start of the twentieth century, were also asked to approve a change in the city's charter. But unlike in 1900, when a massive charter overhaul appeared on the ballot, the 2009 change involved only a minor provision to eliminate the city's outmoded board of estimate and taxation. Earlier, the city charter commission had rejected more ambitious proposals that would have abolished the Minneapolis Park Board and consolidated city hall administrative functions under a city manager.

Minneapolis, like all of America, faces an uncertain economic future as the first decade of the twenty-first century draws to a close. Over the course of the preceding century, Minnesota's major city was able to shed a stultifying social order that inhibited change and entrenched privilege. A new vitality and receptivity to diversity helped lay the groundwork for a powerful economic system propelled by innovation and creativity rather than by capital and industrial muscle. Combined with its natural, cultural, and intellectual amenities, this sense of vitality—this impetus toward reinvention—will help Minneapolis preserve the urban renaissance it achieved by the end of the last century, even as it faces the new limits and particular challenges of the new one.

# Notes

## Notes to Introduction

1. *Minneapolis Times,* January 1, 1900, 1.
2. Minneapolis *Star Tribune,* January 1, 2000, 1S.
3. *Minneapolis Journal,* January 1, 1900, 1.
4. Mary Lethert Wingerd, *Claiming the City: Politics, Faith and the Power of Place in St. Paul* (Ithaca, NY: Cornell University Press, 2001), 4.
5. Wingerd, *Claiming the City,* 4.
6. Jon C. Teaford, *The Twentieth-Century American City: Problem, Promise, and Reality* (Baltimore, MD: Johns Hopkins University Press, 1986), 5.

## Notes to "Struggle over Structure"

1. *Minneapolis Tribune,* November 3, 1900, 8.
2. *St. Paul Pioneer Press,* May 4, 1898, 4.
3. Minneapolis Charter Commission, "Orientation Pamphlet for Minneapolis Charter Commissioners" (March 1982), Special Collections, Minneapolis Central Library, Minneapolis, MN.
4. *St. Paul Pioneer Press,* April 27, 1900, 3.
5. *St. Paul Pioneer Press,* April 30, 1900, 4.
6. *St. Paul Globe,* May 1, 1900, 4. *St. Paul Dispatch,* May 2, 1900, 5.
7. *Minneapolis Journal,* October 5, 1900, 4.
8. *Minneapolis Journal,* November 3, 1900, 4.
9. In 1900, several important charter reform advocates, including W. J. Dean, Edward Decker, O. C. Wyman, and George Christian, became founding members of the Citizens Alliance.
10. *Minneapolis Times,* November 4, 1900, 6.
11. *Minneapolis Tribune,* November 3, 1900, 8.
12. *Minneapolis Tribune,* November 3, 1900, 8.
13. *Minneapolis Journal,* October 16, 1900, 4.
14. Wingerd, *Claiming the City,* 88–89.
15. Wingerd, *Claiming the City,* 88–89.
16. Wingerd, *Claiming the City,* 90.
17. *Minneapolis Journal,* January 21, 1929, 14.
18. Carl Solberg, *Hubert Humphrey: A Biography* (1984; St. Paul, MN: Borealis Books, 2003), 109.
19. Solberg, *Hubert Humphrey,* 110.
20. *Minneapolis Tribune,* May 31, 1960, 4.
21. *Minneapolis Tribune,* May 30, 1960, 1. *Minneapolis Tribune,* May 31, 1960, 13.
22. *Minneapolis Labor Review,* May 19, 1960, 1.

23. *Minneapolis Tribune*, June 2, 1960, 6. *Minneapolis Tribune*, June 1, 1960, 4.

24. *Minneapolis Tribune*, June 8, 1960, 4.

25. *Minneapolis Labor Review*, June 9, 1960, 1.

26. This author served on Don Fraser's staff in Congress and later worked for the Minneapolis Community Development Agency, established during Fraser's term as mayor.

27. *Minneapolis Star*, May 22, 1980, 1A, 5A.

28. Minneapolis *Star Tribune*, January 29, 1988, 1A, 6.

29. Minneapolis *Star Tribune*, January 29, 1988, 6.

30. Minneapolis *Star Tribune*, January 29, 1988, 6.

31. Minneapolis *Star Tribune*, January 29, 1988, 6.

32. Minneapolis *Star Tribune*, January 29, 1988, 6.

33. Minneapolis *Star Tribune*, January 29, 1988, 6.

34. Minneapolis *Star Tribune*, January 29, 1988, 6.

35. Minneapolis *Star Tribune*, January 29, 1988, 6.

36. Don Fraser and Dennis Schulstad, interview by the author, January 2005.

37. In 2003, Minneapolis's municipal structure was reworked through the consolidation of the city's planning and development functions into a new Department of Community Planning and Economic Development (CPED). But that consolidation dealt with only one aspect of city government. A cartoon in the December 5, 2004, Minneapolis *Star Tribune* depicted that government as a Rube Goldberg machine, with more than forty different agencies, boards, and commissions each carrying out individual and sometimes overlapping functions. In 2008, one independent city agency, the library board, was eliminated when Hennepin County took over operation of the Minneapolis libraries.

### Notes to "The Shame of Minneapolis"

1. Lincoln Steffens, "The Shame of Minneapolis," *McClure's* (January 1903): 237.

2. Steffens, "Shame," 229.

3. Steffens, "Shame," 229.

4. Gordon Browne, "Hovey C. Clarke: Crusade against Civic Corruption," *Hennepin History* 56.4 (Fall 1997): 24. Iric Nathanson, "The Shame of Minneapolis: Civic Corruption 100 Years Ago," *Hennepin History* 62.1 (Winter 2003): 15.

5. *Minneapolis Times*, January 1, 1900, 4. *Minneapolis Journal Almanac* (Minneapolis, MN: Journal Printing Co., 1900), 1.

6. *Minneapolis Tribune*, November 9, 1899, 1.

7. Steffens, "Shame," 231.

8. Steffens, "Shame," 231.

9. Steffens, "Shame," 233.

10. *Minneapolis Journal*, January 1, 1902, 7.

11. *Minneapolis Journal*, July 1902.

12. Steffens, "Shame," 234.

13. Steffens, "Shame," 236.

14. Steffens, "Shame," 236.

15. Clarke paid a high personal price for his courageous work. In 1903, he suffered a nervous breakdown but soon recovered and resumed management of his successful lumber business. When Clarke died in 1931 at the age of seventy-one, he was remembered for undertaking "one of the outstanding pieces of work for civic betterment in the city's history." *Minneapolis Tribune*, April 11, 1931, 1, 6.

16. *Minneapolis Journal,* June 2, 1902, 1. *Minneapolis Journal,* June 17, 1902, 1.
17. *Minneapolis Journal,* July 3, 1902, 1.
18. *Minneapolis Journal,* July 31, 1902, 1.
19. Steffens, "Shame," 238.
20. Nathanson, "Shame of Minneapolis," 32.
21. Nathanson, "Shame of Minneapolis," 32.
22. Steffens, "Shame," 239.
23. Steffens, "Shame," 239.
24. Fred W. Friendly, *Minnesota Rag: Corruption, Yellow Journalism, and the Case that Saved Freedom of the Press* (Minneapolis: University of Minnesota Press, 2003), 56. Leach was defeated for reelection in 1929 but returned to serve one more term as mayor in 1937.
25. *Minneapolis Journal,* February 17, 1929, 1.
26. *Minneapolis Journal,* February 17, 1929, 1.
27. *Minneapolis Journal,* February 17, 1929, 1.
28. *Minneapolis Journal,* February 17, 1929, 2.
29. *Minneapolis Journal,* February 17, 1929, 1.
30. *Minneapolis Journal,* February 17, 1929, 1.
31. *Minneapolis Journal,* February 17, 1929, 2.
32. *Minneapolis Tribune,* March 8, 1929, 6.
33. *Minneapolis Tribune,* March 17, 1929, 8. Olson had his detractors. Some, including the "scandal sheet" journalists Howard Guilford and Walter Liggett, claimed Olson had underworld ties even as he prosecuted city hall politicians for bribery. Guilford and Liggett were both later murdered, but their assailants were never convicted.
34. Paul Maccabee, "Alias Kid Cann," *Mpls.St.Paul Magazine,* November 1991, 91.
35. Maccabee, "Alias Kid Cann," 91.
36. Dara Moskowitz, "Minneapolis Confidential," *City Pages,* October 11, 1995, 6.
37. Maccabee, "Alias Kid Cann," 160. Liggett's family maintained that Blumenfeld had murdered Walter Liggett even after he was acquitted of all charges. See Marda Liggett Woodbury, *Stopping the Presses: The Murder of Walter. W. Liggett* (Minneapolis: University of Minnesota Press, 1998).
38. *Minneapolis Times,* May 26, 1943, 3.
39. *Minneapolis Times,* May 26, 1943, 3.
40. Hubert H. Humphrey, *The Education of a Public Man: My Life and Politics* (1976; Minneapolis: University of Minnesota Press, 1991), 94.
41. Humphrey, *Education of a Public Man,* 95.
42. Solberg, *Hubert Humphrey,* 100.
43. Solberg, *Hubert Humphrey,* 100.
44. Solberg, *Hubert Humphrey,* 103.
45. Humphrey, *Education of a Public Man,* 97–98. During his two terms as mayor, Humphrey took a tough public stand against known gangsters, but even he had to contend with rumors that his political operatives had ties to underworld figures in Minneapolis. According to Paul Maccabee, "Alias Kid Cann," former U.S. attorney George MacKinnon maintained that one of Humphrey's key confidants, Fred Gates, was a partner in Kid Cann's business ventures.
46. Humphrey, *Education of a Public Man,* 99.
47. Humphrey, *Education of a Public Man,* 100.
48. Corruption has continued to exist in city hall up through modern times. In the early 1980s, Zollie Green, a city council member from the Ninth Ward,

was indicted on bribery charges related to a city bus shelter contract but was later acquitted in federal district court. In the 2000s, three council members, Brian Herron, Joe Biernat, and Dean Zimmermann, were convicted and served jail time on various fraud and bribery counts.

### Notes to "Blood in the Streets"

1. William Millikan, *A Union Against Unions: The Minneapolis Citizens Alliance and Its Fight Against Organized Labor, 1903–1947* (St. Paul: Minnesota Historical Society Press, 2001), 273, 274.

2. "Recollections of Mrs. George Fahr," in Philip A. Korth, *Minneapolis Teamsters Strike of 1934* (East Lansing: Michigan State University Press, 1995), 121.

3. Millikan, *Union Against Unions*, 6.

4. Millikan, *Union Against Unions*, 13.

5. Dunne was known as "Ray" to his friends and coworkers.

6. Korth, *Minneapolis Teamsters Strike*, 29.

7. Korth, *Minneapolis Teamsters Strike*, 25, 60.

8. *Minneapolis Labor Review*, February 16, 1934, 1.

9. Korth, *Minneapolis Teamsters Strike*, 79–80.

10. Korth, *Minneapolis Teamsters Strike*, 80.

11. Korth, *Minneapolis Teamsters Strike*, 81–82.

12. Korth, *Minneapolis Teamsters Strike*, 82.

13. Korth, *Minneapolis Teamsters Strike*, 85.

14. *Minneapolis Labor Review*, May 18, 1934, 1.

15. Charles Rumford Walker, *American City: A Rank and File History of Minneapolis* (Minneapolis: University of Minnesota Press, 2005), 103.

16. Samuel Hynes, *The Growing Seasons: An American Boyhood Before the War* (New York: Viking, 2003), 55.

17. Eric Sevareid, *Not So Wild a Dream* (New York: A. A. Knopf, 1946), 57.

18. *Minneapolis Tribune*, May 22, 1934, 2.

19. Millikan, *A Union Against Unions*, 273.

20. Millikan, *A Union Against Unions*, 274.

21. Walker, *American City*, 126.

22. Walker, *American City*, 126–27.

23. Walker, *American City*, 127–28.

24. Korth, *Minneapolis Teamsters Strike*, 135.

25. Korth, *Minneapolis Teamsters Strike*, 135–36.

26. *Minneapolis Tribune*, July 20, 1934, 2.

27. *New York Times*, July 21, 1934, 1, 2.

28. Walker, *American City*, 168.

29. Walker, *American City*, 170–71.

30. Walker, *American City*, 168–71.

31. *Minneapolis Labor Review*, July 27, 1934, 1.

32. Korth, *Minneapolis Teamsters Strike*, 156.

33. Letter, August 8, 1934, Collection OF 4076, Roosevelt Library, Hyde Park, New York.

34. Korth, *Minneapolis Teamsters Strike*, 159. Haas claimed that Jones had told Minneapolis business leaders that if the strike was not settled within two weeks, the RFC would call in all its outstanding loans to Twin Cities banks and railroads. See Hy Berman interview, *Labor's Turning Point: The Minneapolis Truck Strikes*

*of 1934: A Rank and File Story*, video, produced by John DeGraaf (St. Paul, MN: KTCA Public Television Channel 2, 1981).

35. Jesse Jones to Franklin Roosevelt, wire, August 28, 1934, File 407-B, Roosevelt Library, Hyde Park, New York.

36. *Minneapolis Journal*, August 22, 1934, 1, 2.

37. *Minneapolis Labor Review*, August 24, 1934, 1.

38. *Minneapolis Journal*, August 22, 1934, 2.

39. Local 574, the hero of the 1934 Truckers Strike, underwent a major change in the early 1940s when the International Teamsters Union orchestrated the ouster of Vince Dunne and his allies from their leadership positions in the union, renamed Local 544. Dunne and a group of seventeen other union leaders were tried and convicted of sedition and served time in the federal penitentiary in Sandstone, Minnesota. Vince's brother Grant committed suicide on October 24, 1941, while in jail awaiting trial.

### Notes to "The Curious Twin"

1. Carey McWilliams, "Minneapolis: The Curious Twin," *Common Ground* (autumn 1946): 61–66.

2. Selden Menefee, *Assignment: U.S.A.* (New York: Reynal and Hitchcock, Inc., 1943), 101.

3. *Minneapolis Star and Journal*, October 18, 1946, 18.

4. *American Jewish World*, October 25, 1946, 1.

5. While Minneapolis Jews were often unwilling to confront the more virulent forms of anti-Semitism directly, at least one angry man decided to take matters into his own hands when Nazi sympathizer William Dudley Pelley brought his Silver Shirts brigade to Minneapolis. David Berman, a Minneapolis underworld figure, learned that Pelley had organized a Silver Shirts rally at a local Elks Lodge. He and a group of friends burst into the room and attacked Pelley's followers, driving them out of the hall. Berman is reported to have taken the microphone and announced, "This is a warning. Anyone who says anything against Jews gets the same treatment, only next time it will be worse." See Robert Latz, *Jews in Minnesota Politics: The Inside Stories* (Minneapolis, MN: Nodin Press, 2007), 4.

6. Friendly, *Minnesota Rag*, 47. Ironically, state and local efforts to silence Near's *Saturday Press* led to one of this country's landmark freedom-of-the-press decisions by the U.S. Supreme Court in *Near v. Minnesota.*

7. Friendly, *Minnesota Rag*, 48.

8. Michael Gerald Rapp, "An Historical Overview of Anti-Semitism in Minnesota, 1920–1960, with particular emphasis on Minneapolis and St. Paul" (PhD diss., University of Minnesota, 1977), 146–47.

9. When Rader died in 1952, his son, Paul, succeeded him and continued to operate the River Lake Gospel Tabernacle until it closed in 1968. In 2002, the Minneapolis Heritage Preservation Commission considered placing a commemorative plaque at the site of the tabernacle to recognize Luke Rader's work as a pioneering radio evangelist. The proposal was later scuttled when the Minnesota Jewish Community Relations Council lodged a protest with the commission.

10. Petersen did not use direct anti-Semitic slurs in his campaign but rather made veiled comments about the "Mexican Generals" in the Benson administration, who happened to be Jewish. See Hyman Berman, "Political Antisemitism in Minnesota," *Jewish Social Studies* 38.3–4 (1976).

11. Berman, "Political Antisemitism," 257.

12. Berman, "Political Antisemitism," 262.

13. Calvin F. Schmid, *Social Saga of Two Cities: An Ecological and Statistical Study of Social Trends in Minneapolis and St. Paul* (Minneapolis: Bureau of Social Research, the Minneapolis Council of Social Agencies, [c1937]), 78.

14. Menefee, *Assignment: U.S.A.*, 102.

15. McWilliams, "Minneapolis: The Curious Twin," 64–65. Not only were Jews excluded from participation in local civic organizations, Jewish doctors, including the author's father, were denied admitting privileges in Minneapolis. This exclusionary pattern led to the Jewish-backed Mount Sinai Hospital being established in 1950. See Fred Lyon, *Mount Sinai Hospital of Minneapolis, Minnesota: A History* (Minneapolis, MN: Mount Sinai Hospital History Committee, 1995).

16. McWilliams, "Minneapolis: The Curious Twin," 61.

17. McWilliams, "Minneapolis: The Curious Twin," 63.

18. McWilliams, "Minneapolis: The Curious Twin," 65.

19. Jennifer A. Delton, *Making Minnesota Liberal: Civil Rights and the Transformation of the Democratic Party* (Minneapolis: University of Minnesota Press, 2002), 62.

20. David Brauer, *Nellie Stone Johnson: The Life of an Activist* (St. Paul, MN: Ruminator Books, 2000), 63.

21. Deed for 2732 Forty-first Avenue South, filed May 10, 1927, copy in author's collection. In 1948, the U.S. Supreme Court declared these racial covenants to be unenforceable, but their influence lingered for years after the court decision.

22. Humphrey, *Education of a Public Man*, 99. *Minneapolis Spokesman*, July 27, 1945, 2.

23. *Minneapolis Spokesman*, July 6, 1945, 1.

24. Solberg, *Hubert Humphrey*, 106.

25. See Minneapolis Dept. of Civil Rights records, Mayor's Commission on Human Relations, Minnesota Historical Society, St. Paul, MN.

26. *Minneapolis Tribune*, November 30, 1948, 1. The story was filed by a young Jewish reporter named Geri Hoffner, who later becomes Geri Joseph and a major political figure in her own right.

27. *American Jewish World*, December 3, 1948, 3.

28. *American Jewish World*, February 14, 1947, 8. *Minneapolis Spokesman*, February 7, 1947, 4.

29. See files of the Minneapolis Fair Employment Practice Commission (FEPC), Minnesota Historical Society, St. Paul, MN.

30. Wilfred G. Leland Jr. to J. T. Braxton, June 21, 1950, FEPC files.

31. City of Minneapolis Fair Employment Practice Commission, "Nineteenth Annual Report Covering 1966–67" and "Twenty Year Progress Report 1947–1967," 2, 4, FEPC files. The department store that began hiring nonwhite sales clerks, though not identified in the report, most likely was Dayton's.

32. FEPC Annual Report (1967), 6, 7, FEPC files. The Minneapolis FEPC issued its final report three months after young blacks torched shops—many of them Jewish-owned—along Plymouth Avenue in July 1967.

33. Delton, *Making Minnesota Liberal*, 134.

34. In 2004, Stephen Silberfarb, executive director of the Jewish Community Relations Council of Minnesota and the Dakotas, declared that institutional anti-

Semitism on a national level had all but disappeared even while anti-Jewish hate groups were proliferating. See "Can't Happen Here? Twin Cities Anti-Semitism Past and Present," *Twin Cities Jewish Life* (May-June 2004): 6–8.

35. Delton, *Making Minnesota Liberal*, 110. Delton maintains that the Minneapolis FEPC promised more than it could deliver and did little to deal with the structural problems of black unemployment and underemployment.

36. In 1955, Minnesota enacted an FEPC law that applied throughout the state. Two years later, a statewide fair housing law was passed.

### Notes to "Plymouth Avenue Is Burning"

1. W. Harry Davis, *Overcoming: The Autobiography of W. Harry Davis* (Afton, MN: Afton Historical Society Press, 2002), 159.

2. *Minneapolis Star*, July 20, 1967, 4A.

3. Davis, *Overcoming*, 159–60.

4. Davis, *Overcoming*, 161.

5. *Minneapolis Tribune*, July 21, 1967, 1.

6. *Minneapolis Tribune*, July 21, 1967, 13.

7. *Minneapolis Tribune*, July 21, 1967, 6.

8. *Minneapolis Tribune*, July 21, 1967, 6.

9. *Minneapolis Star*, July 21, 1967, 10A.

10. *Minneapolis Star*, July 22, 1967, 6A.

11. Davis, *Overcoming*, 159.

12. *Minneapolis Spokesman*, July 27, 1967, 2.

13. *Minneapolis Spokesman*, July 27, 1967, 1.

14. *Minneapolis Star*, July 25, 1967, 1B.

15. Minneapolis *Star Tribune*, July 19, 2007, B3.

16. "In 1981 a Jewish Federation Population Study found as many Jews in Minneapolis and its suburbs as there had been 20 years earlier—but only 273 of them were living in North Minneapolis!" See Rhoda Lewin, *Images of America: Jewish Community of North Minneapolis* (Chicago: Arcadia Publishing, 2001), 109.

17. Davis, *Overcoming*, 158.

18. Minneapolis *Star Tribune*, July 20, 1997, A12. "The schism between the Jewish and Black communities resulting from the Plymouth Avenue riots never completely healed despite the efforts of the Urban Coalition and like-minded community religious leaders," former state representative Robert Latz has observed. See Latz, *Jews in Minnesota Politics*, 27.

19. *American Jewish World*, August 4, 1967, 4.

20. *American Jewish World*, August 4, 1967, 4.

21. The Talmud Torah was only one of a long list of Jewish community institutions that left the North Side in the 1960s and relocated in the western suburbs along with a large share of the community's population. Earlier in the decade, the Jewish-sponsored Emanuel Cohen Center on Oak Park Avenue had moved to St. Louis Park and been reorganized as the Jewish Community Center of Greater Minneapolis. Later, major religious institutions including the Beth El, Tifereth B'nai Jacob, and Mikro Kodesh synagogues left as well.

22. Schmid, *Social Saga of Two Cities*, 77.

23. Schmid, *Social Saga of Two Cities*, 78. Minneapolis's black population continued to grow at a rapid rate through much of the twentieth century. By 2000, it

reached just under seventy thousand. For a discussion of the growth of Minneapolis's black community, see David Vassar Taylor, *African Americans in Minnesota* (St. Paul: Minnesota Historical Society Press, 2002).

24. Davis, *Overcoming*, 45.

25. Lewin, *Jewish Community of North Minneapolis*, 107–8.

26. Lewin, *Jewish Community of North Minneapolis*, 116. In February 1968, Rabbi Max Shapiro, the spiritual leader of Temple Israel, devoted a Friday night sermon to the defense of Ron Edwards, the controversial black activist who eventually joined the Minneapolis Civil Rights Commission after his appointment was initially blocked by the Minneapolis City Council. Shapiro was active in a variety of local civil rights efforts, including the Minnesota Council on Race and Religion, the Minneapolis Urban Coalition, and the Minneapolis Committee on Fair Housing. See Rabbi Max A. Shapiro, *Here Am I, Send Me: A Brief Personal Account of Life at Temple Israel* (Minneapolis, MN: Temple Israel, 1980), 22–29.

27. *Minneapolis Tribune*, November 18, 1968, 12. Signaling the importance it placed on the issue of race relations in the Twin Cities, the *Tribune* devoted two full pages to a report on the results of the survey sponsored by the Minnesota Council on Race and Religion.

28. *Minneapolis Tribune*, November 17, 1968, 22A.

29. *Minneapolis Tribune*, November 17, 1968, 22A. Later in the century, this statement would be rejected for its sexist connotations, but the Minneapolis council's survey occurred well before the modern feminist movement had taken hold.

30. Race and its role in America was a national preoccupation during 1968. In February, the National Advisory Commission on Civil Disorders, known as the Kerner Commission, issued its report, declaring, "Our nation is moving toward two societies, one black, one white—separate and unequal." See http://www.eisenhowerfoundation.org/docs/kerner.pdf.

31. Davis, *Overcoming*, 182.

32. Davis, *Overcoming*, 182.

33. Davis, *Overcoming*, 183.

34. Davis, *Overcoming*, 183.

35. Davis, *Overcoming*, 183–84.

36. Davis, *Overcoming*, 184.

37. Davis, *Overcoming*, 184.

38. Urban Coalition of Minneapolis, Statement of Action, Working Draft, December 17, 1968, 3, Minnesota Historical Society, St. Paul, MN.

39. *Minneapolis Star*, September 5, 1969, 6A.

40. *Minneapolis Tribune*, March 20, 1978, 1B.

41. *Minneapolis Tribune*, May 9, 1982, 13A.

42. Through the first decade of the twenty-first century, two local organizations spun off from the coalition have continued to play an active role in Twin Cities community life: the Metropolitan Economic Development Association (MEDA), which provides technical assistance and access to capital for minority-owned businesses, and the Greater Metropolitan Housing Corporation (GMHC), which has played a key role in addressing the foreclosure crisis of the mid- and late 2000s.

43. *Organization of American Historians Newsletter* 35 (February 2007). See http://www.oah.org/pubs/nl/2007feb/stenvig.html. Minneapolis voters demon-

strated some ambivalence in their voting patterns during the late 1960s and early 1970s. While they elected and reelected Stenvig as mayor, they also returned Don Fraser, an avowed liberal, to Washington as Minnesota's Fifth District congressman.

44. *Excelsior-Deephaven-Minnetonka Sun,* June 5, 1969, 5B.

45. *Minneapolis Tribune,* April 30, 1969, 1.

46. *Minneapolis Tribune,* June 8, 1969, 2C.

47. *Minneapolis Tribune,* June 9, 1969, 5.

48. *Minneapolis Tribune,* June 11, 1969, 8.

49. *Minneapolis Tribune,* June 16, 1969, 4.

50. *Minneapolis Tribune,* June 20, 1969, 1.

51. *Minneapolis Tribune,* July 8, 1969, 17.

52. *Minneapolis Tribune,* July 8, 1969, 17.

53. *Minneapolis Tribune,* July 18, 1970, 4.

54. Jeffrey T. Manuel and Andrew T. Urban, "The Backlash as a Conflict over Expertise: The Ideologies of Government in Mayor Charles Stenvig's Minneapolis, 1969–1977" (unpublished paper, copy in author's possession), 3, 4.

55. Stenvig campaign brochure, 1971, Special Collections, Minneapolis Central Library, Minneapolis, MN.

56. Davis, *Overcoming,* 223.

### Notes to "Reimagining the Riverfront"

1. Jonathan Raban, *Old Glory: A Voyage Down the Mississippi* (New York: Simon and Schuster, 1981), 31.

2. Larry Millett, *AIA Guide to the Twin Cities: The Essential Source on the Architecture of Minneapolis and St. Paul* (St. Paul: Minnesota Historical Society Press, 2007), 57.

3. Schmid, *Social Saga of Two Cities,* 14–18. Also see Victor G. Pickett and Roland S. Vaile, *The Decline of Northwestern Flour Milling* (Minneapolis: University of Minnesota Press, 1933), 16–18.

4. Lucile Kane, *The Falls of St. Anthony: The Waterfall That Built Minneapolis* (1966, St. Paul: Minnesota Historical Society Press, 1987), 173.

5. *Minneapolis Tribune,* September 22, 1963, Upper Midwest Section, 1.

6. *Minneapolis Tribune,* February 14, 1971, "Home and Recreation," 1.

7. Kane, *Falls of St. Anthony,* 187–88. Despite her pioneering efforts to bring people to the riverfront, Weston became a victim of the public push to redevelop the area. In the early 1980s, the Minneapolis Park Board condemned a large part of Fuji-Ya's parking lot to make room for an extension of West River Parkway. Lack of parking delivered a lingering and ultimately fatal blow to the restaurant, and it closed in 1990.

8. *Minneapolis Tribune,* June 10, 1978, "Saturday Shelter," 15.

9. *Minneapolis Star,* April 26, 1974, 1A, 3A, 1B.

10. *Minneapolis Star,* August 18, 1981, 1C.

11. Kane, *Falls of St. Anthony,* 187. Adam Regn Arvidson, "A River Runs Through Them," *Architecture MN* (November-December 2007): 37.

12. Minneapolis Planning Department, "Minneapolis, Mississippi," 1972, 45.

13. Linda Mack, untitled talk (Mill City Museum, Minneapolis, MN, November 1, 2007).

14. Minneapolis Planning Department to Ed Dirkswager, memo, December 31, 1980, Special Collections. Minneapolis Central Library, Minneapolis, MN.

15. *Minneapolis Star and Tribune,* June 13, 1985, 18A.
16. *Minneapolis Tribune,* August 21, 1978, 1.
17. *Minneapolis Star and Tribune,* June 13, 1985, 18A.
18. Soon after it opened, Nicollet Island Inn encountered financial difficulties and was forced to close in March 1986. The following year, new owners purchased the property and reopened the inn.
19. *Skyway News,* August 1, 1978, Special Collections, Minneapolis Central Library, Minneapolis, MN.
20. *Minneapolis Star,* July 26, 1978, 19A.
21. *Minneapolis Star,* February 8, 1980, 1C. *Minneapolis Tribune,* September 15, 1978, 6A.
22. DeMars was succeeded as council president by Fourth Ward alderman Alice Rainville in 1980. That same year, Don Fraser succeeded Al Hofstede as mayor.
23. *Minneapolis Star,* March 27, 1981, 1A, 7A.
24. Boisclair Corporation, marketing brochure, 1984, Special Collections, Minneapolis Central Library, Minneapolis, MN.
25. *Minneapolis Star and Tribune,* August 16, 1987, 1D, 3D. By the mid-1990s, St. Anthony Main and Riverplace regained financial viability by being converted to office buildings.
26. *Minneapolis Star and Tribune,* August 16, 1987, 1D.
27. Minneapolis *Star Tribune,* October 31, 1993, 11A.
28. Minneapolis *Star Tribune,* September 29, 1997, 1B, 3B.
29. Mack, talk.
30. The Depot opened to rave reviews in 2001 and garnered several awards, including the prestigious honors designation from the Minneapolis chapter of the American Institute of Architects.
31. Minneapolis *Star Tribune,* February 28, 1991, 3B. Dick Brustad and Peggy Lucas, interview by the author, December 10, 2007.
32. Brustad-Lucas interview.
33. Brustad-Lucas interview.
34. Brustad-Lucas interview.
35. Brustad-Lucas interview.
36. Mack, talk.
37. Steve Brandt, Minneapolis *Star Tribune,* May 1, 2000, 1B.

#### Notes to "Downtown Revival"

1. *Minneapolis Tribune,* October 7, 1956, 2F, 26SD.
2. *Minneapolis Tribune,* October 7, 1956. George Draper Dayton was a founding member of the anti-labor Citizens Alliance during the early years of the twentieth century. His grandsons represented a new generation of postwar business leaders who took a broader, more progressive view of their civic responsibilities than did their forebears.
3. Judith A. Martin and Antony Goddard, *Past Choices/Present Landscapes: The Impact of Urban Renewal on the Twin Cities* (Minneapolis, MN: Center for Urban and Regional Affairs, 1989), 59–60.
4. Alan Altshuler, "A Plan for Central Minneapolis" (New York: Inter-University Case Program, 1962), Special Collections, Minneapolis Central Library, Min-

neapolis, MN. Donald Dayton found a way to straddle the suburban-urban divide. While his family was developing their suburban shopping centers, he continued to play an active role in the Downtown Council.

5. For an overview of the Gateway Urban Renewal project, see Iric Nathanson, "Housing and Redevelopment Authority: Clearing Urban Blight," *Hennepin History* 57.1 (Winter 1998): 4–23.

6. *Minneapolis Star*, August 27, 1962, 1B.

7. For a history of the Metropolitan Building, see Larry Millett, *Lost Twin Cities* (St. Paul: Minnesota Historical Society Press, 1992), 222–25.

8. *Minneapolis Star*, June 16, 1959, 9A.

9. Larry Millett has called the demolition of the Metropolitan Building "perhaps the most inexcusable act of civic vandalism in the history of Minneapolis." *Lost Twin Cities*, 225.

10. The insurance building, designed by the famed Japanese architect Minoru Yamasaki, is one of the few original Gateway developments to survive into the twenty-first century. Northwestern National Life became Reliastar and then was acquired by the Dutch firm ING in 2000.

11. Greg Bownik, interview by the author, July 31, 1997.

12. Sam H. Kaufman, *The Skyway Cities* (Minneapolis: CSPI, 1985), 1.

13. Kaufman, *Skyway Cities*, 5, 8.

14. Kaufman, *Skyway Cities*, 44. One of the most elaborate skyways, spanning Ninth Street and connecting the Medical Arts Building with the Young Quinlan Building, was intended to evoke a bridge over a Venetian canal.

15. *Minneapolis Tribune*, November 27, 1972, 1B, 2B. *Minneapolis Star*, April 29, 1974, 11A. Architectural historian Larry Millett has noted skyway pros and cons: "[They] have undoubtedly helped the central core remain vibrant, providing an all-weather connection from one end of downtown to the other. Yet they have also sucked life up and away from the street. As a result, ground-floor retailing has become a dicey proposition in much of downtown." Millett, *AIA Guide to the Twin Cities*, 33.

16. *Skyway News*, October 13, 1987, 11.

17. *Minneapolis Star*, February 13, 1964, 1B.

18. *Minneapolis Tribune*, November 11, 1967, 10M. In 2002, the *Mary Tyler Moore Show* was memorialized with a stature of Mary Richards installed on the mall at the corner of Seventh Street.

19. *Skyway News*, March 28, 1989, 1.

20. Minneapolis *Star Tribune*, September 2, 1991, 2B. Minneapolis *Star Tribune*, July 4, 1993, 1F.

21. While downtown's population did not reach the "Metro Center" goal of 55,000, a figure "above 40,000" is expected to be met by 2010. See Jack Fisher, Brita Gill, Candace Lothian, Vichit Sayavonongkhamdy, "Downtown Minneapolis: A Peer City Analysis" (Denver: University of Colorado, Fall 2006), http://www.denverinfill.com/images/special_topics/peer_cities/minneapolis_report.pdf.

22. Keith Ford, interview by the author, December 14, 2007.

23. *Minneapolis Star*, June 3, 1977, 1A, 3A.

24. Ford interview.

25. *Minneapolis Tribune*, December 19, 1979, 13A. During the 1990s, the retail

mall at City Center faltered and gradually the shops were converted to office use. Only the section that originally housed Donaldson's department store maintained retail sales through the first decade of the twenty-first century.

26. NRP, launched in the early 1990s, represented a grassroots, neighborhood-based approach to development. During its initial ten-year phase, the citywide program received $20 million annually in funding, generated in large part by cash flow from the major downtown projects, including City Center.

Ford interview. City Center's architects at the New York firm of Skidmore, Owings and Merrill had initially planned to build a windowless facade for the project along Nicollet Avenue, but a young city planner, Tom Martinson, rallied Minneapolis's architecture community to successfully demand design changes, including the addition of windows along Nicollet.

27. Over a twenty-year period, Minneapolis paid millions of dollars in legal fees in an ultimately successful effort to turn back court challenges from LSGI and local property owners who claimed they had suffered city-inflicted damages when the development project was cancelled. The city was more successful with development initiatives at the south end of downtown. In 1990 a new city-funded convention center opened at Grant Street between First and Third Avenues South. That same year, construction began on a city-assisted Hilton hotel at Tenth Street and Marquette, with a skyway connection to the convention center.

28. Phil Handy, interview by the author, October 18, 2007.

29. Handy interview.

30. Handy interview.

31. Handy interview.

32. Handy interview.

33. Minneapolis *Star Tribune*, June 5, 1991, 7B. Minneapolis *Star Tribune*, October 26, 1991, 10E.

34. Handy interview.

35. Handy interview.

36. Minneapolis *Star Tribune*, December 6, 1993, 2B.

37. In 2005, the Minneapolis City Council approved a complex transaction with the entertainment giant Clear Channel involving a thirty-year joint operating agreement with the Hennepin Theatre Trust for the Orpheum, the State, and the Pantages. At the end of the thirty-year period, ownership of the theaters will revert to the nonprofit trust.

Block E, at Sixth and Hennepin, had long been occupied by seedy bars and restaurants that cast a blighting shadow on downtown. The block was eventually redeveloped as an entertainment center over the objections of some city leaders, who maintained that the project's developers were receiving an excessive amount of public subsidies.

In 2006, the Shubert took a major step forward in meeting its $37 million fund-raising goal when it received an $11 million bonding allocation from the state legislature.

38. Minneapolis *Star Tribune*, August 10, 1993, 1A, 10A.

39. Minneapolis *Star Tribune*, December 16, 1988, 1A, 6A.

40. Jackie Cherryhomes Tyler, interview by the author, November 8, 2007. In 2001, Cherryhomes and Sayles-Belton were both defeated in reelection bids. "State of the City 2000" (Minneapolis: City of Minneapolis Planning Department, January 2001), 33, http://www.ci.minneapolis.mn.us/cped/soc00/4-economic.pdf.

## Notes to "Roads and Tracks"

1. See unpublished 1976 report by K. P. Fletcher for the Hiawatha Avenue Citizens Advisory Committee, in author's collection. The proposed route departed from the project that Metro Transit actually built only when it reached downtown. Fletcher had shown the transit line swinging north and west onto Washington Avenue and then tunneling under the Nicollet Mall and ending at the Minneapolis Convention Center. The Hiawatha line eliminated Fletcher's tunnel and entered downtown on Fifth Street rather than on Washington Avenue.

2. Wally Bratt and Jim Tennessen, interviews by the author, May 2004 and December 17, 2007. Federal Highway Act, 1974.

3. *Minneapolis Tribune*, January 21, 1975, B1.

4. Bratt-Tennessen interviews.

5. Bratt-Tennessen interviews.

6. Kathy Mackdanz, interview by the author, May 2004.

7. Fletcher, unpublished report, 2.

8. *The Catholic Bulletin Magazine*, May 28, 1976, 13. Microfilm available at the Minnesota Historical Society, St. Paul, MN.

9. *Minneapolis Star*, August 17, 1976, 1C.

10. Bratt-Tennessen interviews.

11. *Minneapolis Tribune*, May 1976.

12. Bratt-Tennessen interviews.

13. *Minneapolis Star*, October 14, 1975, 6A.

14. *Minneapolis Tribune*, June 12, 1976, 15A.

15. Bratt-Tennessen interviews.

16. Bratt-Tennessen interviews.

17. Mary Losure, *Our Way or the Highway: Inside the Minnehaha Free State* (Minneapolis: University of Minnesota Press, 2002), xi.

18. *Longfellow Nokomis Messenger*, August 2004, 1.

19. Minneapolis *Star Tribune*, January 17, 2001, 1A.

20. Peter McLaughlin, interview by the author, May 2004. Minneapolis *Star Tribune*, January 17, 2001, 1A, 8A.

21. McLaughlin interview.

22. McLaughlin interview.

23. Martin Sabo, interview by the author, May 2004. Minneapolis *Star Tribune*, December 14, 2001, 35A.

24. Minneapolis *Star Tribune*, April 4, 1991, 1B.

25. Minneapolis *Star Tribune*, April 4, 1991, 1B.

26. Minneapolis *Star Tribune*, February 8, 1991, 1B, 5B.

27. Minneapolis *Star Tribune*, March 9, 1994, 9A.

28. Minneapolis *Star Tribune*, March 29, 1996, 1B, 6B.

29. McLaughlin interview.

30. McLaughlin interview.

31. McLaughlin interview.

32. McLaughlin interview.

33. Carol Flynn, interview by the author, May 2004.

34. Minneapolis *Star Tribune*, January 15, 1998, 2B.

35. Flynn interview.

36. Minneapolis *Star Tribune*, April 23, 1998, 2B.

37. Minneapolis *Star Tribune*, May 30, 1998, 1A.

38. Minneapolis *Star Tribune,* February 2, 1999, 3B.
39. McLaughlin interview.
40. Flynn interview.
41. Minneapolis *Star Tribune,* March 13, 1999, 1A, 15A. Minneapolis *Star Tribune,* April 6, 1999, 1B.
42. Minneapolis *Star Tribune,* September 28, 1999, 1A.
43. Minneapolis *Star Tribune,* September 29, 1999, 1B. 5B.
44. Minneapolis *Star Tribune,* May 6, 2000, 1B.
45. Minneapolis *Star Tribune,* January 14, 2001, 1B, 6B.
46. Minneapolis *Star Tribune,* January 18, 2001, 1B.
47. Minneapolis *Star Tribune,* June 20, 2004, 1A.

### Notes to Epilogue

1. Minneapolis *Star Tribune,* September 12, 2001, 1.
2. Minneapolis *Star Tribune,* March 31, 2000, 3D.
3. Metropolitan Consortium of Community Developers newsletter (Spring 2008), MCCD office, Minneapolis, MN. Minneapolis *Star Tribune,* November 20, 2006, 1A.

# Index

Page numbers in *italic* refer to illustrations and captions

page 18
*Minneapolis Journal,* October 19, 1900

page 22
*Pioneer Press,* April 22, 1900

page 23
*Minneapolis Journal,* November 2, 1900

page 31
*Twin Cities Reader,* 1988

page 37
Minneapolis *Star Tribune,* December 5, 2004

page 65
*Minneapolis Tribune,* July 1902

pages 116, 118, 126, 131, 142, 148, 155, 158, 198
Courtesy Minneapolis *Star Tribune*

page 168
Robert Jackson

page 181
Diane D. Brown

page 185
Bill Stern, Bloomington, MN

pages 187, 193
James K. Hosmer Special Collections Library,
    Hennepin County Library

page 205
Minneapolis *Star Tribune,* 1984

page 211
Brian M. Gardner—gardnerphotos.com

*Minneapolis in the Twentieth Century* was designed and set in type by Will Powers at the Minnesota Historical Society Press. The text type is Miller. The display types are Iris and Interstate. Printed by Sheridan Books, Ann Arbor.